Dedicated to
Eagle, White-throated Sparow,
Grasshopper
and
All My Relations
With deep gratitude for how they have
wondrously altered my life.

Acknowledgements

My heart-felt thanks to all those two-leggeds who have spirited this book and me along.

In particular - my early editorial support team of Sue, Susan, Kae and, later, Jack, and then finally the pro editor John Stevens, who encouraged me to search for fairy tales that echoed my life and my path in this book.

Tom Thumb and the Ugly Duckling re-entered my life and cast their mark.

Table of Contents

Part I   **Introduction**

Chapter 1 Seawall Ceremony 1
            2 Eagle 3
            3 White Cougar Woman and Animal Medicine 6

Part II   **1989**

            4 New Tools in Play 13
            5 Animal Communication Workshop 16
            6 White-throated Sparrow 21
            7 Laughing Eagle 26
            8 Candle 31
            9 Fall Wrap-up 36

Part III **1990**

           10 Medicine Walk 45
           11 Smudging Stone and White-breasted Nuthatch 47
           12 Pine Siskin Chorus 50
           13 Native Elder 56
           14 Grandmother Twylah 60
           15 The Bear Tribe 64
           16 Sacred Sites 70
           17 Re-entry and Snake Medicine 73

Part IV   1991

18	Day-to-Day Life	83
19	Vision Quest: Preparations	86
20	Departure Jitters	90
21	The Program Begins	94
22	Vision Quest of a Heroine	97
23	Diary of a Summer	104

Part V   1992

24	The Year of Searching	115
25	How to Serve	120
26	The Garden Power Place	123
27	Listening to Nature and Ceremony	128
28	Emotions and Obstacles	131
29	Brooke Medicine Eagle	137

Part VI   1993

30	Creativity Blossoms	141
31	Preparing the Soil	148
32	Grouse Wing and Act of Power	152
33	Afterwards	160
	Epilogue	169
	Glossary	170
	Bibliography	171

Part I *Introduction*

1
Seawall Ceremony

I WANT A SIGN, permission to carry out the ceremony that brings me back to the Stanley Park Seawall this drizzling April morning. I near the Douglas firs, smell their fragrance and the salty tang of the ocean. Suddenly, not 40 feet away, down swoops a mature bald eagle, snatches a fish in its talons and flies off. Tears cascade down my cheeks. *Oh what a sign and oh so close this time.*

Tears of gratitude continue to well up from the well-primed pump of my heart as I slowly walk on, thinking of the people in my upcoming ceremony. Mom and Dad and my brother, Jon. All my close family and several good friends as well. All dead. Sadness sweeps over me. Even my footsteps are heavy.

Pelagic cormorants are building their nests on the cliff face. Pigeon guillemots are flying off shore. As I watch them, my mood lightens again. The tide is well out and I stop and catch myself grinning as I watch a glaucous-winged gull tackle a purple starfish breakfast.

The rain stops. I can do without the swish of my pancho. Off it comes and I listen instead to the call of the chickadees. Their chatter warms my heart and brings a smile to my face. By the time I approach where I anticipate holding my ceremony, the drizzle recommences, hardly noticeable, so gentle it is. *This area is more cleared than I remember from my last visit. Will I find a suitable place?* Birds are flitting about a cluster of bushes slightly down the slope. *There may be enough shelter there at the base of the tree with the bushes in front of me.*

I gingerly work my way to the spot, not wanting to damage the vegetation. I select a small stick en route for digging holes. I don't have cornmeal and miss its gritty feeling on my fingers. Instead, I scatter tobacco around a small circle. I sit, smudge myself with sweet grass, filling my nostrils with its sweetness and immersing my body in the smoke, and prepare myself and my gear. I dig two holes at the base of the tree beside me and spread out some tin foil in front of me.

Nature joins its drizzle to my tears and sadness. This is just enough to make it a challenge to burn my give-aways on the tin foil. Occasionally one smoulders and smokes and I frown, concerned that someone may notice. When I burn a photo, the smell is as rotten as the death it symbolizes. One bursts into flame and I shelter it carefully so that none of the vegetation burns. Another of these difficult moments occurs just as a police car passes by. I tense, then relax. *Have more faith: the Spirits are not going to let me be disturbed.* I plant my forget-me-not seeds in honour of those who are dead and tamp down the cool earth over them with my fingers.

When I have finished giving away the painful memories of family and friends, it is time for the

"Fly like an eagle" finale. As I retrieve my tape recorder from my backpack, a park employee, driving his lawn mower along the Seawall walkway, stops, and with his ears muffled to block out the noise, begins mowing below me. So even my song is solely for the Spirits and me. I sing along lustily with my head thrown back, ending the ceremony.

    I descend again to the Seawall. As I am about to leave this little bay, I look to see if an eagle is anywhere about. In a tree nearer the other end of the bay an immature bald eagle faces me. *It has been there all along. Thank you Eagle for your presence and acknowledgement of my ceremony.* Eagle is my symbol for my close friend, Sharon. My heart is full and I carry on. A great blue heron close to the shoreline brings a big grin to my face. Heron is the symbol for Dad. I halt, enjoy his presence and then become aware of the sense of pain lifted from my heart, more confirmation of the significance of the morning. *Thank you Great Spirit and all my Relations.*

    I choose a rock on which to sit and gaze out over the ocean. I think back to how the form of the ceremony had come to me back home in the east as I was crossing a small parking lot. First and foremost this ceremony was a give-away of the pain and sadness that I had not yet relinquished over the death of family members and close friends, even though some were long gone. I had got to wondering. *Is part of the need to hold on to that pain my old fear that I wasn't capable of "love?" Is it also demonstrating to myself my loyalty and not forgetting my loved ones?* My head was beyond those old tapes, but maybe I needed to formalize that change.

    I decided to burn and bury the pain symbols of those family members and friends – pictures of them near the time of their deaths, letters written near that time, whatever would symbolize the associations with pain. In their place, I would have new Nature symbols representing the gifts of these people that I could carry instead of the pain. Then I would plant the package of wildflower seeds that had come in the mail some time ago and was still somewhere on the kitchen table–turned out they were forget-me-nots!

    Later, back home, I'd realized it was time to draw Medicine cards. What supportive and exciting messages they offered. One was Turkey, the other Raven.

    Turkey's heading in *Medicine Cards* is "Give-away": "Giving is without regret and with a joyful heart, or the "give-away" has lost its true meaning. . .You are being given a gift. This gift could be spiritual, material or even intellectual." (p.162)

Raven says:

> "Raven is the guardian of ceremonial magic and *in absentia* healing. . . Raven is the messenger that carries all energy flows of ceremonial magic between the ceremony itself and the intended destination. . .Magic is in the air. . .It is the power of the unknown at work, and something special is about to happen. . .You are about to experience a change in consciousness. This may involve walking inside the Great Mystery on another path at the edge of time. It would portend a signal brought by the Raven that says, 'You have earned the right to see and experience a little more of life's magic.'" (pp.101-102)

How could there be two more appropriate guides to have for this undertaking?

    Then my thoughts flashed back farther yet to five years earlier when I'd made this same walk. November 12, so fittingly just after Remembrance Day. It all began then.

2 Eagle

IT WAS EIGHT at night on a dreary November 11 when I finally got up, squeezed Sharon's small hand, held in my tears and left her hospital room. I got down to her Honda, slid in, and started to sob. I'd spoken to Sharon days ago, telling her she could let go, that it was time for her to move on. So grief had been with me for days. But suddenly now, as if the thumb was removed from the hole in the dike, my grief was pouring out as I sobbed with all my body for the friend I loved so deeply. All the way back to where I was staying with friends, I cried and cried.

Before heading inside, I dried my eyes and tasted the salt of my tears. My friend's son Johnny was there, sensed my pain, and offered to show me the slides from his recent African trip. So he dragged me away from my pain to the wonder of elephants, lions, wildebeasts and my favourite giraffes.

The phone wakes me at 6:00 a.m. Sharon's aunt to say that Sharon died at 5:00. I thank her for calling. There is nothing else to say. Our vigil is over. I lie back in bed. Somehow, in spite of the sadness, a load has lifted: Sharon's pain is finally over.

I look out. The sun is touching mountain tops in the distance. Sun. The first day in three weeks, it seems. Suddenly I know what I have to do – walk Sharon's favourite Seawall walk in Stanley Park. I dress hastily, eat a quick breakfast, leave a note for my friend and am back in the Honda again. As the glorious early morning unfolds, I play a Richard Clayderman tape that Sharon gave me when I arrived three weeks before. My lungs are bursting as I join in with all my being to the song, "Chariots of Fire." I soar with the music. Sharon is free, and so am I. She is spirit now, whatever that means, but free from her body and cancer and torment.

I park near the children's wading pool, our usual spot. I set off, caught up in the beauty of the morning, sun shining, mountain peaks glistening with new snow from the last night's rain, fresh salt smell of the ocean. I soon sight a harlequin duck, the season's first for me and one of Sharon's favourites. No wonder, with its tapestry of slate blue and rich mahogany. I enjoy its beauty for both of us.

Rounding the point past the Lion's Gate Bridge, I think of Sharon's family's desire for an open casket. How strange that seems to me, so glad that she is freed from that body, free now in spirit, bringing her closer to me than living 3,000 miles apart. My peripheral vision catches movement out over the water. I turn in time to see a bald eagle swoop down and come out of its dive just before hitting the ocean. Then somehow it vanishes. Never have I seen one out there before.

The symbol and its timing plunge into me. I am open, vulnerable and I pay close attention. Important symbol to the Cree. *Protection?* I'm not sure but I know it is more than coincidence. I carry on.

Near Lost Lagoon, a third bird of the morning catches my attention, a mandarin duck. That's an Asian species, stunning golden cousin to our wood duck. My heart beats faster. *Blown here in a storm? Escapee from captivity?* Either way, another wonderful symbol of Sharon, a Japanese Canadian. My heart is the bud of a day lily bursting into bloom. I return to my car and all that is now to be done.

* * * *

Let me describe the person who walked the Seawall that November day in 1987. Until the age of five I lived in a small community. There were woodlots on three sides of our home. We moved to Toronto where, other than vacation trips and visits to cottages, I had little time in Nature. Later in graduate school, I was introduced to hiking in the Lake District of England. From then on hiking and camping became an important part of my life. Gradually birdwatching became the goal of hiking and the distances walked shrank while the places I visited burgeoned. No wonder then that birds have so frequently been symbols and messengers for me on my spiritual path.

My parents were well-educated and firm believers in science, logic and reason, as was I. Morality was very much a part of our lives but religion was not. The desire to fit in with my friends took me to church in my teenage years but I was turned away by Christianity's belief that theirs was the only way. A bird tour to Thailand brought me a fresh awareness of Buddhism. What I read of oneness, the common essence in all living things including humans, appealed to me. The Buddhist emphasis on the suffering in life didn't ring a strong chord but I was drawn to Tibetan Buddhism and the Shambhala path within it, which talked of the spiritual warrior and focused not on suffering but on discovering the magic in life.

That is a snapshot of me, a 47-year-old woman reaching out to a spiritual path for a new sense of purpose that I was finding less frequently in my job. I remained well grounded in my physical world, skeptical of astrology and anything mystical. I was intrigued by my native colleagues' beliefs. Yet some of what I heard from them about the spirit world sounded eerie to me. I did not reject them outright even then, but I definitely found them eerie.

* * * *

I suppose I could have overlooked the significance of the bald eagle sighting, although somehow I doubt it. In any event, to remove all doubt, I saw eagles again. It was the morning of Sharon's funeral. I was to read the "appreciation" for her later that day, join others in honouring our friend. I was having my breakfast with another of Sharon's friends. Suddenly, I noticed two bald eagles flying over the house. I was speechless, knowing once again that this was a message for me. Somehow Sharon was with me in the eagles, had chosen to show she was with me by selecting that bird we both loved. It didn't feel crazy at the moment. I accepted it and so my life was changed, for I took those visits as invitations to new directions, a new connection with the Universe.

That first year, as I turned to Lynn Andrews' books, recommended by my native colleague, a whole new world started to open before me, as I let go slowly but surely of my tenacious clinging to reason, my steel cage cover of intuition. The eagles brought reinforcement through the year that followed.

In January I visited a long-time friend and mentor, Isabel, in Mill Village, Nova Scotia. She had been Superintendent of a women's prison where I began my working career as the psychologist. She was aging and in poor health and I hadn't seen her in over a year. As I drove from Halifax to Mill Village, I caught a broad smile on my face as I thought of her. Such a smile had not been there since Sharon's death two months before. As fast as it came, the smile changed to tears. *Would I see a bald eagle?* Not impossible, although on my numerous visits I never had.

I arrived. Within minutes Isabel told me that visitors the previous day had sighted a bald eagle in a pine near the road. *Would it be there for me?* We drove out by the sea that afternoon. No eagle. We drove along the Medway River late in the afternoon. No eagle. Almost off the icy road in the effort, but no eagle. We headed home as the sun was casting its golden glow. As we rounded the last curve before the turn into Isabel's drive, we both spotted it: white head, white tail of a mature bald eagle in the pine at the end of her drive.

Binoculars up quickly, though scarcely needed. A good look and it lifted to fly across the road to the river on the other side. Not one but two! They circled, danced, airborne in the golden glow, and we watched, entranced and ensnared in the web they wove in the sky. The dance over, they flew up the river and out of sight. There were small pearls of tears in my eyes and my heart was so full it hurt. Sharon was with me once more.

In April, wanderer I, I headed south to Rockville, Maryland to visit another friend. Like Sharon a year earlier, Hillary had recently moved into a new condominium. The parallel hit me hard and I thought of Sharon. A morning later I took my thoughts out with me to the Pennyfield Locks of the C & O canal – a lovely escape from Ottawa in April. I searched for signs of spring and came upon an opening where a bluebird darted here and there for insects. Apt the phrase, blue bird of happiness. But not alone: I found the first returning warblers alongside too. My heart became airborne with them. As I started on, a woman, also with binoculars, approached. We shared our "finds." "Had I seen the eagle's nest a mile away?" My heart thumped. Never had it occurred to me that this could be a home to bald eagles. Next morning I found the nest, found the two adults close by. One eyed me as I eyed it and as Hillary and I returned to the car, one flew directly overhead. For me, it was the presence of Sharon again.

Natives speak of the Medicine Wheel, place the four directions on it, see four in the cycles of the seasons, four in the cycles of our lives. This eagle cycle of mine completed its circle when I returned out west in July 1988 and visited one of Sharon's friends on Whidbey Island. Three of us retraced the route we had followed on our last trip together with Sharon the summer before her death. As I got out of the car at Deception Pass, I yelled at the others to hurry. A bald eagle flew over our heads, circled and glided off in the direction our trail would take us. We were silenced by its visit, each taken to inner thoughts about Sharon. But the cobalt blue sky and the sun on our backs drew our thoughts back to the present. In due course, we sat and munched our snacks on a rocky promontory clothed behind with pines. A gentle breeze cooled us and we drank in the salt air. As we prepared to head back, a sharp cry interrupted us. An eagle lifted from the trees behind, flew over and sailed out across the water. I said goodbye to Sharon.

White Cougar Woman and Animal Medicine

THE CYCLE OF EAGLES took a year. What else was cooking, what steps on this new path? Reading was primary that first year. Reading Lynn Andrews' *Medicine Woman, Jaguar Woman, Crystal Woman*. The books gripped me. Sometimes I was on a bungee cord, leaping into the unknown with her. This wasn't fiction. It was the story of a spiritual path, the path I was choosing to take. Some of the events she described seemed impossible and yet my inner knowing now said, *No, it's real. Take it in, digest it, accept it.* I read on, went back to the Carlos Castaneda books I had read in the early '70s. Castaneda, an anthropologist, had studied in Mexico under Don Juan, a *nagual* or sorcerer. Castaneda learned to shift his level of awareness and thus, for example, saw things that weren't there to the eyes of others. What he wrote had to be fiction, symbolism, I had thought at the time. Now I knew that it wasn't fiction that touched me then, that had awakened something far within. I had read of other levels of awareness in books about parapsychology but put it aside, not part of my world yet. So the stories simmered within, a world out there, real, very different from mine, not yet mine.

September 1988. The next step came. A friend suggested going to a special sports film. The tickets were on sale at a sports store in the market area. I went there but they were sold out. I was sent two streets over to another sports store. The tickets were there, saving me two dollars from the front door price. The clothes that I bought in the store, however, cost far more! No, that's not the step. Next door was Sunnyside Bookstore. Books for the development of consciousness, their bookmarks say. And so it was for me, a source of books for years to come. But that's not all. In the hallway were flyers and cards plastered all over a very large bulletin board, advertising massages, workshops, channeling, and, somewhere there, "teachings on the medicine path" by Kristine Nickels, White Cougar Woman. This sounded like native teachings, just what I sought. I noted the time and place of her meetings. At last, my first teacher after eagle had come my way.

We smudged at that first class. Kristine had an abalone shell in which she had put sage and sweet grass, sacred plants to natives, she said. She lit this mixture, used a wing of a hawk to fan the embers, keep the smoke coming. Brushed some of the smoke over each of us in turn. Said it would cleanse our negative thoughts and energy, help us be more receptive and present. The mixture was called "smudge" and the process of brushing the smoke over us was "smudging." The smudge smelled sweet, fresh, hard to define, strange like her, like the room in which we sat on cushions. She was thin, long blond hair, deep circles under her eyes, full of energy, body and thoughts leaping from one topic to another.

Kristine was not native but spoke of Swiftdeer, her Métis teacher, connected in some way to Don Genaro, one of the teachers of Carlos Castaneda. My eyes opened wider, if that was possible. She spoke of sun dances, of medicine wheels. She drew circles, marked the cardinal and non-cardinal directions. Then she spoke of where we sit on the wheel, our core place determined by our date of birth. May 11th made me a Taurus sitting in the east. Beaver, the animal there in her teachings, beaver, builder of dams and lodges, hard worker, family important. And so it went. I reeled like a drunken sailor from what I heard. She seemed flippant at times. She knew a lot but did she respect what she knew? Over time I concluded she did.

I kept coming back. Homework, too. Our first ceremony in October was what she called a "flowering tree" ceremony. We were to go outside after dark to a tree of our choice, offer prayers there, sit in each of the directions, wait for answers to questions she gave us to ask at each place.

I drove to Mer Bleue, part of Ottawa's Greenbelt. On foot, I followed a side trail to a huge beech, a foot in diameter, tall, strong, right next to the path, leaf-covered ground around it. The full moon couldn't get through this woods very well. Flashlight in hand, I read the prayers. *This sounds like gobbledy-gook, weird.* I asked my question for the east as I sat with my back to the tree, facing east, compass with me to sort that out. My body was tense and alert, a lookout awaiting the enemy's approach. I heard noises. *Not used to this. What was that?* I shivered. Nothing happened. No answer. *How long do I wait?* I sat longer. Still nothing. *Well, on to the south.* Asked my question, changed the direction I faced. Waited, listened and so it went. My feet and hands got cold. I completed the ceremony, none the wiser, doubtfully put down tobacco in thanks and trudged back to the car, disappointed and skeptical too. Nothing to report in class. I listened to the others. More had happened for them. *Something to it after all.* Kristine wasn't concerned that some of us felt little or nothing had occurred. "Don't worry, just try to relax more next time and it will come."

Two weeks later another ceremony, this time inside. I chose my bedroom, sat on the floor with candle, water, earth on hand. Faced each direction and jotted down what I saw, tried not to focus on anything in particular. I noted the photo of my Dad on my dresser in the west, the direction of death, of change. Something there that seemed like pyramids. Didn't make sense then, but now, looking back, pyramids are tombs. Dad died later that month. Coincidence? Probably not, the beginning of new ways of seeing, new connections to reality.

Others in this group attended workshops on crystals, sessions on channeling. I noted later, "I stuck to my one course, aware that my attempt at openness could only go so far!" Kristine smoked a special pipe from time to time, an Indian pipe, long dark brown wood stem, pipestone bowl. Special prayers went with it. Something about the pipe and prayers moved me, touched another chord, a chord still off key, but awakened, quivering slightly, like my first encounter with Carlos Castaneda's books.

One last event in 1988 stands out. I went to my first workshop touching on any of this new venture. It was called "A Celebration of Women," co-led by a gentle Métis woman and a highly organized psychologist. The psychologist kept the show on the road, the Métis opened our hearts. On entry we chose a name for ourselves for the weekend. I chose Eastern Sun, reflecting a new life rising with the warmth of Grandfather Sun in the spiritual gate of the east. This was applying symbols of the Medicine Wheels that Kristine was teaching me.

During the weekend I was introduced to visualization. We sat or lay on the floor with our eyes closed and tried to see where the leader led us as she described a path we walked and then left us to have someone, or animals, appear in the scene we imagined. I witnessed others experience this but saw nothing myself. In another exercise, we had partners. With eyes closed and concentrating on the partner, whom we didn't know, we waited for some image to come to us, which would relate to the partner in some way. My body and mind were ramrod tense with fear of failure. Again I drew a blank. I was disappointed and frustrated, feeling I had let my partner and myself down. Not a very likely candidate for this path I was choosing, was I?!

The gift of the weekend for me came in the evening during free time. A fellow participant, Lady Hawk, true to her name, was a messenger for me. She had brought Animal Medicine cards and the accompanying book, *Medicine Cards*, by Jamie Sams and David Carson and introduced me and others to this tool. What is meant by "medicine?" Kristine used it too. The book states that "it is anything that improves one's connection to the Great Mystery and to all life. It is also anything which brings personal power, strength, and understanding."(p.13)

As the book suggests, Lady Hawk had me select seven cards from the deck of 44 and these she said were my totem animals, there to guide me through my life.

The first, for the east, was Porcupine, described as exemplifying trust and innocence. I warmed to Porcupine. So much so that at the naming ceremony at the end of the workshop, North Star, our Métis leader, named me Little Yellow Porcupine, capturing my newness to the path, the yellow of my eastern sun and Porcupine's innocence and trust. I liked that name. It represented me well right then.

There were six other totem animals. Honoured to have Buffalo, abundance, one who shares all that others may live, sacred animal to the tribes whom it clothed and fed and sheltered. *But so many rodents* - Porcupine, Opossum, Badger. Only Porcupine familiar, welcome. I liked what I read in the book, the emphasis not on the quills but the trust. There was Turtle, too. *O.K., I guess*. The book speaks of being grounded to the Earth but I wasn't enthusiastic about Turtle's plodding pace. I was not at all sure about Spider. *Medicine Cards* says "Spider is the female energy of the creative force that weaves the beautiful designs of life." (p.210)

All fine and dandy but I'm not keen on spiders. Why not Dolphin, Wolf, or Mountain Lion? They sound special. Now Moose. I like that.

"Two others, I knew myself or would come to know," Lady Hawk said. Eagle for sure, no doubt of that. The ninth. Beaver, my place in the east? I was not sure, I'm still not sure.

So, I drew these cards. So what? What do they mean? What kind of hocus-pocus, tell me pray. My love of Nature drew me though. We all can learn from Nature, I felt sure. Kristine was stressing that natives saw animals as teachers. And most of all, Eagle had helped me find this path. So why not others? Nature, reflecting our being, our potential, our weaknesses, ready to offer guidance to those who seek.

What did *Medicine Cards* say about Eagle? First card in the book, subtitled "Spirit," starts with:

"Eagle medicine is the power of the Great Spirit, the connection to the Divine. It is the ability to live in the realm of spirit, and yet remain connected and balanced within the realm of Earth... If you have pulled this symbol, Eagle is reminding you to take heart and gather your courage, for the universe is presenting you with an opportunity to soar above the mundane levels of your life." (p.41)

Medicine Cards speaks not just of those who guide us through our lives, these nine totem animals, but tells how to ask for help at any time. You will see how I used the cards as time went on. They are a tool to help us city slickers progress. They taught me to open my eyes when I'm out and about, as I had done for Eagle. Who shows up today? Out of the ordinary? Look for a message. Check what *Medicine Cards* has to say about the animal. That's what I learned that weekend.

As 1988 came to an end, I now had some tools for my spiritual tool kit. I had joined in the prayer of smoking a pipe; I had followed a couple of ceremonies; and, strongest by far, I had noticed Eagle for more than just a beautiful bird on each of the occasions it visited me.

And now I had the Animal Medicine cards and my own totem animals to help me develop a new connection with Spirit and Nature. *Medicine Cards* speaks of the animals, their habits, their gifts, and offers suggestions to what they might mean for us. It encourages us to study each animal, learn more for ourselves, expand the teachings the animal offers us. I carried this gift into my life and cherish it still. Since then another book, *Animal-Speak* by Ted Andrews, has given me similar information for a wider range of animals, birds, insects and reptiles.

In this way a door opened for Nature to enter my life and guide me. Opening my eyes to Nature in this new way also helped me to discover more of the magic in Nature, simply through paying more attention. Both these opportunities are open to each and every one of us, wherever we may live. Acknowledge the tree that is closest to you. Begin a new relationship with it. Touch it, sense its energy and thank it for its presence.

Meanwhile, I was moving from book-learning to tools I could apply to my life. I was poised for a new year and a shift in the pace.

Part II   1989

4
New Tools in Play

NEW YEAR'S RESOLUTIONS: use the Animal Medicine cards daily and record my dreams.

At first, as usual, I attacked the cards in a flood of enthusiasm. Who says Badger is not a basic part of me? The subtitle of Badger in *Animal Medicine* is "aggressiveness." That was I, wasn't it?

Well maybe badger's not so bad after all.

On January 2, 1989, I started drawing a card a day. The first was Hummingbird, subtitled "joy." That night I dreamt that I was looking at someone's slides. One was not clear until I noticed the shimmering of a hummingbird. It moved in the slide, kept catching the light as only a hummer can do. I put my thumb on the slide to show someone else where it was. I saw its bill protrude out of the slide, a long, partly red bill. Joy at seeing it, both during the dream and on waking. Birder that I am, I added in parentheses in the journal "probably Rivoli's or magnificent hummingbird." Magnificent it was, no doubt of that. My heart was light yet full all day, reinforced by reading one of Mary Summer Rain's books and coming on a passage in which she, too, watched a hummingbird with joy.

Next day I drew Owl and noted that Owl is deception of yourself or another. My *Animal Medicine* bible said: "The message is to befriend the darkness inside of yourself. Look deeply and the bright light of dawn will illuminate you." (p.122) That night in a dream, I was watching a baby boy coming on his back towards me through fairly shallow water. No fear on the part of the child as he laughed, splashed and kicked. I reached out to the child. While I could not fully interpret the dream, it seemed linked to the message of Owl, somehow bringing to the surface something hidden deep within me, a fearless, happy child I don't remember but must have been and to whom I was now reaching out.

By mid-week it was clear that I, with Turtle medicine, working best with the slow pace of Turtle, couldn't keep up to a card a day. I wanted time to see what the message might be and try to apply it. I was responding through dreams but how was I to bring Hummingbird into my life? How could I go about that in just one day? I opted right then for a card a week throughout that year, sorry to have cut off Hummer at only one day!

This was not the only way that I used the cards in the course of the year. As we proceed, you'll see how they influence me more and more as I move along my path. Are you getting interested in this book, *Medicine Cards*? If so, why not treat yourself, open this door for yourself.

Dreams. "Some of them are important," Kristine said. "Work in fifth dimension, the dream dimension: that can materialize into third dimension, this reality." This concept of different dimensions of reality was part of my new teachings.

Physical reality was all I thought there was. One of the other important dimensions is the dream dimension, labelled the fifth. Controlled dreaming, access to learning, access to travel. There are techniques that can help us to have some control of the subjects of our dreams and even our actions in them. "Keep a dream journal," Kristine said in the fall of '88. January 1, 1989 I began recording, in a bright lime green dream journal, not only my dreams but also the day-to-day events, since the dreams might reveal their meanings in that context. Where I could, I added my interpretations in parentheses.

January 1, no dreams recalled. January 2 the same. Then January 3, 3:45 a.m. the dream of Hummer. What a wonderful beginning for my dream journal.

Dream symbols. *How do I interpret my dreams? Can books help? Are there techniques?*

I didn't look, wanted to discover my own symbols in due course. Some dreams were related to the Animal Medicine card of the week. Barn owls, magnificent heart-shaped faces peering out at me, came in Owl's week.

On January 6, I cleared letters of past years from my computer, keeping only those I wrote to Sharon. That night I dreamt that Sharon was to be my guide on a route familiar to her. "Portal Way," she called it. Follow it and we couldn't get lost, an arch like the *Arc de Triomphe* at the end. One left turn to make but follow Portal Way.

What a lighthouse beacon that message was. *I've passed through some gateway and I'm clearly on my path. The left turn must be turning to intuition. And Sharon will continue to be with me to guide me.*

January 15. I dreamt of travelling and having a problem with a tire. I took the car to be fixed. A man with a beard in a white coat helped. In real life I drove to Lac Philippe to cross-country ski that day, fluffy fresh snow on the pines and cedars and very few people. Hard to beat that. I skied leisurely, gliding smoothly and easily through the new snow to the end of the lake. There a stream of open water played its tinkling melody to me. Several white-breasted nuthatches "yanked," a downy and a hairy woodpecker pecked, and chickadees "dee-dee-deed." Back to the car and spotted a nail in a tire. *Take it out or leave it in?*

I took it out and the air poured out like a spouting whale. *Now what?*

Quickly I got in and drove to the park entrance visitor centre. Two men, one a ski patroller in a white jacket, came to my rescue and changed the tire. Back home in Ottawa I went to Canadian Tire to get the tire repaired. Two of the workers had on white coats and one had a beard. Later that day as I wrote up my journal the relevance of the dream suddenly leapt to the fore, preview of the events of the day. A first for me, not since repeated in so clear a way.

One other dream, I'll note right now. On March 10th, on my way home from opening night of Ichebana International, a display of delicate Ichebana Japanese flower arrangements, I listened to Sharon's tape and the Chariots of Fire poured forth just as I reached my garage. Tears trickled down my cheeks as I listened. Came inside, smudged and asked Dolphin, my card for the week, to show me through whom Sharon would continue to talk with me. Oh me of little faith. That night I dreamt I was on a high promontory with water straight below. Something in the water. *My dolphin?* Twice an eagle flew by gracefully, very close. *Eagle. Sharon flies with eagle still.*

On waking my heart was overflowing with awe and pleasure. My journal doesn't signal the connection, jump with joy. I'd missed the link between my request and the dream. Seems so obvious now, worthy of note.

Calling in a dream, my first conscious request for a dream that was answered. Strange thing about this path. Big moments, sometimes not fully grasped as such at the time, or downplayed. *Couldn't be happening to me. It must be a fluke.*

You know that refrain too, don't you? Not just mine, I'm sure. Calling in. This tool can either be consciously asking for something or merely being receptive to messages that your spirit at some other level calls in for you.

It was a dream that I had called in then but it wasn't only dreams I was learning to call in. Late March I went back to Hillary's in Rockville, Maryland near the Potomac, saw Eagle on its nest and a young one barely big enough to see.

Next new step, or recognition of it, came down there. Twice as I followed a trail by the Potomac, I suddenly "knew" wood ducks were present. I didn't stop soon enough the first time, flushing three wood ducks close by. Carried on. Some time later, the same knowing came upon me. I halted this time, eyes alert for movement, and immediately saw a wood duck dead ahead. Then three more appeared 8 - 10 feet away, not flushed this time. I drank in their beauty. They are just like hummers in disguise for me.

The next morning, driving back from a Potomac outing, I suddenly thought of Opossum, one of my totem animals, and wondered if I'd see one here in possum land. Turned a corner, saw a road kill and stopped. *Not a squirrel. Could it be a possum?*

Needed confirmation from someone else. Yes it was. "Often found as road kills here," he said. Was I impressed. It made me look at this event and the wood duck sightings in a new light.

First of all, with the wood ducks, I had experienced using my intuition or sixth sense, allowing being in tune with Nature to bring me close views of shy birds. It had happened before but I'd written it down to coincidence. **Now I saw the need to acknowledge that more than coincidence was at play.** I was in tune with my environment and open to sense what was there. More than that in the case of the opossum. Just following my birding outing, still in tune with Nature, I had thought of opossums. Calling one in? Or synchronicity, an occurrence not there by chance? I "knew" in that moment it wasn't chance, not aware of the term "synchronicity" then and certainly not ready to see I might have had a hand at some level in calling it in. Here was another opportunity falling closely on the others that helped me grasp that much more is possible than my belief systems had ever imagined. At very least, I was ever so impressed by that power so much greater than I, whom by then I was calling Great Spirit.

So two new tools were added to my spiritual tool kit. I was learning that dreams could have meaning and that I could call in dreams on particular topics of importance to me. I was also discovering that my inner knowing or intuition could guide me to connect more fully with Nature if I paid more attention to my internal cues. Not only that, such an awareness could aid me in spotting synchronicity, enabling it to bring new meaning and opportunities into my life.

Do you give free rein to your intuition or do you tend to stifle yours as I had done? Why not start looking for it more often, encourage it to emerge? If there is something concerning you deeply right now, before falling asleep ask for a dream to help guide you.

The next turning points came in May. Lynne, a friend of Kristine's and fellow apprentice of Swiftdeer's, ran a workshop entitled "Animal Communication" and, of course, I had to go. If that wasn't enough, Lynne and Kristine were running what they called a Vision Quest weekend on Manitoulin Island later in May. I registered.

4

Animal Communication Workshop

MAY 5, 1989, my last day as a Parole Board member. I was retiring early, leaving a government job that relied heavily on reason and facts. No regret, time to go, but I was leaving that security for what? Well, I wasn't worried about money. Between my own savings and the estate that my mother had left to me at her death, I was financially secure for at least a year. (In fact it turns out I still haven't returned to full-time work.) But employment had also represented purpose in my life. So far I'd attended some classes, read books, attended one workshop and gained some new insights. Time for new directions, new purpose.

It was a day of endings and beginnings all in one. That evening I began a new venture, Lynne's workshop entitled "Animal Communication." I left work, came home, changed, headed off to Lynne's in the Gatineau for a Friday evening, all day Saturday workshop. Two of us attended. Suited me fine. Lynne and Louise planned to fast, fluids only, and I joined in. Never tried that before. Smudging, teachings, imaging, that was the evening fare.

Saturday morning, sunny, cool. Our turn to work. We are to seek guidance from Lynne's four horses, two burros, three dogs and all of nature. Theme: ask them to teach us of our negative attachments such as being overly drawn to chocolate or to hoarding things. Two hours or more we have to wander, ask, seek answers. I set off focused on seeking my attachments, left out the "negative." So I see it now, realize it was my pattern. I found it hard to concentrate on negatives. *What negatives? Mine? Who, me?* I shied away from that. Much safer to generalize than look at just me.

The gentle breeze is cool on my cheeks. I cross the road, visit the horses, note the birds, stroll down the road. Back for a break part way. Take a flower essence, tincture drops under my tongue that are cool and sting from the alcohol base. (This was new for me. It was supposed in some subtle way to help us be open.) I encounter Jenny, the mother burro, and on and on. As I proceed, I record my notes, orderly, capturing each and every turn I and the morning and Nature take.

We three meet, sit down, sip mandarin orange herbal tea, with its hint of cloves. In turn we speak of what we wrote. It's then I hear the task "<u>my negative</u> attachments." Too late now. I tense, seek vindication. We search a dictionary. Attachment: "thing attached." Attach: "fasten (thing *to* another), join oneself (*to* person, company, expedition)." No judgment there, not all negative. Some of mine out there, not related directly to me and yet reflections of how I view attachment, how it touches me. I read my list, presented in the order and the context of the day. My interpretations at the time are in italics.

1. A pair of cowbirds flew in and landed on the telephone wires above me. The second had barely landed before the first took off again and the second followed. I sensed reluctance on the part of the second bird to take off again so immediately: *attachment can curtail independent choice and timing of action.*
2. I approached Chetan and Ablaysa (two of the horses). What struck me was how tied up in knots their manes were: *too much attachment to anything can tie you up in knots.*
3. A pair of tree swallows darted around the field in a lengthy courtship chase: *a free flying, care-free display of the joys inherent in the attachment of courtship.*
4. In the still early morning, I was halted by the spell-binding exquisiteness of water droplets on the needles of a pine tree. They offered a brief moment of sheer beauty before passing on, providing sustenance below: *the beauty in attachments needs to be appreciated in the moment, for the moment may not be enduring.*
5. A small moss with a red flower was attached to a stick: *sharing strength can bring life to others.*
6. The two burros and the two puppies and I were all close together. The young burro started exploring the puppies and Max, one of the puppies, got between my legs and, from there, started exploring the burros: *attachment and closeness allow more courage to explore.*
7. The horses carried on munching their hay and seemed to entirely ignore me: *food is a more basic need than attachment and communication.*
8. Some of Raven's (horse) winter hair was hanging loosely, ready to fall off completely: *when you no longer need something, let go of it.*
9. A flock of blue jays flew in. After a brief stop all but one headed off in one direction and shortly after the last departed in a different direction: *while there is attachment to and within a group, there is always a member that wants to do its own thing, and that's O.K.*
10. As I attempted to write my notes, one of the horses approached closer. I stiffened and drew my notes in to me: *others interested in my writing can frighten me and make me stop writing.*
11. I went over to check out the bluebird box but there was no sign of its occupants. As soon as I backed off to a reasonable distance, both landed on the box: *attachment brings out a need to check the safety of things important to you.*
12. Even though I was outside the fence, the horses attempted to put their faces through and make contact: *don't let barriers block communication, they can be overcome.*
13. More attention from the horses as I was writing my notes: *others want to share my thoughts and what I write.*
14. A snipe went into its courtship display overhead: *there is a time, place and way to let others know of your attachment to someone.*
15. Immediately after taking the flower essence, I had the most emotionally powerful message. Jenny, the burro, was near me and came so close she nearly knocked me over. I wanted to back off from such closeness but then found that I did not need or want to do so: *attachment can be safe and feel good.*
16. The young burro was still frightened of me and moved to the other side of Jenny, clinging close. Jenny gave her a nip to force her to move off: *when you're still too scared for new attachments, a good mother won't let you depend too much on old ones.*
17. A small spring stream of water was gently flowing on: *change is ongoing, a factor in any attachment.*
18. The horses were munching on their hay with sporadic brief pauses: *attachment is something to "chew" over and examine from time to time.*

19. As I watched the horses, one of them snorted: *in all attachments there is a need to breathe out, with the freeing up that that entails.*
20. The horses were looking for a goody from me and I had nothing to offer: *attachment entails giving and sometimes you have to accept that there are demands that you are unable to meet.*
21. The horses wanted attention even though I was trying to write my notes: *attachment requires paying attention even if it interrupts what you are doing.*
22. All of a sudden, Max appeared from nowhere: *attachments reappear when you least expect them.*

In the afternoon, we worked with the horses, leading them on a halter around the field, riding one of them bareback and visiting two calves in a neighbouring field. Finally, to end the day, Lynne had us build our Medicine Wheel, by reflecting on what we had learned and where it belonged on the wheel. Once again I jotted down my images and thoughts. While I didn't spot teachings for all the wheel directions, the approach brought me a new way to view the whole. Here is what I wrote:

> Trust issues represent the South. I had a lot of reaction to the closeness of the animals. With the burro, I initially feared closeness and yet enjoyed it when it happened. With the horses, I was surprised at how close they wanted to come when I was leading them. I was very aware of my need for space and developed a recognition and respect for their power that necessitated leaving room for their flight reaction if surprised. The most important trust teaching, however, was that messages would not only come from the animals, but that I could focus the topic of those messages.
>
> The touch experiences of the West that came to mind were the velvety softness of the horses' noses, the burro almost knocking me over, the floppiness of the burro's ears, the silkiness and power of the horses' necks.
>
> Rules and laws and philosophies and beliefs (NW and North) ran together for me. I learned that the friendliness of a horse doesn't change its need for space. From the calf I learned that a quiet, gentle approach doesn't necessarily eliminate the instinct of a young male to charge. From leading the horse, it became evident that left turns are not always more difficult than right turns!
>
> Choreography of energy (NE) lessons included my recognition that when I could feel my inner fibres, my whole being, directing the way the horse was to turn, the results were better. My energy was clearer when I was under a certain degree of pressure, self-imposed when the horse was resisting me. Importantly, I discovered that I could be open and receive messages where I had selected the topic through intent.
>
> In the East I was aware of my sense of oneness with the young animals, particularly. Their hesitant attempts at exploration and the self concept message (SE) seemed to be that I still remain more leery of closeness than I realized but enjoyed it when I allowed it to occur.

The workshop came to a close but its teachings had just begun. I had had my first experience at putting a Medicine Wheel into practice. Native Americans of all tribes make use of Medicine Wheels. A circle represents the seasons, the four directions, and even the cycle of life as we spring from the womb and return to the womb of Mother Earth. Meanings associated with the various directions on the wheel vary from tribe

POWERS OF THE FOUR DIRECTIONS

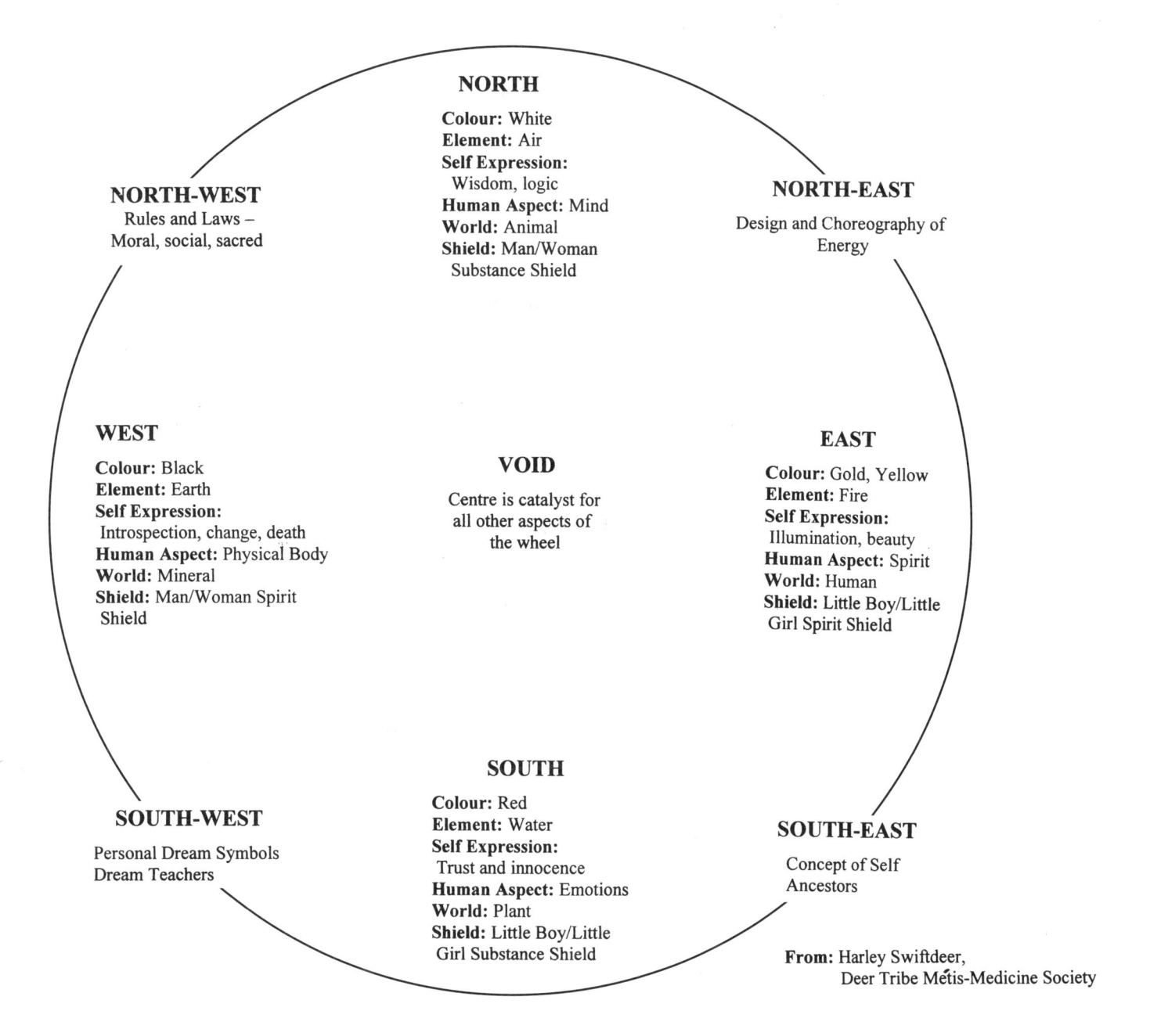

NORTH
- **Colour:** White
- **Element:** Air
- **Self Expression:** Wisdom, logic
- **Human Aspect:** Mind
- **World:** Animal
- **Shield:** Man/Woman Substance Shield

NORTH-WEST
Rules and Laws – Moral, social, sacred

NORTH-EAST
Design and Choreography of Energy

WEST
- **Colour:** Black
- **Element:** Earth
- **Self Expression:** Introspection, change, death
- **Human Aspect:** Physical Body
- **World:** Mineral
- **Shield:** Man/Woman Spirit Shield

VOID
Centre is catalyst for all other aspects of the wheel

EAST
- **Colour:** Gold, Yellow
- **Element:** Fire
- **Self Expression:** Illumination, beauty
- **Human Aspect:** Spirit
- **World:** Human
- **Shield:** Little Boy/Little Girl Spirit Shield

SOUTH-WEST
Personal Dream Symbols
Dream Teachers

SOUTH
- **Colour:** Red
- **Element:** Water
- **Self Expression:** Trust and innocence
- **Human Aspect:** Emotions
- **World:** Plant
- **Shield:** Little Boy/Little Girl Substance Shield

SOUTH-EAST
Concept of Self
Ancestors

From: Harley Swiftdeer, Deer Tribe Métis-Medicine Society

NATURE SPEAKS: I LISTEN

to tribe. Since my earliest teachers were apprentices of the Métis, Swiftdeer, the Medicine Wheel of his teachings has guided the symbols I still use on the wheel. The workshop and many ceremonies to follow rely on this wheel. The illustration shows you a wheel with some of the symbols associated with the various directions.

The shields need explaining. Each of us carries within us four beings in one. As adults we manifest to the world our adult substance shield. This is how we present ourselves in our most mature way in the physical world. Hidden, or not so well hidden within us, is our little child substance shield, which inevitably still carries some wounds and scars from childhood. These pop out in our not-so-mature actions and speech. Each of these shields corresponds to our sex, male or female. We also hold within us two other shields that are of the opposite sex to the two substance shields. So I, for example, have a little boy spirit shield, a playful, adventurous spirit child who is able to do anything. This is the child who was laughing, splashing and kicking in my early January dream. The other, also spirit rather than the substance of this physical life, is my male spirit shield, or Dream Warrior. This is my wise adult warrior being and perfect mate.

The substance shields are part of this physical reality, which Swiftdeer labels third dimension while the spirit shields belong to the spirit and dream reality, which he calls the fifth dimension.

Many of the Swiftdeer ceremonies aim to help us heal the wounded child substance shield as well as to come more in touch with the spirit shields. In this way we learn to bring our adult substance shield into better balance or centredness. Medicine Wheel teachings in general start with the premise that we begin our life at one place on the wheel, determined by our date of birth. In the course of our lives we must learn the lessons of all directions. Doing so brings us closer and closer to true balance and the centre of the wheel. We journey into the various directions numerous times, the lessons of some directions being harder for one individual than another. And there is always more to learn as we work our way round the wheel again and again, lessons learned bringing us more and more to the centre.

With the symbols available on the wheel, I had another tool, like the Animal Medicine cards, through which I could learn and seek guidance.

In addition and most important of all, I had now discovered during this workshop that I could set a focus, such as we had done, and then go out into Nature and ask for guidance and insights. Such a simple, powerful tool that Spirit and Nature offer us. Many more examples will come as my journey continues and it is something you may like to try yourself.

Now on to the Manitoulin Island adventure.

6

White-throated Sparrow

EARLY MAY. I was champing at the bit, eager for spring to burst forth. Warblers with their joyous spring songs were just coming back. The ever so soft green needles of the larches were just about to emerge. The surge of new growth in the offing. And here I was truly launching in to my new spiritual growth.

The Manitoulin Island weekend workshop with Lynne and Kristine was just a couple of weeks away. An overnight Vision Quest was billed as the highlight; reaching out to Great Spirit, asking for vision. I was seeking vision and guidance.

Are visions possible? Part of me believed they were.

But am I ready? Me, worthy of a vision? Not me, but I want it so much, want connection, want purpose and direction. How do I get ready? This isn't just a fun weekend somewhere I've never been. This is my spiritual quest, what quitting my job was all about. Will anything happen? Am I really on the right track? . . . But even if I fail, it will be an adventure just to go there.

I had a channeling with Kristine. The previous fall channeling was not yet within my realm of possible realities. I'd been with her in a group, saw her touch chords with those around. She caught my interest, opened me a crack, chipped at my disbelief, enough to rouse my interest. By May I was more open, still skeptical, but not wanting to miss an opportunity for more new learning. My venturing side took over and I arranged for a personal session. Sue, my closest friend, came along to listen, to discuss it afterwards, adding her helpful insights.

The session was taped. A brief prayer by Lynne, there to assist Kristine, and then Kristine closed her eyes and went into a trance. She spoke with the voice of a different person as she answered my questions. Part way through the session, I asked how to prepare for the Manitoulin Island workshop. Was there anything special for me to do? There most certainly was. Laughing Eagle was my name and the name of a Medicine man in the Spirit world, the voice explained. I was to do a ceremony to gain the power of the Bird Tribe. I would need a beaver staff to which I would attach feathers: Eagle, Owl, Heron and Crow. Detailed ceremony provided, all the steps outlined, exactly what to do and ask.

Whatever lingering doubts I still had about channeling, I certainly took this ceremony, my own special ceremony, seriously. Besides, now there were preparations to which I could turn. Restlessness and mind chatter dissipated. I had something concrete for Taurus to do. At Lac Philippe I found the staff, a three-foot-long stick neatly stripped of its bark by a beaver. I ran my hand over its whiteness, much of it so smooth, but the beaver's teeth had etched the wood at either end, and removed all the twigs and smaller branches. *How appropriate to have a stick from Beaver, the animal Kristine says sits on the same direction as I on the Medicine Wheel.*

Crow feather, owl feathers, those I had. No eagle feather, no heron feather but extra crow or other feathers could stand in.

I prepared notes for what to do and laminated them in case of rain. My busyness held my eager anticipation in check. There was a chunk of anxiety, too, that I tried to hide. Hand in hand: excitement of adventure, fear of the unknown and doubt whether I was ready and worthy.

The weekend arrived. The first evening brought introductions, teachings and, finally, instructions for a Flowering Tree ceremony that we were to carry out first thing the following morning. This ceremony would help us prepare for the Vision Quest that night.

I was nervous all right, and my mind was racing a four-minute mile. My experiences with ceremony up until then had not produced much. Could this be different? I ran over what I now knew. The directions are important. The direction of the flight of birds, what appears and where, colour, and numbers. Anything and everything can be significant. So I had my notebook and pen, ready to take notes of all that happened. That comforted me: I could do that.

We were to find a tree to which we felt drawn. The ceremony would take place at its base.

6:30 a.m. I walk along a path beside the water, searching for my tree. I concentrate on my search for the tree, try to ignore the uneasiness in my tummy and the back of my mind about how much the instructions for the ceremony focus on my looking at myself. As I approach the area where I select my tree, a rabbit scampers off. Fear is a characteristic of Rabbit in *Animal Medicine*. I beg Rabbit to take mine away.

I choose a birch with three trunks merged into one. The tree is close to the edge of the escarpment, with Lake Huron in the background and some distance below. The water laps softly on the rocks below and the gentle breeze rustles the birch tree leaves in welcome. I hardly notice since, at this point, I realize that I have forgotten to bring tobacco. I want to kick myself. All I have are a few grains in a special pouch I have with me. So the opening tobacco offering becomes the miniscule amount of tobacco, and water from my water container. In view of the day's inclement weather, the latter is bringing coals to Newcastle.

This is my first big ceremony. I re-read the instructions. Each feels crucial. My throat goes dry. The focus is squarely on me. I squirm like a worm on a hook. *This is hard.* I ignore my body reactions, take refuge in the safety of my mind. I talk to myself. *This isn't the main ceremony. Answer the questions as best I can and take notes of what's happening around me. That's my focus. Look for the messages out there. Besides, change is what this is about. Go for it.*

At 7:00 a.m. I'm ready and a crow, an omen of change, flies in from the West, the direction of change, and goes off to the Southwest, the place of the dream. A flicker, symbol of beauty and creativity, calls from the North. I'm taking notes already. *But let's face it. I've got to turn to the questions.*

I start with the South and sit with my back to the birch in an uncomfortable position. Inadvertently I mirror part of the answer to the first question, which is "What am I leaving behind and how am I feeling about it?"

My brow furrowed, I mull this over and start a list:
- security of a career: scared and yet a sense of completion and a need for change and a new purpose;

- the known: scared and excited;
- reputation: freeing me, but how much did I rely on it for defining myself?;
- full sense of control of my life in respect to habits, routines.

My retreat into mental analysis is suddenly jolted by a sound like galloping hooves. The answer to how I feel about what I have left behind surges through me. The fear of the unknown grabs my stomach. I quickly turn to see what is there. Nothing. But I miss the point, don't see the connection right then.

A bird appears, circling with an unusual flight. I can't identify it or resist going for my binoculars in my backpack. It is too late to identify the bird but not too late to recognize this less threatening message. *Not everything has to change. Some parts of my habits and routines carry forward in the same or slightly different ways.* My shoulders relax like a boiling kettle unplugged, and a sense of calm comes over me. I'm able to add to my list.

- reliance almost exclusively on 3rd dimension and reason: a sense of groping and needing practice in the new techniques and approach.

Enough on this question. I discover that half an hour has already passed.

I move on to a position facing North and the North question, "What are my attachments to routines, cycles, habits, the familiar and the known?"

My list becomes very practical:

- physical needs: lots of sleep, being warm, regular meal times;
- psychological needs: to be out in nature regularly, to see beauty, to feel tranquillity;
- not looking at this question. I check my watch and only seven minutes have gone by. So I sigh and persevere.
- not voice opinions until I feel confident in them;
- a considerable degree of order and structure, things in their place, timeliness;
- non-openness about sharing my hesitations or what I perceive as weaknesses.

By 7:45 my back nags at me and I've had enough of the South question. I stand and lean against the dead third of the tree and my sore lower back is against a part of the tree that is spongy and flexible. *Comfort!*

I work my way through the West question and on to the East, "What am I doing to limit my creativity?" I now sit facing Lake Huron. The sun's reflections on the water are framed by branches of my tree for a picture that satisfies the photographer in me.

- want too much structure? But can flow with instinct framing things in ways I know

Finally I move away from simply lists. I focus on the reflections in the water. They suggest a tight collar on the throat - *not giving voice to my creativity.* In time, the collar I see in the water loosens completely and expands, becomes more golden and sparkling. I think about the image.

Perhaps the expression of my creativity can be by voice or words instead of music as suggested in Kristine's recent channeling.

Song sparrow appears and Loon calls from far off. *Well, yes, bird song is music to me.*

The next question is "Who am I? What is my dream warrior?" I hit my head when I stand. *I'm taller than I'm aware,* quickly downplayed by *but not really big by any means.* A cool breeze from the North brings a few goosebumps and its direction reminds me that I'm driven by mind and intellect.

I'm facing a sentinel cedar on the edge of the escarpment, with smaller trees near it. It's a loner group on the edge and near water. *That represents determination and tenacity.*

A very big fish jumps, like a small whale. Later I looked up Whale:

"Whale medicine teaches us to use the sounds and frequencies that balance our emotional bodies and heal our physical forms. . .Before the advent of speech. . .the language that was understood was the sounds of Great Spirit's other creatures, the animals.

"You are being asked. . .to allow yourself to be sung to by those who have the original language. We are the only creatures who do not have our own unique cry or call. Find yours." (p.202)

My attention comes back to the cedar. *The cedar also represents that I am able to take my own stand, provide shelter, support and a model for others, voicing spiritual truths, guided by feathered songsters in particular . . . That sounds pretentious.*

The wind is gaining momentum, *I shall become stronger in time. My cedar is weathered on the North and East but growing well in the South of emotion and West of change. That's more like it.*

I proceed to the North-East and the question, "How does my dream warrior act in 3rd dimension and in 5th?"

- 3rd dimension: Takes careful observations; gentleness, patience, objective. Looks for and is open to symbols in Nature, is spiritually aware and has a solid base of sacred rules and laws. The wind is blowing in my face. *My reason blows forcefully.*

- 5th dimension: Calls in nature symbols and guides. Great Blue Heron flies to me from this direction and turns off to the South. The wind direction has changed more to from the South-East. I made no interpretation at the time but it hit me ever so forcefully as I wrote this years later. Heron is reflective, the writer, according to Kristine. Writing is an important way that I access 5th dimension but I didn't know it then. South-East is the position of self concept and identity. So it heralded the coming of writing as part of my path.

At 8:42 I proceed to the North-West, "Ask yourself about your dream(where, who, when, what and why."

- Why? To grow taller, more centred and more comfortable. I note I have a better seat here.

- Where? A little inland, first trees are mostly coniferous, including larch, spruce and cedar. Gulls calling and flying by. *So not far from water.*

- When? Four killdeer give voice while flying over in one complete circle, with me in the South-West of its circle. *Four years?*

Move at 9:10 to the South-West and the last instruction, "Step into dreaming state and develop a symbol that you use for power."

Hear White-throated Sparrow with its "Yes, I'm right here" call and then another more persistent and louder.

For my symbols, I draw a bare-branched dead tree and a young green one coming into leaf, a five-sided shape and the notes of the calls of the two white-throated sparrows. The trees represent letting go of the old, no longer needed parts of the past, to make room for the growth of a young, healthy tree. A five-sided shape is out of the ordinary. Unbeknownst to me at the time, the number five is associated with positive qualities of versatility, change and activity. And the bird calls? Well, they just feel good and are what I heard as I sought out my symbols.

Blue Jay calls as I leave. I thank it, recognize it as a symbol of connection to Spirit. I feel calm and satisfied, no tummy nervousness as I had at the start. I've done what was asked, even using what

Nature has brought me as symbols a number of times. I have my notes. I don't know what all of it means right now but that is O.K., not nagging at me.

The only tension in my body now is because I'm chilled. I put my hands in my pockets to warm them. My pace is much quicker than when I arrived. The cold wind is in my face and I bend my head and lean forward to protect myself as best I can. Time for a hot drink, but no meal. We are fasting today. So far I'm not at all hungry.

More teachings, and a visit to Dreamers' Rock, a nearby sacred site that was, and is, used by natives as a site for Vision Quests lay ahead in the afternoon. All this was leading up to the highlight of the weekend, our own overnight search for a vision.

7

Laughing Eagle

MY OVERNIGHT Vision Quest ceremony is to include the special Bird Tribe ceremony from the May channeling as well as the ceremony we have been given here. I have my feathers and the beaver staff for the Bird Tribe ceremony and I have gone over the steps many times in advance.

Well before dark, we are sent out to find our circles. I walk purposefully along the dirt road towards the point. My body is tense. My shoulders, in particular, are as knotted as the mane of Lynne's horse. My mind is in overdrive. *I so badly want this to go well. What can I do to help make it go well? I want a spot not completely in the open but fairly close to the road to ensure that it won't be difficult to find in the dark. Since I'll be sitting there for a number of hours, I'd better consider comfort as well.*

An area sheltered by clumps of cedar catches my attention. The ground cover is low-lying juniper, spongy underfoot. On my way in, I pick up a couple of the eight stones I'll require for placement in the cardinal directions, two for each direction. *Even whitish stones will be hard to find in the dark.*

Tension slips away like a snake as I set to work. I search for sticks that will be easier to locate to mount with the stones. I add an additional stone in the centre of the circle. I even use my compass to establish where to place my four pairs of stones. Finally, satisfied with my preparations, I note a cluster of large stones at the edge of the road that mark where I am to turn off for my circle.

My boots are now wet through and my feet are damp. *Thermal socks and rubber boots will be the footwear of preference. Will I be able to keep warm? Will I get really hungry?*

So far, I'm still not hungry. This surprises me: it can't last. Anxiety and mind in overdrive take off in these new directions.

By 11:30 p.m., we complete an indoor snake dance ceremony, for which we have painted our faces and hands. It is time to set off. I'm not scared about being out overnight: I've done enough camping to be comfortable out on my own. My heart is beating faster with excitement but there's tightness in my chest too. I'm still anxious about doing it "right" so that maybe, just maybe, I'll get results.

I remember to obtain cigarette papers for the smoking part of the ceremony, don my backpack, with all the necessary pouches and items for the ceremonies inside, along with emergency rations if I can't make it through the fasting period. The instructions for the ceremonies are in the pocket of my jacket, the newest instructions not covered in plastic. I grip my large flashlight. A tiny one for reading is in my pocket.

Although partially overcast, it is the night of a full moon, and not nearly as dark as I anticipated. I locate my turnoff markers with no difficulty. I come upon some of the rocks of my circle. *Which ones are they?* I'm confused over the stone in the centre versus those in the four directions. My flashlight picks up tall pale coloured grasses better than my dark sticks. *How can I be bungling this before I even get started?*

Desperation and panic set in. The harder I try, the more confused I get. I'm rattled and tense, like a construction worker drilling concrete. I even resort to using my compass. Who knows how much time I took just getting my bearings!

Finally my frantic activity comes to a close and I think I'm ready. About to start the opening prayer, I suddenly remember it is important to spread some of my blue cornmeal around the edge of the circle for protection first. With difficulty I trace my way around my newly constituted, dubiously shaped "circle." It starts to drizzle. *Oh no, I don't need this too.*

In order to cope I prepare all the items for commencing the ceremonies, especially the cigarette that I'll smoke. Rolling the cigarette in the dark is a challenge for a non-smoker, but I take my time and patiently prepare it. I place it carefully back in the top of the tobacco pouch. I cover the backpack, beaver stick and feathers with my pancho, since the jacket I'm wearing is also rainproof.

Time to start again. There is an initial prayer, as well as a banishing ceremony in which we call on all negative energies to stay out of our circles. *Do I begin with the banishing ceremony or the prayer? Why didn't I think of this before now?*

I sigh and settle for banishing before inviting guests to my circle. Both require smoking at the conclusion. *Do I do that once or twice?* The non-smoker opts for once, after concluding the prayer. Out comes my tiny flashlight to make absolutely sure I banish everything that needs banishing as per my plastic covered instructions. *Foresight paid off in that respect!*

I then continue on with a thorough and satisfying prayer of welcoming everyone into my circle. Tension is easing out of me like sand through a fine sieve. Time for the smoking to round it out. Over to the pancho and a search for the tobacco pouch. It I find, but the rolled cigarette has tired of the waiting and is nowhere in sight. The calming effect of voicing my prayer abruptly departs. I take another of the papers and try again, more hurriedly. There is more tobacco in my mouth than in the cigarette but finally I have what I grudgingly accept as the semblance of a cigarette. I smugly take out my safety matches. Lots of sparks, but only once or twice do I get a match lit. But there's no way I can coordinate lighting it, and getting the cigarette to it before it goes out. *Will nothing go right?* I struggle and then sigh deeply and give up, making it clear to Great Spirit and the guests that at least the intent is there.

On to the Bird Tribe ceremony. It, too, is already somewhat bungled because I'm not prepared to take my feathers to the cardinal points and leave them out in the rain, as the drizzle gains momentum. So they stay in the circle centre, facing their appropriate directions.

I call in some more special invitees for my ceremony and offer more corn meal in keeping with my ceremony notes. By this time my well-rehearsed ceremony was far from being at my finger tips and my notes are crucial!

I move to the South and ask for my dream from the place of the Dream Warrior. I then sit on my still rolled up, plastic-covered foam and wait for the response, like a heron poised before striking. I'm reasonably comfortable in spite of the rain. Nothing happens. Little wonder, given how wound up I am from all my struggle to get properly started! *How long do I wait? What if I don't get anything?*

Time passes as I anxiously wait, nervously wringing my hands to warm them. Then I recall that in the channeling I was told not to worry if I did not recall the dream for it would come back to me in waves of memory in the waking state.

So I proceed to the North and call on Laughing Eagle, asking for my sacred bird name so that I can speak to this teacher and ask him for guidance to clarify my dream. I sit again on my foam, even more uncertain of how long to wait for answers in the rain. *This one is really important. If I don't have results, how do I carry on when some of the steps that follow are dependent on them?*

My leather gloves are wet now to my cold fingers within. My toes are cold too. Resignation or discomfort or both step in. It occurs to me that maybe I'll have more success in the dream state in any event. Relief. The thought gives me permission to speed up the process and I carry on to the East.

The East comes easier. My notes say I am to seek guidance about the best posture for my meditation, see the image of Crane's dance and get my body in rhythm with the sound and movement of the bird. Without waiting for the guidance on posture, I leap to the image, vivid for me, having seen cranes dance in Australia. I join the movement, bobbing my neck, flapping my wings and hopping. Now on to the West. *How on earth does one speak to the ancestors of the West about the vision that I haven't yet seen?!*

That escapes me and, resigning myself again to failure, my visit to the West is brief. I return to the centre, tie my feathers to the beaver staff and complete the ceremony in the South with my oath to the ancestors to carry on walking the path and asking for guidance in the path of beauty for all women. Deep disappointment envelopes me and my shoulders droop like a wilted flower, but I've done all I can.

Time for the second ceremony. In this ceremony I'm to call on Great Spirit to help me find my spirit guide, an ancestor who loves me, who will help me see my vision. I presume that this will be Laughing Eagle once again. I'm to ask the wind to carry the message of my intent out to the universe and bring back the answer. I'm to cry from the heart to all four directions, representing my death song and call on loved ones, spirits of friends and teachers to gather round and witness me dying. At least that was what is in my notes. It's too wet to do anything but remember as best I can.

I huddle under my pancho and, if other things are to stay more or less dry, this means that I'll stay put in the centre of the circle and do the ceremony from there. My pancho has been inside out. So when I put it over me its wetness joins the wetness of my jacket. Cold water drips down my neck like a leaky faucet, but otherwise I'm dry underneath. By now the leather gloves I'm wearing are soaked right through. *No one ever said dying is painless.* I put my head on the foam and lie there on my spongy juniper death bed for the ceremony.

I forget to call on the wind to carry off my message until it suddenly comes up strong in the nearby cedars. I'm surprised that it is perfectly calm where I am, only ten feet away. I also forget to cry out to each direction and merely talk quietly to them. I forget to call in the spirits of friends and loved ones and get on with my death accompanied by all those who remained from the first ceremony. By now the rain has stopped. I lie there, somewhere along the line having cast off the frenzied effort to "do things properly." I'm tranquil and reasonably comfortable. Rigor mortis hasn't set in. As I lie there I begin to enjoy the stars and the clouds rushing by up there. *If this is dying, it isn't so bad.*

I'm not to call for my vision until close to dawn, still a long way off. It is now partially clear. The moon pokes through from time to time, and the occasional bird gives a phrase of song, as though in mistaken belief that dawn is on the way, but I know better.

To the South where Grandmother Moon is making her odd appearance and the clouds scuttle by at a fast clip, it is as though there is an outdoor movie screen with a science fiction movie in progress. I watch, fascinated. A very clear bright number 7 is inscribed by clouds and I appreciate the reminder that dream symbols are a possible entry for me to my vision. But I'm far too wide awake to sleep. The cedars protect me from some of the wind. I finally unroll the foam to have part of it under me, the rest wrapped cocoon-like back over me. Fortunately the wind is not blowing as hard at ground level as on my movie screen. I dig into my pack for the woolen liners to my leather gloves and make an exchange. Too bad I haven't mended the holes in the thumbs. More stars break through to complement my movie screen. I finally look at my watch, to find that it is now three o'clock.

Somewhere between four and five o'clock, I allow myself to doze, resting on my side facing my movie screen. I awake to a single call of White-throated Sparrow, "Yes, I'm right here." I open my eyes and the clouds in my direct vision are clearly delineating the profile of the head of an Indian. Laughing Eagle is showing his presence. I gasp and stop breathing. I'm so awed it never occurs to me to pose my questions. I just watch, speechless, no thoughts, not even tears of joy. The clouds dissipate. Later as I doze on my opposite side, White-throated Sparrow again calls once. I open my eyes to the profile of the head, again clearly etched in my direct field of vision. It's too much for me to take in.

As the sky lightens, I sit up, watch and wait. False dawn has arrived. One of the other participants passes by while I glimpse another gather up her belongings from a nearby circle. Fox comes towards me, turning quickly once aware of my presence. Clouds over the eastern horizon, as well as trees, partially obscure my view of where the sun may appear. After the enormity of my Indian head clouds, there is no way that I'll leave early. I patiently continue to wait, fully relaxed now, and eventually decide it is time to make the final request that my vision be shown to me. The despair and desperation of the earlier hours are long gone. Now instead, hope and eager anticipation fill me, like a child waiting for Santa Claus.

A large rainbow arch of small fluffy clouds appears. The sky becomes a soft powder blue in the arch and the clouds are a mixture of white-gold with others of a soft gray. The beauty of day's arrival takes my breath away, brings tears to my eyes. This is my vision. It's the mural over the entrance way to the centre that I'm occasionally thinking that I may some day be meant to open. I'm learning so much that seems important to self-healing and spirituality. And so I'm beginning to consider the need for a centre where this kind of teaching and experiencing can flourish. I think about the name for the Centre, perhaps the Nagai Earthwalk Vision. . .I suddenly realize that Sharon's last name "Nagai" is not far off "*nagual*," the name for Carlos Casteneda's teachers, and I couldn't help thinking that grounded as Sharon was, she also reached the level of the "*nagual*" at times in her "knowing."

My quest is over. My head is spinning. My heart is hurting. I'm so overwhelmed and awed by it all. And cold. I gather my gear, slip into the shoulder straps of my back pack, and carefully make my way through the juniper bushes and back to the road. I walk slowly, absorbed in the wonder of all that has transpired. I return to our cabin for a welcome hot shower and drink. Oddly enough, I feel no hunger pangs and don't break my fast until breakfast is served a couple of hours later.

After breakfast, we gather to share with one another something that has happened from which we recognize a teaching for ourselves. I tell the tale of the complete and utter botching of my ceremonies by someone who relies on being organized and how much better I felt when I let go. I'm laughing so hard at times that I can hardly carry on with the story. Tears are even running down my cheeks and I have to wipe my eyes. A second teaching comes in the telling of the first. I have never laughed so hard at myself. And that feels great.

Powerful as all this was at the time, it was not until several days later that it dawned on me that one of the power symbols that I had chosen in the Flowering Tree ceremony was the song of White-throated Sparrow. Furthermore, Whale had admonished me to seek my own unique cry or call. White-throated Sparrow had brought me that tune. It remains a powerful Spirit Song that I still sing when I most need to centre myself.

The power of ceremony was truly brought home to me. How far I had come since my first Flowering Tree ceremony just eight months earlier. I now had my own spirit song and the beginnings of a personal vision of a teaching centre.

There was another big lesson embedded in those Manitoulin ceremonies. It was many years before I fully discovered and appreciated it. I had set out wanting to connect with Spirit in a big, striking way. That's how I thought it was supposed to happen. Well, I got my Indian head in the sky and it was glamorous. But what did it mean? I assumed it was Laughing Eagle but that didn't have any real impact on my life. It demonstrated forcefully, however, that there was some force out there far greater than I. That was what I thought I was searching for and I needed such evidence to build my trust. But the biggest gift I received that weekend came in the form of the small white-throated sparrow, which most of us don't even recognize. As a birder, it caught my attention, however, and offered its song as a huge gift, bringing me a personal way to tune in to the spiritual, not out there, but inside myself.

8

Candle

IT WAS SEVERAL MONTHS since my Vision Quest on Manitoulin Island. I felt more confident: I'd got an overnight ceremony under my belt already. It was back at Lynne's in the Gatineau.

We had found our circles during the afternoon. Lynne told me of rocks and a viewpoint close to the area I had in mind, across the valley. Much of the circle was the hard, solid rock of the pre-Cambrian shield. The large trunk and thick boughs of the white pine at the back of the circle gave me an impression of stockiness. I stroked its rough, shaggy bark and was surprised at its warmth. *Thank you, I feel welcomed and protected in your presence.* Its needles, abundantly covering the outcrop of rock, softened the surface and, over the years, had helped create thin pockets of soil here and there. It was more open than I had planned but its view of the valley and the sky, and the site itself, appealed to me and I prepared my circle.

The Night on the Mountain of Fear was the first of what are called Gateway Ceremonies in the Swiftdeer teachings. A night to face our fears, label them, go beyond them, let Nature speak to us, help us as we seek to know ourselves. Lynne gave us pages of written instructions for the ceremony.

"This was our chance to learn, have Nature teach us one way or another," Lynne had said. Told us of another on this path who had undertaken this ceremony. As soon as she started she had to poop. Couldn't leave her circle, didn't want to step in her poop in the dark, collected it up in a plastic bag, carried it with her all night. She was disappointed the next day. Nothing happened, nothing matched the stories others told. She took Lynne aside, poured forth her disappointment. Lynne asked what had happened, heard about carrying the poop all night and burst out laughing. "You got your message," she finally got out. "When are you going to stop carrying all your shit around with you?" Crude, blatant message, but powerful.

It is time to set off. *So no expectations, no Indian head*, I think to myself. I've read through the instructions. This sounds much harder than the previous Vision Quest. It is more like the Flowering Tree ceremony, focusing on examining ourselves, both the Light and the Dark, poking hard at the Dark. I prefer to avoid that part of me, hardly know it at all. I'm scared of it, don't want to admit what may be there, even ashamed in advance.

I trudge up the hill, the uneasy part of me fearing the unknown that looms overhead like a huge black cloud. My mind is racing. But it isn't just uneasiness. I'm partly eager for the adventure, still secretly hoping for an Indian head of some sort. It's dark but I have no problem finding the circle or knowing which stones are in what directions. *What a pleasant contrast to the beginning of my Manitoulin Island ceremony.*

Still, I want to do it just right, need to do it all, like it or not. But oh so long it is. Halfway through, the notes read "I'm picking up steam now." I add *Oh yeah?!*

Yet before this point I'd found my teacher. I had not recognized many of its messages, but note taker that I am, they were there later. I had touched in, seen my teacher while I was looking for my Light side, not the Dark. At that moment I had been striving to reach my Child Spirit Shield, the little boy within for whom there are no limitations, no fears, no dark mirrors.

Boy, did I want this badly. It sounded so positive. I wanted that buoyancy to envelop me, let me escape from the self doubt that hovered over me right then and so much of the time. My focus and intent were clear. I struggled, so anxious to feel my Child Spirit, not just imagine I was because I wanted it so badly. I wondered, *How on earth will I know? Will I discover the symbol that indicates I have done so?*

Time passed and so did the struggle. I somehow lost myself in the wait, even my shoulders reclined. I let go. Something inside of me shifted. My body and I felt on top of the world. As I realized that I was experiencing a glimmer of the world of my Child Spirit, my candle started to hold a strong, confident flame for the first time all night. *This must be the symbol.*

Up until then the candle had held my attention, mainly for sputtering or going out, never strong like this. So there it was, the candle, my message giver and teacher throughout the night, the candle mirroring me. Oh how it struggled to keep alight all night. I helped it along as best I could, sheltering it, relighting it, cupping it with my hand. But it struggled as I grappled with my Dark side, had as much trouble facing it as I was having to answer the questions laid out. At times it went out. Any old time? Oh no. Key moments linked with the questions asked. Meaning clearer later, thanks to time and my notes.

The first time is startlingly clear. I was coming up blank on my spiritual fears as a child. Blank, completely blank and the candle went out. No meaning to me then. Later, I saw it. My spiritual life went out as a child, snuffed out when my brother died, my hero, my protector, my teacher. He was 10, I was three. He was rushed away in an ambulance, siren blaring out distress. Jon died of a ruptured appendix–his life snuffed out, my spirituality snuffed out, too.

So my candle mirrored the Dark for me that night, but what I caught out there was its mirrors of the Light. First came this strong confident flame for the Child Spirit in me. Doubting Thomas though, I needed more magic than that, wanted another symbol to indicate that I had truly touched in to my Spirit Child. So just to be sure, I asked for a shooting star. As I raised my head, pondering in which direction I would request it, one descended directly in front of me. What more could I ask?

The night goes on, as does the ceremony. More struggle and then another chance to soar. The questions turn to what would happen if I accept myself completely, live what I say I believe in, let go of childish, immature behaviour, and am an impeccable warrior, the ideal me.

I gaze intently at my candle. It is in a position where a large buildup of wax is between me and the flame. Occasionally the wind, cool on my face, blows the flame within view beside the wax but mostly I view and drink in the extraordinarily beautiful inner glow of the flame. It answers the question as fully as anything could answer it. That glow is what I had touched and felt in my Child Spirit earlier. I warm inside and out as I watch it.

If that isn't enough, I next ask what I have to offer life and others and know enough to look to my candle. From my new direction it takes on a different mantle, new message. A priestess, hands in a praying position. *Can this possibly be me? Surely that's well beyond me. . .How wondrous that would be. Hands not only for writing, but for prayer as well.*

It is too much to accept and yet part of me resonates in harmony with it.

The final step of the ceremony entails looking at my circle as my circle of life, where I take my power, not give it away. I am to exit from the circle, not looking back, and re-enter my world.

It isn't yet dawn when I reach this step and I plan to stay until then. So I put out my candle. I open my foam and spread my pancho over me, using my backpack as a pillow. I am covered fairly well except for my face, which I want out for viewing the universe. Suddenly I become very aware of mosquitoes. They are persistent. I swat at my sweatshirt and am aware of a spark of light. The mosquitoes bizz and I make a swat at the pancho. There is a shower of sparks like fireworks. The mosquitoes win, even over my curiosity at the sparks. I pull the pancho right over my head. Then I discover that a mosquito chorus is a symphony of different tones not just one chord, and definitely off key. While I am intrigued with this new discovery, their bizzing has me on edge waiting for that moment when the noise stops and one lands. It's evident that sleep and dream symbols are not close at hand. I sigh, sit up and lift my face out again. The false dawn has clearly arrived and I settle for considering it dawn.

I gather my belongings, re-light my candle, regard my circle of life, and make my vow not to give away my power anywhere or to anyone. Suddenly I realize that exiting the circle and not looking back will be considerably easier said than done. I have extended my circle as far as possible over the open space. The edge drops off and I have to go around outside it from the North-East to almost the South-West for my route back! A bat squeaks for me. I grin to myself, thinking that it would be too much to have a ceremony run smoothly. So the final challenge, as I bungle my way out and back down the hill, echoes my vow not to give away my power by taking myself too seriously.

To this day, a piece of the candle rests on my altar, a constant reminder of the Night on the Mountain of Fear. No wonder when a flame came later on as a dream symbol with my smudging stone its meaning was clear: my spiritual being is a candle flame, confident, glowing. Nature speaks - I listen - some of the time.

I was beginning to learn another important lesson on my path. Ceremonies bring glimpses into ourselves and our potential, but it takes time and effort to unravel the messages received and carry them into our lives.

The highlights of 1989 were mostly the ceremonies. Parts of them stood out in their meaning as clearly as the shooting star, right as they happened. For other parts the meaning was there but I found it hard to interpret or I noted the symbols, their meaning unknown. Sometimes I teased them out soon after, sometimes not, or new meaning appears on re-reading years later. Great Blue Heron's connection with writing in the Flowering Tree ceremony on Manitoulin Island was not clear to me at the time but I understand it now.

I started early on to write up special events shortly afterwards to catch their meaning and feeling. So it was with The Night on the Mountain of Fear. I struggled for meaning as best I could, insights coming one by one. That ceremony included identifying what was called "fox's tail patterns." Know what a fox's tail pattern is? I didn't. I discovered that if a fox catches sight of its own tail, it often begins to chase it and goes round and round in circles in the process. In the Night on the Mountain of Fear ceremony this concept is incorporated to describe unproductive behaviour patterns that lead the person in useless circles. These patterns are usually learned early in life and hence often are carried-over methods of attempting to cope with situations that recall negative childhood experiences. Thus identifying such fox's tail patterns is a step in being able to recognize them when they occur, or are about to occur, and to have the choice of giving them away and learning more appropriate responses.

What I learned about my fox's tail patterns occurred a couple of weeks later. I was swimming with the current that day, akin to how I felt during the ceremony when I was the very strong, unwavering flame of my candle. I had spent considerable time writing up my experiences, thoughts, and feelings during the Night on the Mountain of Fear ceremony. I was puzzled by the apparent contradictions in my answers to the various requirements of the ceremony and was disappointed that I had not managed to put my finger on any of my personal fox's tail patterns.

Late in the afternoon, I had really enjoyed my Tai Chi class and, for once, had not taken myself too seriously. I had joked about how easy Tai Chi was when I watched advanced students on the ground floor and how difficult it became when I went up to the second floor where we were the students. Still in that open, accepting-of-myself frame of mind, I decided to do lengths in the pool when I got home. I became surprisingly exhausted, hardly able to drag myself through the water, no swimming with the current then. By bedtime, I was developing a sore throat and took vitamins in an attempt to stave it off.

Before going to bed, I smudged and asked Owl, my medicine card for the week, to bring me a dream that would enable me to see one of my fox's tail patterns. The dream was short. The strong, unwavering flame of my ceremony was in cupped hands. Someone said that in getting rid of my sore throat I should avoid letting the candle go out.

When I awoke and recalled this dream, I immediately sensed its significance. I became flooded with examples of incidents linked to it. It was no struggle to find an interpretation that would fit the symbols, there was simply an immediate "knowing": don't allow welcome and comforting nurturance to snuff out my inner glow and zest.

I recalled that whenever my adventuresome little boy Child Spirit attempted an activity that had the potential for hurting me, Mother would preach caution either before or after the event. This had curtailed my little Child Spirit's confidence in his ability to be able to do anything daring. One example occurred when I was three or four. I was supposedly "lost" - Mother didn't know where I was, and I was eventually found where a creek came out at Lake Ontario, far from home. I was scolded in no uncertain terms that it was far too dangerous to go there. What had felt exciting and right was dangerous, frightening and not to be done.

At some stage, I incorporated this fear into myself so that Mother was no longer the person responsible for instilling the over-cautious approach. I took it upon myself, or felt guilty after the fact when I had not done so, and this became a fox's tail pattern.

Fortunately the adventuresome little boy Child Spirit has never been completely subdued in me, witness my love of travel, love of trying new foods, venturing forth on this path. Following whatever short time it took for all these thought associations to occur, I found myself crying with gratitude.

I was tested on this new learning immediately. Two nights later, Kristine asked if I wanted to go to Kitchener on the weekend to see a crystal skull. *That's a long way to go to see a skull. Am I tuned in enough to be able to feel the energy it emanates?* On top of that my sore throat was still like a rasp. By the following morning I realized that this trip represented a test of what I would do with my new found insight into a fox's tail pattern. Any doubt about going dissolved. I experienced a buzz of energy run through my hands and body from the crystal. I also had a good time.

Further afterthoughts surfaced. I noticed on a number of occasions when I thought about the concept of the fox's tail, that I had a tendency to say "tiger's" tail rather than "fox's" tail. The image that came to mind was of the ever-bouncing Tigger, the epitome of the child spirit substance shield, in *Winnie the Pooh*. The image included wanting to grab hold of Tigger's tail and go with it. Here was an opportunity to turn fox tails into tiger tails and new adventures in my growth.

Thus the ceremony of The Night on the Mountain of Fear was another important step on my path. It was the first time in which I saw clearly how ceremonies using the Medicine Wheel teachings could help me to understand myself better in order to change old patterns that no longer served me well and to awaken me to my inner being, the brightly glowing flame, the Spirit Child who knows he can do anything.

My spiritual quest was no longer only a search for connections "out there." I now realized it was also a journey within to uncover the Dark, but also to free the Light. It's that Light within that brings the connection, the Oneness with what is "out there."

8

Fall Wrap-up

THE FALL BROUGHT the first step, in the form of writing, towards new purpose and productivity in my life. It also introduced a new tool to my spiritual tool kit, and a trip to Europe and Africa, as well as more doubts.

I can write. Seems like I always could. Dad, logical thinker, clear writer, gave me E.B. White's *Elements of Style*, my writing Bible. Research reports were torn to shreds when I failed to follow E.B. White. Later on, as a National Parole Board Member, I wrote reasons for decisions, day in and day out, to deny or grant release from prison. My bread and butter, writing. Writing personal letters, the honey. Writing yes, but stories, books? No, never tried my hand at that.

In the fall of 1989, a new beginning, a new release of energy and power. I turned to creative writing. Writing was in the air, my destiny before that day. These new beginnings in my writing were first announced in the "Flowering Tree" ceremony in May. "How does my Dream Warrior Act in 5th Dimension" was the question. *Calls in nature symbols and guides*, I noted. And there it was. Great Blue Heron flew towards me from the North-East of choreography of energy, with the wind direction changing to the South-East. In my interpretation, noted much later, I concluded: "Heron is the writer and writing is an important way that I access 5th dimension but didn't know it then. South-East is the position of self concept and identity. So it heralded the coming of writing as part of my path." The message not understood, nor acted upon at the time.

The next message was August 27. That evening Kristine held an open group channeling. I asked about my healing powers. The voice spoke of using my hands to write. I puzzled over that. Didn't seem like a healing power, not my concept of healing power. But there it was, using my hands to write. Automatic writing, the voice suggested. The channeling in May had talked of writing, too.

August 28, I tried automatic writing. I was reading Jane Robert's *The God of Jane* and some of her writing was non-stop, free flow. *Can I do that too?* Well, yes, mine reflected her style somewhat, but <u>my</u> writing, just letting thoughts flow on paper:

An Excursion into Automatic Writing: August 28, 1989

> The mind,
> A source of thoughts, insights, and problem
>   solving,
> Can also block the way to other worlds.
> It guards the portals of these worlds
> Like a bristling guard dog.

They say the way of entry is through fear:
No doubt the Guardians muster fear,
But it is not that fear one seeks
But one so much greater as to render
The Guardian Dogs an apparition
Lowly as a Mouse.

I try to slip by Ninja style,
Silent, invisible, already on the Path
And through the doors.
That takes a sense of calm.
Pact with nature
Achieved but fleetingly
When captivated with the glimpse
Of inner beauty of
A plant, a moth, a rock, a tree,
The sound of water or
The orchestra of Nature's
Winged ones and creepy-crawlers.

The dog that yaps next door
That breaks the flow of
Consciousness
Becomes a Guardian Dog
Despite its meager size and harmless
disposition.
How little does it take to jolt the mind
To rejoin its comforting, yet limiting,
Sovereignty.

They say that automatic writing
Can be learned and leads us well beyond
Our often dreary, mindful thoughts.
This hardly seems to meet the tests
Described above and skirts or cheats
The mind. Oh, the games mind plays!
Why not a mirror of its ways?
Outfox the fox. Set it off in
Circles, quicker still and quicker,
To catch its own elusive tail.

First step taken. I wrote again two days later. Over a week passed. Then September 11 I had a dream. I was writing a book and was printing up its pages. Never wrote a book in a dream before. Preparation, working in the dream dimension to bring it forth in this reality. No excitement at the time, no puzzlement, just noted down the dream as usual.

Four days later, Louise, a friend I had met through Lynne's classes, and I were down by the Ottawa River early in the morning to usher in the day with ceremony and prayer. As we began, Grandmother Moon was full and still up. Then she disappeared and Grandfather Sun made his appearance. A great blue heron flew across the river from North to South-East and a crow cawed in the South-East. Note taker jotted it down, attaching no meaning then. Now, looking back, this was close to a repeat of the message in May. Heron or Crane, symbol of writing, coming from North, the place of wisdom, to South-East, the place of self concept and identity in the Medicine Wheel I used then. Writing coming into my sense of self and Crow, keeper of Sacred Rules and Laws, cawed there, acknowledging the rightness of Crane's foretelling.

Writing was written all over those days, I just did not truly grasp it. Then on the 16th it was thrust like a spear into me by Lynne. I was on the hot seat, centre of the circle. I had spoken of my powers including writing. Now members of the circle spoke to me. Lynne's turn. She saw an image of an eagle at sunrise over an open expanse, wings raised more than half way. She then challenged me to write a story with birds as characters for her next class. With no thought at all, I said *"yes."* The image she gave is in my notes but I failed to note the challenge. Strangely enough, big moments and key events are often missing from my notes or journal. It is as though when I act from an altered

NATURE SPEAKS: I LISTEN   37

state of consciousness, I'm not always able to record it right away.

I didn't forget about the story however. I thought about the characters and sat down on the 25th and wrote. Not a completed story then and there, but a beginning. Seven birds, Owl, Eagle, Dee, a black-capped chickadee, Pic, a hairy woodpecker, Crane, a great blue heron, Crow, and Hummer, a ruby-throated hummingbird, decided to meet together and share their experiences, each taking their turn at starting the session. Later on, I made Dee the central character and told the story from her perspective.

My journal notes "quite fun!," nothing more. Three days later I read it in class. A cryptic note in my journal again, "Read my story with great pleasure!!" That's all.

So far so good. The class liked it. "Next chapter, next week," said Lynne. "Whoa," I said, "not sure I can. I'm going away for the weekend, off to Europe and Africa soon after. Won't promise, I'll see." I was hyped up though. During the 40-minute drive home, I thought of the birds, worked on the story, the only time I "worked" ahead of writing.

Two days later, the day I left for the weekend, my fingers said "Write, not meditation." I wrote, chapter completed in less than two hours. Now the excitement creeps in. Journal entry actually underlines: "Parts just burst forth as I'm writing it."

The signs were there, the opening came, I picked up the glove, donned it and began a new career. Dare I use that word? First time I have – Jan. 20, 1994. And yet it is. As the dream suggested, I printed up copies of the book, *The Bird Tribe Gathers*. One hundred copies scattered about to friends and friends of friends. Not sold in bookstores, no publisher, but my writing career was launched. New beginnings, new expression.

Expression of inner thoughts, inner views, a form of healing, self-healing, through my hands, my writing self. And I now had another important tool for my spiritual tool kit.

Next came finger testing. Here's how I learned about it. September was an eventful month, some pain, some joy. The pain came first: itchy bites on my upper legs that didn't go away. Then one night in a booth at Nate's Delicatessen with Lynne, drinking cup after cup of hot water and lemon, my substitute for coffee in those days, I brought myself a teaching. The bites got worse, itchier, not bites, hives. *Food reaction?*

Maybe so. My arm came out in angry bumps, my chin too. I was a case of full-blown teenage acne. What a mess. A month before I leave for Kenya. I seized up with panic. *What if I'm like this there, in a hot climate with no medical care?*

No appointment with a dermatologist materializes. Not meant to be. Instead, my friend Louise comes to the rescue. She takes me to my kitchen, gets my left arm straight out to the side. I hold firm. She pushes down. Good resistance, I'm strong.

"Take a lemon," she says. I put one in my right hand. "Place it under your chin."

I hold firm, left arm out straight. She pushes down. My arm squirts to my side. I don't believe it. I couldn't hold it up. *What happened?*

"Wash your right hand," she says and I obey. "Now try an onion."

I take an onion, love onions. *Hold firm*, I think, *concentrate on holding firm*, onion under my chin. Louise pushes down. My arm descends not quite so fast but down it goes. *Oh dear. No onions anymore?*

We try an apple. Arm holds firm. *An apple a day. Can I get apples in Kenya?*

And so it went. My body reacted to spices, chicken, tomatoes, and on and on. OK for bread,

38   Fall Wrap-up

rice, bananas, a shorter list for sure. My world of food closed down. My body cleansed itself, then allowed a taste of this or that - no citrus fruit, no hot spices but some onion, a little tomato. My body knew its wants. I, consciously unknowing, could ask my body, find out its needs, and respond.

There was a shortcut Louise taught me that I could do alone. Since then I've learned others. Here's the one I find simplest. Form a circle by touching the tips of your thumb and baby finger together. If you're right-handed, make the circle with your left hand and vice versa if you're left-handed. Then place the first finger of your other hand into the circle and try to break the circle. It should hold firm. If not, reverse hands. That position is your body's response of strength or "yes" to "yes"-"no" questions. Think of a question or the item you want to test. I think, "Am I allergic to penicillin?" My fingers won't budge. The answer is "yes". I already know I'm allergic to penicillin: my body is adamant too. Am I allergic to apples? My fingers burst open.

Sounds bizarre, you think. Maybe you deigned to try it, maybe not. If it really works, why does it work, you wonder. Well so did I. "Why Louise, what is this all about?" I asked.

"Kinesiology," she replied, "energy movement" but she couldn't help much more than that.

Later on in my path, as a new part of my journey planted its seeds, I found my answer. Machaelle Small Wright has ventured this way too. Her path is gardening, not everyday gardening but co-creative gardening, working hand in hand with Nature and Nature Spirits. She also connects through kinesiology and here is how she explains it in *Perelandra Garden Workbook*:

> "Simply stated, if a negative energy (that is, any physical object or energy vibration that does not maintain or enhance the health and balance of an individual), is introduced into a person's overall energy field, his muscles, when having physical pressure applied, will be unable to hold their power. For example, if pressure is applied to an individual's extended arm while his field is being affected by a negative, the arm will not be able to resist the pressure. It will weaken and fall to his side. If pressure is applied while being affected by a positive, the person will easily be able to resist and the arm will hold its position." (p.15)

One day, not long after I learned this technique from Louise, I saw a ruffed grouse a long way ahead of me on the Dewberry Trail of Mer Bleue. It entered the woods. I moved forward some distance and was no longer sure where it had left the path. *Was it beyond that tree?* My fingers said "no." *Was it closer than that bush?* The answer was "no." I scanned between the two and there stood the grouse. No sooner had I searched it out, then, mission over, it departed.

And so I tried my new connection on everything, not just food. *Am I to go for a bike ride now?* "Yes," they say. I go. *Do you want a second helping of rice?* "No." Harder to accept. I turned to my fingers so often that I, with my Badger aggressiveness, quickly had a sore finger.

Before I left on my trip, I undertook another Gateway Ceremony. The Night on the Mountain of Fear was still fresh with me. I was eager for more. I chose a spot on the other side of the valley with an open view once again. There were fewer sheets of directions for this ceremony with stones, the Rock People. I'd not had much experience with stones and was ill at ease. My body, inside and out, was fidgety. *Why no time for preparation and practice with stones?*

Out I go. As I choose my stones for my circle, White-throated Sparrow calls. I consider it my spirit song and now take it to mean "Centre yourself."

NATURE SPEAKS: I LISTEN   39

Do I hear the message? Not well enough. During the opening parts of the ceremony Great Horned Owl hoots. *What is this wise one saying?* I note, but since it's not a stone, I pay no heed.

Into the ceremony. In keeping with instructions, I choose a stone, then call out my fears for that direction. That done, I test the heat of the chosen stone. "Am I ready to let go of these fears?" is the question I ask of the stone, following my instructions. If the stone feels warm, the answer is yes. I can't tell. I grit my teeth. One stone is warm to my cheek and cool to my hand, another the reverse. No confidence. Still not centred.

No shooting stars this night but northern lights instead, somewhat faint, pale green. "Pay no attention to distractions," the instructions say. I've only seen northern lights once before but I try to concentrate, not on them but the ceremony.

Near the end. "Command the fears to enter an area of my circle so I can face them," the instructions read. I call and call, louder and louder. Nothing comes. My frustration mounts and mounts. Finally I burst forth, "You're no damned big fear!"

Great Horned Owl hoots. I laugh and my tension dissolves. Owl's agreement is so loud and clear. Ceremony ends on the most positive note of the night. I return to my tent with a smile on my face and a much lighter step.

The lesson on fears was clear: I make mountains out of molehills. There is no damned big fear. Yet I wanted to connect more with the Stone People. No lesson from them that time but it kindled a desire in me to work with them more.

Now a diversion came, a continuance of my former life, a bird tour. I took my new life with me but concentrated mostly on the birding. The kinesiology finger testing I had learned allowed me to cater to my weakened digestive system while on the trip. I was away six weeks that fall, two in Wales and London, and four in Kenya.

The desire to connect with the Stone People went with me on my trip. In Wales a friend and I walked beaches gathering stones, small coloured stones, amber, greenish. Larger ones, odd shaped, a shoe, a whale, some gray, some striped, some rough, others worn perfectly smooth. I kept the size and number partly in check, respecting the long trip ahead and heavy cases already.

On to Kenya. I needed a smudging stone. Bird tour it might be, but smudging and prayer were a part of my life now, not every day but often. I found my flat pink Rift valley stone mid-way through the trip on the Masai Mara. I found a rounded reddish stone as well, with a flat bottom that sits warmly in the palm of my hand. Two African stones to add to those that were waiting for me in London. The Stone People entering my life, me entering theirs.

I was home again in Late November. Giraffes (my favourite), elephants, leopards, hornbills, vultures, magnificent starlings, all behind me. Not much emphasis on my new path. Now it's time to turn back more fully to it. *Is it really my life? Can I re-enter it? Most of all, can I still write?*

Dec. 3. Time change, temperature change, uncertainty and doubt all affected me. Slept to about midnight and from then on got nowhere in spite of how tired I felt. My mind raced, my body was like a twisted rope, and I tossed and turned. Finally decided to read and Evelyn Eaton's *The Shaman and the Medicine Wheel* called me. From the introduction alone, I could tell that it was the book to get me back on track. She said:

> "[This book] might be called an attempt to travel the Shamanic Journey into a realm of experience we usually believe belongs to specialists, Medicine Men and Women,

Lamas, Saints, Enlightened Ones. We are not to leave it respectfully to them. It is the journey all of us will take when the time is right, and the time may be right for many who do not realize it, now." (p.1)

No tossing and turning now: I was fully absorbed. By page 15, I shifted and sat cross-legged in my bed. A paragraph later I read:

"'Sit down', the Medicine Man said, 'set up a squawk. The Grandfathers hear.'

'Sit down' does not mean recline in a comfortable armchair with a cigarette, a cup of coffee or a glass of wine. It means sit cross-legged in a sacred manner on our Mother Earth for a long time, many times, a posture unfamiliar to most westerners."

She proceeded to talk about stones and their importance in her path. I read it as a clear message to me who had come home laden with stones, whose last ceremony focused on stones. She talked of healing stones, describing the most common shape. It was the shape of the roundish red African stone. I had been receptive enough for this particular stone to call to me. Here was more evidence that I had taken my new life to Africa with me.

That week I finished reading *The Shaman and the Medicine Wheel* and turned to *The Good Red Road*, well written, filled with insights and glimpses of mid-west America, native and non-native.

Doubts continued.

Dec.8. Feeling uncertain about my "path." *The Good Red Road* made it clear it was not an easy path. No wonder my dreams are about routes this week. A quote from the book:

"As you find your way home, the spirits say they are protecting you; for your home is within you, and the Spirits are in it. Your offering and your prayers are being answered, accepted into the holy winds; and the Wanbli, the eagle, stands over you to guide, and protect, and take you down a good road to when you come to him forever."

It was a message as much to me as it was to the author. I smudged that morning, feeling inadequate and very humble.

Reading, reading, and more reading that month. I turned to Lynne Andrews' *Windhorse Woman*. It brought together my native leanings and my Shambhala Tibetan meditation practice. I cried, overwhelmed at its timing just as a Shambhala weekend training was coming. Then on to the book, *Kinship with All Life* by J. Allen Boone.

Dec.14. I finished reading *Kinship with All Life*. It gave various examples illustrating my belief that animals aren't necessarily less intelligent than humans - everything is endowed with universal spirit. Very reassuring and challenging to find what I believe in theory carried out in practice.

And so the year came to a close. Still very much on my path, doubts and all. In finger testing I had acquired a significant new tool for my spiritual kit and I had rapidly put it to use. I still had not really grasped the idea that stones and animals could communicate beyond being the symbols they represented for me. I fully acknowledged that they were intelligent and endowed with universal spirit but I wasn't yet truly ready to take in that animals and stones could communicate, let alone with me.

Part III *1990*

10

Medicine Walk

TIME TO BEGIN a new year, to capture the next full year of this voyage. 1990. New growth, new developments once again. As I write now in 1994, is it time for a change in how I present the year?

Why not a Medicine Walk today? I'll ask Great Spirit and the Nature Spirits of this place to guide me in how to proceed. I smudge indoors, breathe deeply of the dried sage from my garden. Sage, sacred plant, cleansing, centering.

I don my jacket, mitts and boots and out I go. Snow melting, my initial path well packed now. *Will I get my snow shoes? Don't feel like using them today. Perhaps this snow will hold me. Let's try.*

I get to my Power Place. Power Place, that's part of 1990. I repeat my purpose to Sister Pine and the Nature Spirits and sprinkle tobacco.

I start off, and soon pick up a likely walking stick. Sturdy, but it breaks through the snow more than I, its path slightly off mine. Snowflakes drift down for a minute or two. Not many, enough to notice, not big wet ones, smaller, more sense of purpose. My mind is in gear. *New approach: no skis or snow shoes for the first time in weeks, first time since my winter writing began. Weather changing, snowflakes, cleansing.*

On I go, noting my tentative stride, not wanting the sudden jerk as I sink. That jars my back. *I get off to a slow start*, I note to myself. *Not sure of my footing*, I add. The snow, as I walk through the pines, balsam and hemlock, is littered with twigs, needles, branches. I'm glad I'm on foot, not on skis. I reach a section of deciduous trees, more open here in winter. The snow on the ground looks fresher. I move more freely, gaining confidence, though my hands are still cold. *I need to move with more purpose.*

Fresh chips to my right, close to the path. *Has Pileated woodpecker found a new tree?*

I look up. Two tall maples with four-to-five inch trunks, and up 30 feet, they are stripped clean of bark for a good three feet. I look for tracks below. One set, almost like Fox, a pretty straight line, no sign of a dragging tail. I puzzle over this. *Doesn't seem like Porcupine. Could Woodpecker do this? Not Pileated, no deep gouges. Something new, quite different. Has to be a message here. Getting closer to the core, stripping off the outer trappings? Time to go beyond just story telling? Time to describe a Medicine Walk, show how it works?*

I proceed. As I near the top of this trail, I sink a bit once again. On I go, over the brush and branch fence, on to the next ski trail. It's much less firm here, used less often. I stop. Check with my fingers. *Is it time to turn back?*

"Yes," they say.

Main message received already, I figure.

My pace quickens. I'm flowing now, hands warmed up, very comfortable. I stop at the chips for another look. This time I see inch-long, oblong feces amidst the chips. *Never seen feces like these before. Not dogs, that's for sure, not rabbit either. Rules out woodpecker work up above.*

I settle on Porcupine, my first sign of it out here. *Porcupine, trust. What's new, trust the flow of my writing. Trust my guides are there, Porcupine is one of them.* (I smile fondly as I write now. Good friend is Porcupine. Good teacher.)

Satisfied, I make my way back. But wait. I note one of the sunken prints where my foot sank deep on the outward trip. It's full of black flecks, almost like soot. I look closer. They're moving. Something alive. I've seen them before in March in Mer Bleue, a sign of spring in the air. *New life, new creativity. What does that imply for my writing?* No idea. *Trust. Not easy, but trust, it's all I can do, what I'm asked to do.*

I stop at Sister Pine, thank her and the Nature Spirits, offer tobacco. Medicine Walk completed. Messages received, noted, taken in, I trust.

And that's why I start the year of 1990 with the Medicine Walk. A new way to begin as the Medicine Walk suggested. So I've let you witness how a Medicine Walk can come into play in daily life. Visualization and meditation is not yet my way. Dreams sometimes, writing, ceremony. And Medicine Walks are sacred for me. Medicine Walks are not daily events but there to help when I feel stuck. They are a joyful way to seek guidance, one of my unique ways.

I spell out my purpose clearly, voice it out loud. Seek help and then the walk. Alone with Nature, opening my eyes, ears, heart to her voice, how she will choose to talk to me. I cry out now for a closer, deeper connection with Nature. I want to hear in voices. Yet I hear their voices now in sign language that I understand. It seems I'm never satisfied and always want more.

I learned at the Animal Communication workshop how Nature could answer the questions I posed. I had used it again since then. But it was in 1990 that I learned that such a walk had a name, a Medicine Walk. My new tool was something natives have used for a long, long time.

Medicine Walks and Power Places are part of the year of 1990. In that year my fingers guided me to drawing an Animal Medicine card every three months. First one this year was Lizard, bringer of dreams, dream helper. And the dreams came. I was recalling them nightly. Not just one dream, often several, once six. Interpretations sometimes clear, often not, but all were recorded in my journal and some on computer too. Now on to what happened.

11

Smudging Stone and White-breasted Nuthatch

I SPENT MUCH TIME spent with my friend, Louise, early this year, including several days in January at a cottage. She introduced me to Runes, new helpers on my way. Symbols carved on small chips of a hard material with interpretations in *The Book of Runes*, by Ralph Blum. A tool, like the Animal Medicine cards to use when I was looking for guidance.

By mid-February a cycle began so full of events in a 10-day period that I wrote it up as a special event. Let me turn to the train of dreams and events as they happened.

Feb. 15. It all started innocently enough. At Lynne's class, one item of our homework was to choose a stone or gem, research it through library books, meditation or whatever, and share what we learned with the class the following Tuesday.

When I arrived home I was curious to see if the gem was already in my possession. I checked with my fingers, trying the stones that, in my estimation, came closest to gems - crystals, obsidian, kyanite and crisicola. None of those were to be used. *Is it something else on my altar shelf?*

"Yes." My African smudging stone was the one.

Now while I think this stone is precious, I had no idea what information I could share with the class. There was no point thinking about it anymore that night and I went to sleep.

Feb. 18. My fingers insisted on my transferring my 1989 dreams from my journal to the computer. As I did so, I was impressed with how much was coming to me in dreams. I rediscovered that, on several occasions, I had asked the animal of the week for the answer to a specific question through my dreams and received answers. Prior to going to sleep that night, I called on Lizard, my animal for the quarter, to help me with information on my stone for the class.

Feb. 19. I had a dream of my stone. There was a small but strong flame coming up from it. Then a much bigger, even stronger and brighter flame came to it from the east and joined forces with it.

In the dream and on awakening, my heart was full. I knew that the flame that approached the stone was my own. At first I linked it to the little boy spirit flame in my Gateway Ceremony of the previous July. Then I realized it was the flame of that ceremony that responded to the question of my role in life and with others – a flame of spiritual healing as signified by its coming in from the east. A glow of warmth welled up in me. This was a teaching for me as well as the class. I was well aware of how much this stone brought to me as a smudging stone. It had never occurred to me, however, that by asking it to perform such a role, I brought it fulfillment too. What an exciting and marvelous feeling that fosters, a lesson that applies in all relationships with Nature.

Feb. 20. Right at the end of the class, I eagerly shared my rock teaching with the group. Again its lesson filled me with joy and warmth.

Feb. 21. Louise came over in the evening. She taught me to balance her chakras, after she had done mine. I sensed heat with my right hand, but it came and went, my confidence level low. Last thing for the evening, we each drew a rune. Mine was Thurisaz (21) reversed. *The Book of Runes* stated:

> "A quickening of your development is indicated here. And yet even when the growth process accelerates, you will have reason to halt along the way, to reconsider the old, to integrate the new. Take advantage of these halts. . . Do not attempt to go beyond where you haven't yet begun. Be still; collect yourself, and wait on the Will of Heaven." (p.126)

Feb. 23. I woke shortly after midnight, wide awake and energetic. I was imbued with the desire to run workshops in the spring. I decided to contact my first workshop teacher right away. The title of a workshop popped into my head: "Touching the Magic in Nature." I even made planning notes for the workshop. I would also speak to Lynne about co-leading a workshop on Communication with Nature and I would offer a part day out for some of the Shambhala group to which I belonged. For varying reasons, each fell through and, much later, I looked back at the wisdom of the rune: "Do not attempt to go beyond where you haven't yet begun. Be still; collect yourself, and wait on the Will of Heaven."

Feb. 24. One of my dreams was of particular significance. I, and a man beside me, were at a gathering of psychics. Another man asked him what he had studied. He said, "Oh, lots of things. The key is getting attuned and then just waiting. If something is not happening weekly, there is a tendency to be impatient." This man was quiet, had blue-gray eyes and emanated a sense of calm and assurance. My fingers indicate that he is one of my Guides, the first time that I have been conscious of him and recognized his bringing me a lesson. Another step forward.

It is sunny, bright and very cold. I can't resist a short ski in the Gatineau. It is magic. The sky overhead is a deep summer blue, contrasting with the heavily laden branches of pure white, heavy snow with ice crystals tossed here and there. The day and I are radiant, confident, champing at the bit. On the way back, facing the sun, ice crystals glisten on branches and the snow crystals on the ground are a rainbow carpet.

As I near the end of the trail, I notice a white-breasted nuthatch at one of the empty feeders. I want to put out some of my sunflower seeds for her. In the process of reaching the feeder, for the first time that day, I fall and fall clumsily like a clown. Much of the seed reaches the ground not the feeder. Nuthatch returns. She stops at a sapling closer to me than the feeder and winds her way down still closer to me, uttering a strange mewing sound repeatedly. I sit up, as best I can, smiling, and encourage her to fly to the feeder. Instead, she flies closer to the trail, indicating a route for me to follow. So I rise and ski towards her, stopping part way. She returns to a tree near me, repeating her earlier performance. She takes off but not to the feeder. I follow her route to the trail and then watch her head to the feeder and fly off with a seed. My fingers say she has been thanking me but has also been concerned about whether I had hurt myself.

How hard it is to really accept what beings in Nature are capable of expressing. How right Jane Roberts is about the beliefs that are incorporated so deeply in us, even if we now are consciously rejecting those beliefs. Science had drilled into me that animals couldn't have feelings. Well Nuthatch wasn't motivated by fear or by hunger, whatever else I can or can't attribute to her. The teaching in my fall was the concern of Nuthatch for me. But then it was also aware of my concern for it - to apply the rock teaching to this event, again there was reciprocity.

Feb. 25. A significant dream: I was driving around a residential area that looked down on water. I was pleased with how much I had done, still before dawn. I saw two great-horned owls where I was planning to park. I interpret this as describing my psychic development and how I felt about it before getting to daybreak. *Full daylight will be ushered in by two external teachers. They will guide me while I spend time with them.*

I read in bed before getting up. My fingers didn't want me reading what I had on hand and guided me to a pile of eight or nine books on my bedroom bookshelf. They then said "no" to each book, but assured me it was one of these books. Puzzlement registered on my face as I cocked my head to the side. Eventually I figured out I was to locate the particular book without relying on my fingers. Using heat in my hand was acceptable. I reduced it to two and finally I chose *Bear Tribe's Self Reliance Book*. My fingers signaled agreement. I was to open it at the correct place. I returned to bed, prayed to Great Spirit and opened the book at the beginning of Section III: "Communities" in which the Bear Tribe community and Twylah's Wolf Clan Lodge were described.

I cried, overwhelmed. It corroborated my sense that I needed to live in a community with teachers for a period of time. There were two owls in the dream and two specific places, with two specific teachers in the book. In addition, my fingers were instructing me to learn additional ways to touch my inner knowledge; they would guide me.

Not only was I being pointed in new directions, but I was learning to rely more on my inner self for guidance through my dreams and finger testing. Have you ever followed up on such seeming whims of your own? I was Tigger bouncy with excitement, also on edge with all the unknowns. Excitement won out and I wrote letters to the Wolf Clan Lodge and the Bear Tribe.

12

Pine Siskin Chorus

FEBRUARY BROUGHT all the symbols of new ventures, yet the need for patience, too. As it turned out, there were other new beginnings before my visits to the Wolf Clan Lodge and the Bear Tribe. I was preparing myself, my dreams leading the way. The month of March opened with this dream:

> Young man in jail. He was starting to be allowed some things. Others and I had calculated he was being held illegally and had already completed his sentence. Someone told him they thought we could get him out. He said he would just as soon stay in. I poked my head around a corner and said I wanted to invite him to stay with me. He said he would sleep better in a familiar and less formal place. I said it wouldn't be formal since there would just be him and me. He came over and offered his hands in thanks and I pointed out it was he being formal and that I could have him out within a half-hour.

I see myself as the young man as well as the "I" in the dream. The imprisoned part of me needed encouragement to reach out, take new steps. And that was March when I was introduced to both yoga and reiki. On March 29 I experienced a profoundly moving visit to "Sharon's waterfall" on the Mackenzie King Estate. There, what I was reading in *Talking with Nature* came alive in my life and I reviewed it the next day in automatic writing.

Mar. 12. A series of dreams augur something coming.

1) I was to quietly let something come all over me.
2) I was at a place near water where two men were close to an explosion of fire. One was always near a blue flame that was dangerous and would cut his life span significantly.
3) A car was going around a racetrack. As the driver passed me, he had his eyes closed. Just after the car passed me I saw a flash under its tires and it exploded.
4) I was at an airport. I had the ticket for Highers but I had left my purse and tickets in the taxi.

While the first dream indicated that I am to go with the flow, the remainder suggested that the flow in this instance is going to be an explosive and difficult one, rather than anything easy, but I did have the ticket for "Highers," which I viewed as progress.

Mar. 13. Louise and I went to our first yoga class in Hull. The teacher was a woman in her 70s, who looked much younger, and could fold herself up unbelievably.

The exercises challenged my back. I gingerly tried more even after my fingers said to quit. I finally stopped, close to tears of hurt pride, failure and frustration. I leaned against the wall and took deep breaths to gradually centre myself. Our teacher finished with an excellent relaxation meditation, which I did from a sitting position.

After lunch I decided to walk the trail by the Ottawa River. I frequently sank in the snow and my back rebelled to such lightning bolt hits. It became a Medicine Walk. I asked Nature to bring me a teaching about my back. Chickadees caught my attention. Their repertoire of calls was varied. There was the two note "phoebe" call, as well as the stranger almost mewing sound, both complementing the more familiar "chickadee-dee-dee." My fingers agreed that my message was with the chickadees. *It is time for a new, more varied perspective and approach. My whole life pattern has been to do what I can do well and leave other things aside. This has applied physically as well as with respect to creative activities.*

I thought back to a 1989 dream about a dentist who gradually became mobile through doing his own stretching exercises in addition to prescribed ones. *So I choose a few of the yoga exercises on which to work daily very gently to strengthen my back.*

My morning's frustration and discouragement lifted like fog as I shifted to this new perspective. I strode back more confidently.

Mar. 14. Dreams reflected the situation once again.

In the first, someone said there was a warrant out for childhood friends of the family. A big change was going on now and so former things were resurfacing.

In the second dream a former work colleague was the central figure. Two men replayed events in her life as though they had been in it. The process became teachings for them too. There were two words associated with the replay of events. One was "death." I arrived next day and called her by the other word, "blue."

I didn't pretend to have a complete interpretation of these dreams but replaying past patterns was clear. The second dream suggested insight through re-enacting events – perhaps with a different ending than previously.

That evening Louise told me about a Level 1 reiki course that was being offered on the weekend. Reiki is a way of channeling energy from the universe through our body and out our hands to another person. *That doesn't sound like me.*

I pulled back. No decision until morning. As I prepared for bed, I called on Lizard to bring me guidance about the reiki course.

Mar. 15. More dreams. In one I was being taught that it was necessary to hold certain positions in order to maintain power with respect to healing. In another, Louise and I were alternating giving treatments to one another. I poured us tea into very small almost flat containers. Mine no longer held the tea without spilling. Then she ushered me in symbolically, ahead of other women, and I worked on her back.

On awakening, I mulled over these dreams and those from the previous night. I leaned toward taking the course, moving beyond old patterns. I looked out at the neighbour's tree, deliberately searching for a Rune symbol and quickly saw Dagaz. While I recognized it as a Rune symbol, I had no idea of its meaning. It stands for "Breakthrough, Transformation, Day" in *The Book of Runes*. The interpretation is that it marks a major shift or transformation in attitude. The book goes on to indicate that "because the timing is right, the outcome is assured although not, from the present vantage point, predictable." This cast aside any lingering doubt that the course was appropriate and the time for me to take it was now.

I learned that one can send energy and that it happens even if one doesn't know what is transpiring. I gained confidence in the technique and, more importantly, in my doing it. So I came away with a new tool for healing myself and for using with other beings in my universe, human and otherwise. For all of the initiation ceremonies, we held our hands in a praying position. I thought back to the Gateway Ceremony where one of the candles had hands in a prayer position. I previously linked that with the concept of spiritual healing, but perhaps it linked also with reiki as a component, since it is a form of spiritual healing. I had already been applying reiki to my jade plant, although I thought of it more as stroking its aura.

Thus the week offered two new challenges. On the one hand, I had an opportunity to learn a new approach from my past patterns of dealing with my back. My response was yet to be fleshed out and put into practice, but I accepted the challenge. More than that, I had a new thought pattern, seeing myself becoming more flexible than I have ever been, especially physically. In itself, that was an important step forward. On the other hand, I also gained a wider perspective on my ability to use my hands to channel energy.

Mar. 29. One of those special days. The urge came upon me to visit Sharon's waterfall, so named by me in honour of Sharon, who loved water and waterfalls. It was just around the freezing point, but the sun was shining and the breeze was slight. I prepared a pita sandwich for lunch and departed.

After turning on to the Eastern Parkway, I came to a quick halt and watched two gray partridge in the ditch at the side of the road. Later I came upon a ruffed grouse that had been foiled in its attempt to cross the road. *There must be a message from Grouse.*

When I got home I opened *Animal Medicine* at the last page on Grouse at this paragraph:

"Dancing or walking will put you back in touch with Earth and your body. Grouse may then teach you how to notice the energy flows that put you in harmony and balance with body, mind, and spirit." (p.175)

That message was in tune with my plan for the day.

I continued on to the Mackenzie King Estate. Part of the trail was a foot or so deep in snow, while other sections were completely clear. The trail had been packed down during the winter and that, combined with the cold temperature, meant that I hardly left footprints, let alone sank. I quickly reached the brook. It babbled contentedly at the upper level, more noisily where a second branch joyfully reached it a little lower down and downright vigorously when it reached the falls.

The rocks at the upper part of the falls glistened with embedded flecks of jewels that I didn't recall noticing on previous visits. The side of the falls was iced like a layered wedding cake. Patches of ice, on rocks in the brook or at its edges, were either crystal clear or sometimes big foam bubbles gathered together in colonies. What harmony of sight and sound! My African stone sparkled in the setting as I smudged, offering thanks to Great Spirit. I then sprinkled tobacco for Mother Earth, the rocks and the water before opening my lunch. The sun shone warmly in spite of the temperature and Browning's phrase, "God's in his heaven, All's right with the world" burst into my thoughts.

I watched the water flow over the falls, intrigued by how much of it rushed over with great velocity and yet some, in the same area, just slipped down the rocks with a strikingly contrasting gentleness.

The brook had a message for me. "Your path is the gentle one. It doesn't have to be dramatic to reach the bottom of the falls: both paths reach the same end."

I thanked the brook and began the walk back. I stopped twice en route to "pish" at the chickadees and pine siskins. (To "pish" is to make a soft noise that sounds like the word "pish." Some birds respond by approaching.) Both times they dropped down for a lengthy, close visit. The siskins were particularly vocal. Suddenly it became a "pish" from me followed by a chorus from the siskins that was as one note. This continued for as long or as short as eternity. *I've never been part of a bird choir before. I'm going to have to make my "pish" more musical!*

One siskin flew around my head, close enough to hear the flapping of its wings. The same bird followed me briefly when its mates had flown off. What delightful companionship, an energy flow putting me in harmony and balance with body, mind and spirit, just as Grouse had predicted.

I arrived home, bubbling with energy, anxious to commit the happenings and feelings to paper. It occurred to me to include some quotations from Michael Road's *Talking with Nature* that I had been reading before I set out. My connection with Nature was evolving, aided by my reading and my experiences of that day. In the following quotations, I have underlined parts that struck me particularly forcibly. Quotation marks signal the author's view, while italics indicate the views put forth by the river, a plant or whatever.

> "I have learned that this 'connection' with Nature transcends the physical connection, becoming an involvement with the Spirit. Seemingly we are required to stand alone, humble and vulnerable before the Spirit of Nature, which paradoxically is the Spirit of Self. <u>We are no longer required to relate to humanity 'and' Nature, but rather humanity 'as' Nature</u>. Within this framework there develops a union, one of joy, a joy rising triumphant over all outside stress, making the moment whole and complete." (p.90)

A rose tells him: "*My friend, let the heart know truth which the mind cannot yet comprehend. Explanations become useless. Cast aside knowledge based only on a physical reality. You must become attuned to another world, a dimension within and without your own dimension. Let your heart accept, even while the mind paces in its cage of outraged belief.*

When you learn of a physical truth, you accept and believe because you can see it. Do not deny a simultaneous truth vibrating to a higher wisdom simply because it may not be seen.

Place your faith in 'knowing'. Trust your Self." (pp.95-96)

A tree told him: "*Doubt holds you away from your acceptance of Self. I need not tell you that doubt is a lock on the door to greater realities, to extended possibilities. Doubt is the part of your mind which fights to retain control. Doubt seeks to speculate and, from speculation, to walk a known path.*

You cannot do this and enter a higher conscious awareness. There is no room for doubt, no place for doubt to express its fear. Doubt destroys faith. Faith knows not, nor seeks to know, for in faith this moment is complete." (p.98)

Mar. 30.

Impatience

Timba, the dog next door, barked. I crossed to the bedroom window to talk to her. She looked up with interest and stopped barking. I talked. She nosed around, headed to the door, out of sight and barked again. No response there, she came back to look me over. The postal truck drove by and Timba barked vigorously. It must be frustrating to be in an enclosed area where you hear but can't see what or who is making the noise. I explained but that didn't bring satisfaction. She retreated to the door to try again for entry.

Timba has given me some semblance of focus. I want so badly to be more receptive to what Nature is saying. I receive visual and auditory messages that I can interpret as symbols when I'm open. My fingers usually then give me assurance that I'm on track when I need reassurance. But that is so limited compared to the authors of *Kinship with Animals* and *Talking with Nature*. My fingers assure me that I'll expand my receptivity, but oh how impatient I am, like a racehorse at the starting gate, in spite of numerous messages that I need to bide my time. I need strong desire to make progress but I also need faith and ways of dispelling doubt. Somehow the latter are far more elusive, much as I think I'm ready, willing and eager to move on.

This amounts to a conflict of guiding principles, both of which are applicable but which can interact in negative as well as positive ways. Anything worth doing is worth doing well and you can't wait forever but have to take a leap into the unknown. But somehow in all that, gentleness and the need to let go and trust get pushed aside. Without them being an integral part of the learning process, all the pushing in the world doesn't bring much in the way of results. My intellect may grasp what the necessary ingredients are but, like learning a new tennis stroke, converting that correct image in the mind into a physical stroke still requires an additional leap. This leap has to remain nameless because, in fact, it is something that just happens when the time is right.

Funny thing that, as that last sentence came into being all on its own, I relaxed. It is OK. I am doing all the things that I can be doing at the moment. The time still isn't right for the next leap forward. Rather like reading *Talking with Nature*. I read it last summer, liked it but couldn't fully relate to what was too far ahead of where I was. This time around, I'm soaking it up like a sponge.

Road's book does little to rein in my impatience. To the contrary, I find myself champing at the bit, aware that I have already taken, at least at some level, some of his steps. I have come much farther than I give myself credit for. I turn to Nature for guidance far more naturally and frequently than a year ago. In fact, until last May I had never tried at all.

Allowing my fingers to guide me to books or activities is even more recent. And if I accept the message in *Talking with Nature* that it is not humanity <u>and</u> Nature but humanity <u>in</u> Nature, then even this activity of mine is a form of communicating with Nature, in this case my own.

When I look at it all in this light, I am struck by not knowing myself. I have always viewed myself as having enormous patience. And yet as I walk this path, I am constantly confronting my own impatience. Is it a different standard I use for myself as opposed to others or have I confused perseverance with patience? My very strong trait of perseverance can mask another equally strong (and I find myself grinning!) trait of impatience. My now sheepish grin embodies an acknowledgement that I've let the cat out of the bag. OK. What's finally no longer camouflaged should be something I can tackle. Thank you Great

Spirit and the Nature in my fingers for teaching me this today.

Apr. 25.

Malaise

The last little while I have felt a general malaise at times, sometimes sadness, other times more a sense of anxiety although that sounds too strong. Have I had unrealistic expectations about what all this exploration can do in terms of pointing me to my particular path? Is it linked with my impatience?

These feelings don't stay long. Action puts them aside. Is that escapism? Maybe partly. A walk in Nature evaporates them, even though my mind remains open. That action isn't escapism: far more it puts my world into broader perspective, brushes away my impatience, and lets me drink in the energy, beauty and teachings of the Universe in a very "now" kind of way.

So what's new? As usual, Great Spirit, through Nature, guides and supports me, provided I allow myself to be open. What's new is that Great Spirit, through the Nature in my fingers also can guide me to this alternative route of writing. Thank you, Great Spirit. Sitting meditation is yet a third and all are focused on the "now," an approach that is not just action for action's sake.

I was still controlling the topics of my automatic writing but it was leading me to new insights in spite of myself. In *The Bird Tribe Gathers*, however, I was already holding the reins looser.

So during these two months I gained two more tools, yoga and reiki, to add to my tool kit. Yoga, at this stage, was simply a tool to aid my physical being. Reiki could be used that way too but was introducing me to new ways of spiritual healing.

At the same time, I was struggling to take in the changes in how I was relating to Nature. I had been using the Animal Medicine cards, unusual animals I saw, the directions of the Medicine Wheel, and Medicine Walks as sources of symbols that brought me messages that touched my daily life. As I was washing the dishes, for example, I would look out into my small back yard. If I saw Black Squirrel or Blue Jay I thought about how they might be speaking to me right then, which of their qualities I might need in my life. That's what we all can do.

But now I was starting to relate differently to Nature. I had been part of the pine siskin choir and White-breasted Nuthatch had showed her concern when I fell. It was not just what I was reading. These experiences were happening to me. This required a far bigger shift in my belief systems than just seeing Nature as symbols. This leap would take far longer to become truly part of my day-to-day life even though the way I was approaching the ordinary moments was facilitating it.

13

Native Elder

THE NEXT SPECIAL EVENT was a return to Manitoulin Island for a weekend workshop. Had I known what the workshop would entail, I might well not have gone. It announced itself clearly as a Healing Circle but I overlooked the word "healing." My teacher, Lynne, was co-leading it with a friend, who had also apprenticed under Swiftdeer. I focused on that, not Gloria's background in psychology or the word "healing." I had to bring a picture of myself as a child but even that rang no warning bells of how close to group therapy this might be. No, what caught my eye and heart and interest was that a native woman, described as an elder, would assist. That hooked me.

The weekend began formally after supper. We introduced ourselves, giving our name, where we were from, and our personal dream for the weekend. That caught me off guard since my focus was time with the native elder. I struggled to determine my dream. The concept of flexibility, physical, emotional and mental seemed appropriate. As others took the floor, I concluded that was too vague. Then I realized that meeting Lillian, the native elder, was my dream.

Gloria stopped going around the circle three women ahead of me and from then on anyone who wanted to do so took their turn. Two "healings" took place on the spot. In one the woman's hearing improved dramatically. By midnight, some of us, myself included, still had not taken our turns. Suddenly Gloria brought the evening to a close.

It was important to me to state the importance of meeting Lillian. So I took my power and went to her, explaining that time with her was my dream but not sure exactly what I was seeking. She acknowledged what I had to say and the washing machine churning inside me subsided to the gentle rinse cycle.

Mid-morning Saturday, we turned to an exercise using clay with a partner. The eldest woman of the group headed to me. *Thank you, I didn't have any idea who to turn to.*

With eyes closed, one partner told of a death of someone she knew, which had been traumatic for her. While doing so, both molded their clay, the speaker a giveaway, the receiver a gift for the speaker. My partner began with the death of her father when she was three and moved from there to the death of her husband.

When my turn came, I started with Mother but shifted to my brother Jon's death. I cried in grief, heard the ambulance siren piercing my ears and my heart as they took him to hospital, and wrestled with my guilt in having forgotten him. I pounded out a hand in clay in which to dispose of this load. Prior to this occasion, I had touched these feelings only through a tightening of my stomach when I heard an ambulance siren and tears coming to my eyes when I read and identified with the story of Christopher Robin and Pooh in the Enchanted Forest in *Winnie the Pooh*. This was the first time that a "therapy" technique brought me in touch with these feelings. I was amazed yet not surprised at the appropriateness of my partner, for whom the traumatic death had also occurred when she was three. Synchronicity in action once more.

The following morning I was up early as usual, in spite of all the late nights. As I wandered, enjoying the bird song and the freshness of the morning, I recognized a feeling of inner sadness, emptiness, a well run dry. I was puzzled, given the beauty of the weekend in general and the Sweat Lodge healings that had taken place the previous night. *Had I not succeeded in giving away my loss and guilt over Jon?*

I checked with my fingers. That was not the source of my sadness. It was for myself, the frightened young child of three, alone in her world. Not only had I lost Jon, but my parents were no longer the same either, as they struggled with grief. I wasn't frightened now at this feeling of pain. It was a sense of discovery of a hurt that I had no idea I was still carrying. Now as I write, I am aware that I have this feeling each spring, the time of year when my brother died.

I walked, aware of that pain. I was now over by the lake, looking out from the cliff. The sun was not shining where I was, but over near the far shore, the lake was glistening. The result was a narrow, long band of spectacular, brilliant light along the far shore. Next to that band was another of about the same width but very dark. Between that dark band and me the water was much lighter, but not sparkling, which I saw as the undramatic course of my adult life to date. As I took this in, I was instantly in tune with an inner knowing that my pain, hurt and needs following Jon's death were the narrow, very dark band. What struck me was that it was narrow and that the magnificent strip of sparkling light was before it. I was equally sure that this band stood for an experience prior to, or at Jon's death. At that time I must have been blessed with an important message that remains under the surface, just waiting to burst forth in all its brilliance when I'm ready to pass through the pain and tap into it.

The light was blinding and I was filled with warmth. I stood there, wanting to touch in to that light with all my being, knowing that I can and will get there, and the message will once again be mine in my conscious mind. I knew that the pain would not be intolerable and the light ever so wonderful and that it is tied in with why I have some special way of linking with those who are dying or have lost someone. I was enveloped in a shawl of comfort, secure in the feeling that tapping into all this is possible.

Later that morning, we turned to an exercise in which eight of us represented the directions of the wheel. I chose to be one of the eight. We showed our picture as a young child, describing how we viewed it when we chose to bring it, how we thought or remembered we felt at the time and how it looked to us now.

In my picture I am sitting on a stone wall with stuffed animals all around me. It met an unstated requirement that it be of me alone and it showed my early love of animals. Looking at it as I sat in the centre of the circle, I saw the little girl looking guarded, clutching her animals close to her, almost as though they were protecting her as much as she was supporting them. They were her closest friends, a formidable group, two each of bears, elephants, horses, and giraffes! My view now was that the little girl, still within me, doesn't need to hold on to them for protection but nevertheless remains very much supported by all of Nature. She recognizes that Nature includes human beings, and is more open to that support too.

The program ended at lunchtime. The following week when I looked back on the weekend, I was elated by what had occurred. I had been drawn to a healing circle that I might have avoided if I'd focused on "healing circle" rather than "Native Elder to lead a sweat." It was clear to me that I was meant to be there. The healing circle had helped me to touch in to past trauma with my emotions and also to allow Nature to bring me messages about that time too. For some time I had wanted to explore the childhood I had blocked out at an early age and now I was finding an entry into that world. There was healing to be done and this was opening a door.

But the weekend did not end at lunch on the Sunday: what I came to consider a second weekend began. Lillian signaled me to leave the dining room with her. We went around to the side and sat on a fallen tree. Oh for a tape recorder. What I recall is what she considered perhaps the most important teaching her teacher had given her. He told her that she had a foot in the past and a foot in the future and was straddling the most important day. What was she going to do when she had to pee? We need both feet in the now. She went on and told me that she prayed daily, offering tobacco both morning and evening. She prayed in the morning to receive and in the evening to give. The morning receiving called in what was needed for the day and helped focus on the "most important day." The evening provided for thanking for what had been received during the day and giving away any negative leftovers. I realized that it was almost the reverse of what I had been doing. When she finished speaking, Lillian handed me a pouch of tobacco. My heart was too full for words.

As I parted from Lillian, there was no question in my mind – I was going back to Dreamers' Rock, which I had visited the previous year. My travelling companions acquiesced. I told Lillian we were staying over to go to the Rock and asked if she would be free to join us. She was committed to some teaching with a training group but would consult her diary. Next thing we knew we had been invited to stay with her.

That evening, we nibbled away on our leftovers from the weekend. Lillian said we would visit her mother, who had called twice on Sunday before Lillian arrived home, which meant she was feeling depressed.

We were served tea and homemade bread in the kitchen, not room enough for all of us in there at once. Lillian intended to say a prayer with and for her mother before leaving and wanted us to join them. We crowded into her mother's bedroom, sitting on her bed on either side of her, while Lillian offered a prayer in Ojibwe. Two of us gave her mother some reiki and brushed away negative energy from her. I hid my discomfort at being included in something I would have thought of as private and yet I felt honoured that Lillian wanted us there.

The next morning I prayed out back of Lillian's. I inwardly squirmed at focusing on asking for things, but in I plunged. After breakfast, both Lillian and the other workshop participant who lived on the reserve had presents for each of us. I received a sweet grass wreath with flowers and white strips of deerhide on it and a rainbow butterfly magnet. What beautiful, generous people.

We headed to Dreamers' Rock around 10:00. A gentle rain sometimes became heavier. Lillian stayed at the Lodge near the bottom of the trail: we walked on up. I made an offering of tobacco at a pair of trees near the beginning. Expressing gratitude warmed me. I led, thankful to be there. Rain was appropriate, a cleansing for being at this power place.

Within sight of the rock, one of the others burst into the lead. She crawled up the last slab of rock prior to reaching the actual Dreamers' Rock, supporting herself with her hands. I sized it up, knew I was in my power and walked straight up. I worked my way up the Rock, the only one of us to do so. Lillian came out below and called to us. Somehow I felt as though I had spent lifetimes here, part of the rock I stood on.

Then, realizing that coming down was trickier, I took my power again and asked if someone would stay by until I got down. One came over and gave me support for my foot, which I gratefully accepted. We each then wandered off on our own before heading back to Lillian down below.

Lillian said she had been with us on the Rock. She had little notes, including a Medicine name, for each of us. I was Bird Woman and compared to the names for the others, Sacred Swimmer and Rainbow Dragon Dancer, mine seemed ordinary. Later I grew into the name, just as I did with my animal totems. With my love of birds, what an honour to take on such a name.

This second part of the two weekends, the visit to Lillian's home on Birch Island, was the biggest source of my elation back home because meeting Lillian had been my goal for the weekend. I didn't realize then that it was a powerful example of how I was developing the skill of focused intent. I had drawn in what was important to me by the strength of my focus and intent, aided by my actions in seeking her out. No wonder I reached the centredness and balance by Monday that I was aware of and used in my physical body as I climbed Dreamers' Rock.

This signalled a significant shift in focus. So far I had been using programs and ceremonies with detailed instructions in which I could immerse my mind as a way to allow me flashes of going beyond that mind into a different realm. At times my enjoyment of outings in Nature also allowed me to shift, but there the shift was so subtle part of me didn't fully acknowledge just how powerful it all was. Now I had created the opportunity I sought, the time with a native elder.

Whatever I was gaining through my meeting with Lillian had nothing to do with detailed ceremony instructions. I saw myself as reaching closer to my role model, Lynn Andrews, who had apprenticed to native medicine women. That meant far more going beyond reason, led there in numerous ways, ceremony included. It also brought new emphasis on the power of prayer in our lives.

I was now ready for this next step, although I still clutched on to control and mind for security. A part of the fear that held me there, gut-wrenching fear, was the evil people and demons that were so much a part of Lynn Andrews' world and Carlos Castaneda's too. That terrified me. I didn't want that, couldn't even so much as voice my fear. I was poised, even so, on the brink of new adventures.

14

Grandmother Twylah

FEBRUARY 25 I had opened *The Bear Tribe's Self-Reliance Book* at "Communities" and read of the Wolf Clan Lodge and Twylah. Not the first time I had heard of her. Twylah was a teacher of the Métis woman who co-ran the first workshop I attended back in 1988. North Star spoke fondly of Twylah.

Since then I had made my plans, signed up for a weekend workshop and an "intensive" with Twylah on the Cattaraugus Reservation, not far from Lake Erie. I wasn't sure what the "intensive" would entail other than a "stone reading," for which I was to take a small stone that I had found myself.

Twylah's family home was a two-storied house, comfortable looking, inside and out. Huge maples surrounded the house, trailers out back accommodating family and students. Large, open space, perfect for tents, and a round sheltered teaching area. Simple, functional, warm, friendly. Hustle and bustle, coming and going, yet not rushed, room for one and all, room for change and growth.

Twylah Hurd Nitsch, Clan Mother of the Wolf Clan Lodge. Frail and not frail, exuberant, scattered, intense, thoughtful, gray hair, aged wrinkles, Grandmother Twylah. Young people are drawn to her, truly her granddaughters. So she replicated the way some native tribes' children are raised by grandparents through the difficult years. In this way, they avoid the generation gap between parent and child and leap to the less strained relationship between grandparents and grandchild. What a difference that makes - grandparents are special people with views to be respected.

Everyone welcome, living in serenity, believing in inner peace. An aura hanging there, enveloping Twylah, enveloping everyone. Her magic, palpable, expressed in colours, concepts, and clown charts. Magic weaving: the web of life, gently, caringly opened, explored, offered, and lived. My favourite prayer was offered daily:

> Oh Great Mystery, we awake to another sun
> Grateful for the gifts bestowed,
> Granted one by one.
> Grateful for the greatest gift,
> The precious breath of life.
> Grateful for abilities
> That guide us day and night.
>
> As we walk our chosen paths
> Of lessons we must learn,
> Spiritual peace and happiness,
> Rewards of life we earn.
> Thank you for your spiritual strength
> And for our thoughts to praise.
> Thank you for your infinite love
> That guides us through these days.

MEDICINE WHEEL OF COLOURS AND TRUTHS

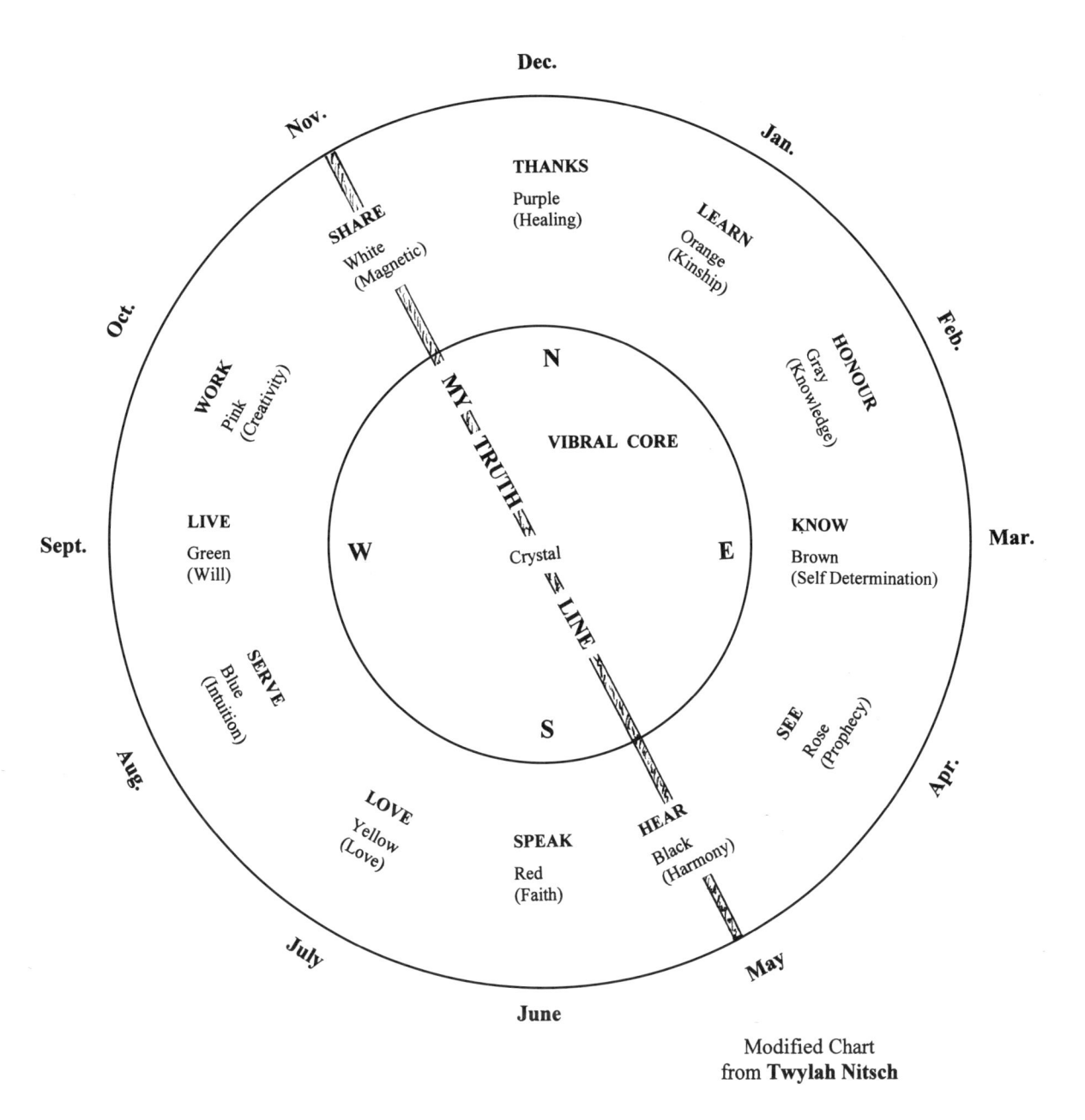

Dec.
Nov. / Jan.
Oct. / Feb.
Sept. / Mar.
Aug. / Apr.
July / May
June

THANKS — Purple (Healing)
LEARN — Orange (Kinship)
SHARE — White (Magnetic)
HONOUR — Gray (Knowledge)
WORK — Pink (Creativity)
KNOW — Brown (Self Determination)
LIVE — Green (Will)
SEE — Rose (Prophecy)
SERVE — Blue (Intuition)
HEAR — Black (Harmony)
LOVE — Yellow (Love)
SPEAK — Red (Faith)

N, W, E, S

VIBRAL CORE — Crystal

MY TRUTH LINE

Modified Chart from **Twylah Nitsch**

NATURE SPEAKS: I LISTEN 61

I arrived at Twylah's in the early afternoon of a warm, sunny June day. The weekend workshop was cancelled; I would join two other women who were in the midst of their "intensive," along with one other workshop participant. The weekend turned into a workshop-intensive run primarily by Twylah.

The teachings focused on three major tools: colours, which represent particular concepts related to "truth," a 12-point medicine wheel on which the concepts and colours are placed, and the animal medicine totems, whose characteristics are also linked loosely to the medicine wheel.

The weekend proceeded on Indian time. In the course of whatever was happening, Twylah would come out with teachings, often those that she had learned as a child. For example, she was sent away to school as a young child. Her first visit home, when they were all around the kitchen table, she was asked to tell them about school. She shared a litany of complaints. Finally, her grandfather suggested quietly that the next time she returned he would be looking to hear about how she had overcome the various obstacles which had confronted her during the term!

Early on, I was helped to establish my own personal colours of the 13 around the wheel. My white, black and crystal caught Twylah's attention as powerful. I came away with confirmation of my intuitive sense that I have much to share with others. Sharing is on my Personal Truth line, and is part of my Black, White, Crystal combination. Furthermore, sharing has even more force given that my birth month, May sits on the wheel in the position of Black, the other end of my Personal Truth Line, which is linked with listening.

The part that fascinated me the most, however, were the stone readings Twylah did individually. The stone was placed in the center of the medicine wheel in the position that the woman found it most comfortable to hold her stone. The number of the sides on which the stone could sit, its colour, the markings on it, the straight lines that it formed, were all taken into consideration.

For some reason, my lingering doubts about the colours and charts lessened in the face of her stone reading. I felt comfortable that the stone could portray a reflection of the person to whom it had been drawn, if one knew how to read it as Twylah clearly did.

Gradually I made some sense of the basic charts, but there seemed to be always something counterbalancing whatever was missing. I wondered if I had tuned into something profound or just a new set of overlapping charts such as delight my teacher, Lynne, but leave me a Doubting Thomas. I had Twylah's permission to stay and sit in on another Monday "intensive," which I hoped might bring me more clarity.

As the weekend drew to a close I was caught between doubt, which made my whole body contract and withdraw like an intruder in hostile territory, and deep warmth for Twylah that expanded my heart and drew me to her. What a contradiction to handle! At that point Great Spirit took over. I returned to my tent before dark seeking my flashlight. Beside the tent door was a largish moth. It was almost two inches long and entirely black and white, not the creamy greyish of many moths. Even the black legs were trimmed with a pure white. The body was such a mixture that it was hard to say whether it was black on white or white on black. There were flecks of black and white all over; even the suggestion of black and white eyes.

At first I was simply struck by its beauty. I was down on hands and knees on the damp grass to observe it more closely. Its location on the tent in relation to the door had it sitting in the place of listening in my truth colour line of black to white. I had come to the tent seeking light. All of this seeped in slowly like melting snow into thawing ground. Meanwhile I passed through stunned blankness to a state of agitation. I was so excited that my heart pounded and I could hardly stay still. I attempted to centre myself by breathing deeply. I just couldn't manage it and rushed off to find others, to share my excitement.

Later that night, restless, too wound up to sleep, I saw this clearly as a message that my truth line was a profound teaching, regardless of how I might feel about the teachings in general.

Monday, the woman coming for the "intensive" didn't arrive. Twylah decided that I should make a medallion of my colours. All that she told me at this stage was that I would be sewing rings of beads of each color around the centre stone. My body and mind freeze when it comes to crafts but this sounded OK, at least no need for me to come up with a design. I worked at it patiently, step by step.

In between busying herself with other chores, Twylah also worked on a medallion in her colours, presumably to keep me company. That is typical of her sensitivity and the unpretentious way in which she manifests it.

It wasnt until Wednesday morning that I proudly completed my medallion and finally honked my horn and waved goodbye. I drove home at the same leisurely pace I had worked on the medallion, accompanied by a contingent of ants, which I eventually tracked down to one of my tent poles. *Be patient about taking in all the teachings.*

I also brought back the saying of a prayer at mealtime. Acknowledging with gratitude the plants and animals that have given their lives for my nourishment helps me remember my connection and dependence on all living things and my need to put forth positive energy in return for the gift of life.

Over time, my Truth Line from her teachings rings true and black and white show up to remind me of it. In fact, however, Twylah's biggest impact on me had nothing to do with the teachings themselves. Twylah believes strongly that learning can happen without having to struggle through demons and pain. It can occur gently and joyfully. This was the energy that permeated her home, the stories she told, and the way she guided those who had chosen to live there and those who, like me, visited briefly. That was the message I most needed to hear. It freed me to open myself to what lay ahead.

15

The Bear Tribe

JUNE 20 I arrived home from my visit to Grandmother Twylah. By July 10, I was on the road again to the Bear Tribe program on Vision Mountain, not far from Spokane, Washington. It was more than just the Bear Tribe program. It was summer vacation with Sue, my closest friend. It was bird watching. It was exploring. It was hiking in the Canadian Rockies. It was visiting Vancouver friends. A tour package full of delights.

Sue and I set off at 7:32 a.m. July 10, just two minutes behind schedule. From then on, the schedule was tossed aside, apart from the days in the Rockies at Lake O'Hara, booked a month in advance.

First destination was Lillian's, Birch Island, memories of the weekend at Manitoulin calling me back. From there we drove along the north shore of Lake Superior with some staggering views of pre-Cambrian shield, of deep blue lake and miles and miles of road. On to the prairies, pancake flat as far as the eye could see. My heart leapt when mountains finally appeared on the horizon. We were headed for Wapta Lake and our base camp motel below Lake O'Hara. I was looking forward to my return to the lake and a replay of a previous hike.

Tucked into a hillside at Lake O'Hara is a closed off crystal mine. Crystals are still to be found on the hillside. I climb the wooded trail slowly, appreciating the rich dark green of the soft moss on rocks along the way. When I come out in the open to the large boulders just below the mine entrance, I hold my breath. *Will I find my rocks? Will the crystals still be there?* Unerring as a bee on the way to its hive, I head to them, remove the rock, feel gingerly in and there they are. I lift them out, view each with love, respect and awe, run my fingers over their cool, smooth sides to their points. I ask permission to take one with me and my fingers say "yes." I smudge, choose one, place the others back, give thanks and leave. That crystal is with me always in a pouch that I made at the Bear Tribe.

As I descend back down the trail, I think back to two years earlier when friends had first brought me here. We had heard the sharp whistle of a marmot and located it on a boulder not far away, splayed out in the sun. What child-like glee as we had picked up small crystals, held them to the light, searched for more, pocketed many. Later that night, it had hit me hard: my disrespect, my lack of ceremony, my improper taking of crystals. Early the next morning, before our departure, I had run back, scrambled up the hill, puffing hard, deposited all my crystals between a pair of rocks, placing a rock at the entrance of the crevice. My self respect restored, I promised myself, the Nature Spirits, and the crystal Devas, to return and properly request one of those crystals another time. How much lighter of heart and feet I was as I ran back down to catch the bus out.

While the difference in how I walked the path this day mirrored the changes in me over those two years, hidden in this visit was a prelude of what was ahead. It was my body, not my mind, that took me unerringly back to those crystals. More new experiences like that were coming.

On to Vancouver where I surrendered the pleasure of Sue's company when she flew home. I stayed on, gorged myself with day outings and friends, waiting for the trigger of the trip, the Bear Tribe program.

But there is magic in Vancouver, my dead friend Sharon's home. While staying with one of her friends, one night the phone rings. An uncle of Sharon's who is visiting relatives, calls to chat. He has news that shakes me, takes my breath away. Relatives of Sharon, living in Richmond, near the ocean, have nesting bald eagles on their land. Bald eagles so connected with Sharon. The next day we eagerly head out to Richmond and there they are, three young eagles in the nest. An adult cries and flies in, so close we hear the flap of its wings. It perches in the pine, not far from the nest. Eagle preens and preens and then I see it, a breast feather loosened by preening, dropping, parachuting lazily down. I rush over, heart in my throat, guide its landing to my outstretched, cupped hands. Sharon's eagle, gifting me one of its feathers. Tears come to my eyes. Magic, Spirit in action.

Aug. 9. Now was the time. I set off early and was across the border by 10:00. After crossing a low pass, I found myself in sage brush country. I stopped and collected some sage, drinking in its sweet aroma, enjoying its light gray foliage. But mostly I drove. The route was hot and much less mountainous than the British Columbia route. Finally, as I was becoming convinced that Vision Mountain was indeed no more than a vision, I saw small hills in the distance, and, yes, that's where I was headed. After entering the hills, I stopped at a lake for the little supper I had. My journal says I was not particularly anxious about arriving but the writing is cramped, anxious, speaking another truth.

I found the turnoff and headed up the rutted dirt road. I saw buildings below me on the left, a garden there. I continued on up. More tracks branching off here and there. It became more wooded, tall ponderosa pines prominent. I reached a building and a parking lot. No sign, but it was the Bear Tribe longhouse. I had arrived, along with 30 others. I discovered that it was tent city beyond the trailer where our program would be. There were two more tents farther off, more isolated. I picked a site on the far fringe from them under a ponderosa pine, capitalizing on the soft ground cover of its long needles. This was home for the next 10 days.

And that's how it all began. Part way through the first afternoon, a short, stocky man with arresting deep brown eyes and a black hat covering his longish black hair joined our group and brought our lecturer to a halt. This was Sun Bear. I'd read one of his books and knew he was of mixed blood, his native heritage Chippewan. As a result of his visions he had searched for this land on which to bring together a group of people to live with him as a community, respecting and living in harmony with Nature. Thus he had founded the Bear Tribe, who were now running summer programs to pass along the teachings that Sun Bear brought to the community. The participants were clearly in awe of Sun Bear. Initially I wasn't particularly impressed. What he had to say didn't seem to have much bearing on the rest of the program. In fact, he didn't truly touch me until the following summer.

It was a tightly packed program, ten days all planned out, revealed to us bit by bit, usually the night before. It included lectures, activities, usually a daily talk by Sun Bear, getting in touch with the land, ourselves and ceremony. There were sweat lodges, chanting, and a ceremony on Moon rocks. It's the activities, not the lectures, that have stayed with me most. Early on we chose our Power Places, drawn there, intuitively knowing where we needed to be. This is where many of our activities took place. These became Power Places for us through the blending of the inherent energy of the place and the energy that we invested there during our frequent visits.

Back to the first morning of the program. We were taken on a tour of the area from which we could choose our Power Places. We had to be able to hear the conch shell blown at the program trailer to call us back in. During that walk, I was attracted to a 12-foot-high slab of rocks among Ponderosa pines.

In the afternoon we seek our Power Places. *This is crucial*. My body tenses up like a cat ready to pounce and my stomach is verging on queasy. It drives me to be organized, let my head be fully in control. (That still allows for me to use my fingers as guides since it's my mind that determines the questions I ask.)

I walk back up the narrow trail to the area where I was in the morning. No difficulty in finding this route. I opt to try out each part of the rock area to find the exact spot for my Power Place. The top looks best and I confidently climb up there first, hug the large Ponderosa pine and ask if it wants me under it. "No."

So much for that idea. The wind is out of my sails and I more meekly work my way back down the opposite side, flushing a nighthawk. This is still not the place. Further down and around to the front, I notice a small ledge. This much more obscure location is my Power Place.

I sit on the ledge with my back against the rock. The surface behind me is rough and hard. I've put my pancho under me for comfort. I reflect on what has happened so far and realize I am uncertain about the proper name for the bird I have just seen. As a bird watcher familiar with the bird, this is disorienting, like losing your sense of direction in fog. Then I try to think of exactly where the tents are in relation to my Power Place. Uncertainty and disorientation once again. *This can't be my Power Place after all: I don't feel in control.*

My stomach tightens, an elastic band pulled taut. But my fingers say that it *is* my Power Place. They add that it is OK to feel disoriented. I breathe deeply and let my shoulders drop, muscles loosen.

A noise at the base of a ponderosa pine catches my attention. *Pine cone falling?* I rule out a pine cone and then spot a chipmunk. The chipmunk meanders closer. Twice it leaps a foot in the air, footloose and fancy free, and just plain enjoying itself. I grin, relax more, feel welcomed and comfortable after all. Over the 10 days my Power Place becomes as much my home as my tent.

Time is up. I descend to the dirt road close by and easily locate the side trail back to the program trailer.

What I was to learn next was that my body could guide me intuitively. Bear Tribe teachers stress how important it is to get out of our minds if we want to touch our true selves and our power. That was so foreign to me. Early on, Matt, one of the instructors, came to me, pointed out that I wasn't yet making that shift. I cried inside, crushed with the heaviness of failure in something that so mattered to me. Yet that elusive shift I was seeking was breaking through now and then. My Power Place took me there several times.

I noted my disorientation during my first visit to my Power Place. Looking back, it is as though my body was deliberately doing some short-circuiting of my "mind hold" on things. The next incident was the following day and was linked with the participant in the program to whom I was most drawn. Carol was a resident of the Bear Tribe and we began our friendship there. Her Power Place was literally on top of mine, without our even knowing it. Carol had chosen the ponderosa pine that I had hugged on the top of the outcropping rock. It was several days before we discovered that we were so close since we were not in sight of each other. Carol, who had been uptight about someone else being near enough to inhibit her, was not uncomfortable about me being far closer! Nor did I feel inhibited: to the contrary, it simply reinforced the positive vibes between us.

On this particular occasion we were to do a ceremony that entailed loud voicing of emotions. It was the one time when Carol and I would have been inhibited by the other's presence. When I set out to my Power Place that day my feet led to a different place. I had no idea where my Power Place was and did the ceremony in this new location. So we both had our own space.

Another similar event was at the end of several hours at night at my Power Place. I was bursting with exuberance on completing the activity, ready to grab my "tiger's tail" and get back to my tent without using my flashlight. But then I had an overpowering gut feeling, without any sense of cowardice, not to do so. When I turned on the flashlight, I discovered that I had forgotten an eight-foot drop that I would have encountered had I proceeded in the dark.

This is that inner guidance, quite independent of mind and reason. Tuning in to this inner knowing and learning to accept and trust it is central to the path I was learning to walk.

One of the activities near the end of the program was for each of our four groups to develop a ceremony focusing on the one of the four elements, air, fire, earth and water. The ceremonies were presented to everyone as part of the program one evening. Our group had fire as our theme. We hadn't got far with our ceremony and no one was taking initiative. I felt we all had a responsibility to prepare a good ceremony but I seemed more concerned than the others. That night, without asking for a dream, I had one in which fire was an element. The dream was of a pajama party around a fire and, later, as I lay awake, I realized that storytelling around a fire is an important element of fire. *How had we missed it in our group brainstorming?*

Then a ceremony just came to me, using a symbolic story about a fire (in both senses of "about") to draw in our intent and lead up to the actions of the group. I was the storyteller in the ceremony and the rest of the group acted out being extremely cold, sending off a hunter to search for fire, his bringing it back and their gratitude for fire and the warmth they then felt. Well-being permeated me from head to toe. It felt so right that I was eager to share it and had no doubt it would be accepted. The ceremony was creative and I performed my role well. Creating ceremony stirred something in me, not just creativity. The same feeling of fulfilment of "all's right with the world" that writing *The Bird Tribe Gathers* was bringing into my life, was also kindled by the fire ceremony. I was discovering my own unique gifts.

Another activity that on the surface seemed unimportant turned out to have significant relevance for me. One morning we visited the Bear Tribe garden that I had noticed on my drive up to the longhouse. I was interested in learning about what they were doing but it turned out that we were divided into groups. Half wouldn't take part in the "tour and lecture" but would work instead. My Higher Self took over and volunteered me for assisting with mulching around young ponderosa pines. I worked with two other women. I focused loving attention on each tree, cared deeply about what I was doing and was grateful for the opportunity to help each one. By the time the hour was up, the idea was already hatched that coming back to work in the garden the following summer would be the right way to return to Vision Mountain for a Vision Quest.

The final key aspect of my experience at the Bear Tribe barely began out there. Frequently during the program, Sun Bear and the Bear Tribe staff spoke of the importance of a pipe for prayer. Pipes could be strictly for personal or family use but they could also be working pipes, smoked as part of ceremony or in response to the request of someone seeking help. They talked of the increasing urgency for more people to have pipes to increase the power of prayer in the world.

I struggled with the issue. Smoking pipes as natives use them was even more sacred to me than a Sweat Lodge ceremony. One had to be worthy and it carried much responsibility too, even, to my mind, for a personal pipe. I couldn't see myself as ready or worthy of owning and caring for a pipe. I talked with a staff member, Moon Deer, who encouraged me, but I remained hesitant.

Early in the week, however, I stumbled on a piece of branch in the grass near the tents that was exactly the shape of a small pipe. It was reddish in tone and totally free of bark, smooth to the touch and comfortable to hold as a pipe. I recognized its coming to me as significant at the time and considered it as perhaps my step in the direction of a pipe.

I looked at the pipes for sale with interest but was even more drawn to those that Mary, one of the residents, makes and was immediately attracted to a design of the head of an eagle. *That is exactly what I would like if I were to have a pipe.* So that was <u>one</u> decision already taken when a dream gave me my answer.

Finally, the issue was of such proportion that when we were to recall a dream for dream interpretation the next morning, it immediately occurred to me to call in a dream about a pipe. My intent was strong and brought forth a relevant dream. In the dream I said, "It is time to turn the sod on a new building even if it won't be completed for some time." On waking, I knew immediately that the building represented a pipe and turning the sod was ordering it to be made. My indecision vanished, as did my mind and body unease over the issue. I approached Mary and asked her to make me a pipe with an eagle's head as the bowl.

Near the end of the program, I and another participant, who was also ordering a pipe, arranged a time to go to Mary's workshop to make our selections of stone and wood. We both zeroed in on the same big lump of white alabaster. Fortunately, Mary felt confident that there was enough stone for both pipes. After my initial inward reaction of "That's mine," I liked the idea of sharing the stone. Then we turned to the wood for the stem. Both of us wanted sumac carved into a spiral like Mary's own pipe. Mary worked out the measurements and lo and behold, we were able to share the same piece of wood as well. Mary left us. Together we smudged ourselves, our stone, and the wood, offering prayers as we did so. Everything feels special about this pipe, right down to the items I planned to attach to it - a "beaver" chip of wood, at my feet during a ceremony that moved me greatly, and Eagle's feather from the nest at Sharon's relatives' home.

How was I changed by the Bear Tribe program? Even years later as I was preparing to answer this question, I was still struggling for more understanding. Suddenly there was a thud as a white-breasted nuthatch crashed into the window beside me. I jumped up and rushed out to where she lay, beak gaping, her head a bit to one side and her wings spread out. I gently picked her up and held her in my left hand, her heart thumping in the palm of my hand. I cupped my right hand over her giving her reiki and my own body heat. We stayed that way for minutes. She closed her beak and moved her head. I removed my right hand to free her, action to mirror what I was saying. She fluttered, then quieted. I covered her again. A minute more. Her eyes darted and she cocked her head. I removed my right hand and she flew off, both of us feeling much better, hearts beating normally once more. Response to my morning prayer for guidance in writing.

When I left the Bear Tribe, I was that stunned nuthatch who had just finished thudding into a window. As you've seen, there had been more than one window in the program for me. The 10 days over, I was exhausted, too dazed and stunned to comprehend all that had happened. First of all I needed warm nurturing to bring my energy back. The return journey offered that in abundance. When I arrived home, that nurturing sufficient, I was ready to fly but still not consciously aware of the shifts that had occurred in me. My actions spoke of change, but I didn't grasp their significance; they reflected my growing awareness of powers within me. I was showing I could use them when I needed them.

16

Sacred Sites

THE RETURN TRIP was entirely different from the trip out. I was alone, eyes, ears and heart fully open. The dove of peace was within me, no concern about such a long journey all on my own. And Nature nurtured me from beginning to end. I lived in the flow of the moment so completely that it was only later that I could step back and look at what had transpired. I was not caught up with interpreting symbols: I was simply connected. I was so balanced, centred, and completely in harmony with the world around me that I slipped into an altered state of consciousness without knowing it. I glided exactly where I was meant to be. I flew with Eagle.

I stopped at unusual places and sacred sites and was visited by special animal "relations." I want you to journey the wonder of that flow with me.

I set out early. There was mist on a lake and clouds hovering around the hills, followed briefly by claps of thunder, lightning and rain. Later, when I stopped to watch a bald eagle soaring over the road, I soared too.

Where I stayed that night, brochures made mention of a Buffalo Jump nearby. I arrived there early the next morning. A circling bald eagle landed on the rocks at the top of the jump, its profile remaining in view against the sky as it watched my approach. Next a busy, chattering rock wren caught my attention.

I picked up a number of small, light, buffalo bones, planning to select just a couple when I sat higher up to enjoy and pray. I carried on up the trail. I jumped back as I came upon a resting snake. My heart beat quickly and was up in my throat. I took a few deep breaths and passed by respectfully! The place I chose to select my two buffalo bones and offer my thanks looked down over a vast area. I watched a northern harrier flying low to the ground, searching for breakfast. Shortly after the eagle flew near the harrier, highlighting the size difference. My heart was overflowing with gratitude for so much big medicine greeting me. Driving back to the main road, the vivid blue of three mountain bluebirds in flight, in the sunlight, took my breath away. I was in love with myself, the day, and the world.

Friday morning my car and I make a very steep climb up to the Bighorn Medicine Wheel. It is still early and **cold** when I arrive. I don mitts and my jacket. Two young men arrive, rush around the Wheel, take a picture and depart. I grin and shake my head. *How bizarre. Just another tourist attraction to add to their list.*

There is a barbed wire enclosure around the Wheel. I'm repulsed by the barbed wire and all the strips of cloth attached to it. It's a fairground with everyone's garbage left scattered and blowing in the wind. Not the greatest of first impressions. It is an enormous Wheel. I wander around, trying to see what line-up of rocks demonstrate a scientist's theory that three particular piles of stones of this huge wheel are lined up with the point where the sun rises on the summer solstice. I can't line up three sets of rocks anywhere.

Finally, off to the side from the Wheel, I sit down and pray to the Sacred Ancestors and Great Spirit. My solar plexus becomes a whirlpool. Soon I'm overcome by a welling up in my chest and heart and I'm close to tears. Now I notice more closely what has been left on the barbed wires. There are feathers, deerhide, antlers, pouches. The "scattered garbage" is a sacred honouring of the site. I, too, have now connected to the Bighorn Medicine Wheel.

Time to move on. I start down, stop for ravens and notice marmots. Next, not 100 feet away, is a coyote. We regard one another, unhurriedly, before it trots out of sight.

A day later I am off early to the Devil's Tower National Monument and acquire a map and advice on the choice of a trail from the Visitor Centre. Not far along my trail, the movement of a stag close by catches my eye. Another with a huge set of antlers is lying at the foot of a tree, eyeing me. It is magnificent. As I continue to gaze at him, I notice a doe lying close to him. No movement, no sound, not even wind in the trees. When I am adequately saturated with deer gentleness I move on, delighted that they have not been disturbed or threatened by my presence.

In a more open area I have a clear view of the south face of Devil's Tower. The sun is beating down even in early morning. I find a large rock boulder with a wee pine tree on it and a bigger pine to the side offering shade to me and the rock. I stay an hour. This is another place for prayers and awe. Devil's Tower is such an inappropriate name. From this angle, Cathedral Tower would be far more fitting. The slope of one side is feminine, flying buttresses: the other side is strong and masculine. After I have been there some time, I shift to a cross-legged position. I immediately feel a strong sexual surge rush through me, clearly associated with the Tower. I realize that its shape from this angle is conducive to sexual thoughts. I welcome the energy and thank Great Spirit. What a gift and how different from my initial physical reaction to the Bighorn Medicine Wheel.

As I continue the circle, the Tower takes on a completely different shape, like the backside of a huge amphitheater. Farther around, it becomes gentler and I am again aware of its ribbing. Suddenly I sense energy rush down the ribbing, across the field between us and enter my second chakra, bringing waves of sexual stimulation once again. As I complete the circuit, there are now numerous climbers on the side of the Tower. I am so thankful that my visit preceded theirs. I have stroked the Tower lovingly, not assaulted it with pitons.

Next morning I reach yet another sacred site, Bear Butte. The instructions are to stick to the trails, one of which leads to the summit. There are many viewpoints along and just off the trail. Almost without fail I see ribbons of white, black, red, yellow and sometimes blue blowing gently in the breeze, constant evidence of the continuing use of the site by natives. Unlike tourists, they are free to use the land for meditation or vision quests. I am frustrated to be restricted to the trail but console myself with the thought that it is good to see that natives are using the site and some of their ways are being respected. I follow the narrowing trail to the summit. Part way up, I stop for a breather, wipe the sweat from my forehead, and enjoy the vista. A raptor lifts up from below and rises directly over me, 20 feet above my head – a golden eagle. Having already prayed for some recognition of the power of the place, I'm overwhelmed, in tears and sobbing. What a statement of power!

I don't stay long at the summit as someone is already there. As I retreat, a falcon zips by. Nothing surprises me any longer. Coming down, I examine the meeting place below more closely. I had seen natives there earlier but they are now gone. I spot the frame of a Sweat Lodge and another still covered, with someone's shorts drying on bushes nearby. All in all, Bear Butte rates as a "living" sacred site in contrast to Devil's Tower.

I pressed on to a petrified forest in the Black Hills, then through the Badlands and across boringly flat and exceedingly hot country. I was elated to finally reach the Missouri River and view a large body of water, lined by tall trees.

My route passed through Pipestone, Minnesota. I arrived early morning at the Visitor Centre. Natives were working at crafts. I was drawn to a man who was carving a pipe bowl, questioned him about the process of making the pipe and about the feathers used in some of the headdresses on display nearby. Neither he nor I knew what part of a golden eagle had feathers that were white with brown for the tip. A park naturalist dug out a bird book and we discovered that they were the tail feathers of the immature golden eagle. Mystery solved, I went back to share my discovery with the native. He laughed, forming a bond between us. That was important because I had decided to purchase one of his small pipes so that I could become comfortable with one before Mary completed mine. I came away with one that Redwing had signed.

Finally I was back with my friend Lillian at Birch Island and Dreamers' Rock. How right that my return journey, which held me so connected with Spirit and all living beings along the way, came to an end at this sacred spot, in the company of Lillian. It wasn't until I arrived home that I fully re-entered everyday consciousness.

17

Re-entry and Snake Medicine

MY JOURNAL noted the arrival home: "Not sad, not glad, a little uneasy about the question of what I'm going to do now – I sure don't know!" A pilgrimage complete but no light shining on a clear path for me to follow. Reality had set in again.

Re-entry to another life. In one way, the life I'd left behind and in another, a new life, a life altered by that pilgrimage. They'd warned us it could be hard. Life carried on while we were gone and our pilgrimage would be hard for others to grasp. No wonder. It was beyond my full grasp, too. My re-entry was easier than most; I lived alone, no job to contend with, and supportive friends.

I phoned Sue. Bad news. Isabel had died, she whom I visited in the year of the Eagle encounters. Ill for some time, painless, slipped away at home. Good news, yet sad, loss of a special friend. Pain and sadness gripped my heart, wringing out tears. How to mark that passing and the passing of my pilgrimage?

This leads me to the first big steps in my re-entry, the first manifestations of the change in me. Next day my trusty fingers step in. Take the new pipe for a prayer. Smoke it in Nature. *Where? Oh, oh, not there to guide me for that.*

I drive to nearby Mer Bleue, my constant hiking location for several years. *How about the beech tree where I undertook my very first ceremony?* That's the trail I take. Before I get that far, chickadee calls and other unidentified noises bring me to a halt. My feet face off to the left of the trail. *Don't be silly. Go on to the beech.*

I continue. A chipmunk scolds out "No, no, no" nearby.

Of course, the beech is right on the trail (no privacy in the daytime. That is enough. I double back and go in where my feet had pointed.

A squirrel chatters angrily and I asks its permission to stay. It stops, one brief grumble, much less angry and that is it.

Acquiescence? I take it for that. A maple, in the centre of a circle, is divided part way up into two equally strong branches. I'm drawn to this symbol of duality. I ask if I may be in this place. No further sense of "yes" or "no" but it feels "right," as my Power Place at the Bear Tribe had.

I lay out my pipe, my smudging stone, the sage, the mixture for the pipe. *Oh-oh, I've left behind my needle for tamping the tobacco mixture.* Right beside me though, is a long rigid stem, dead but not yet broken off. *Perfect. Acknowledgement of my focus and contribution to my ceremony.*

As a precaution, I have along the wooden pipe so that I can carry on my prayers without struggles with matches. I'm not a smoker. The match pile grows, enough for a bonfire, as I struggle to keep the pipe lit. Very hard to pray when all my focus is on keeping my pipe going. But it is worth the struggle. *I like the feel of the hot bowl of the pipe in my hand: the heat is a tangible sign of its life.*

Part way through the prayers, I hear a voice and turn. A man and his doberman pinscher are on the trail. No sign of a leash. My body tenses and I catch myself holding my breath. Yet neither the dog nor its master pay any attention to me. *Am I invisible?*

I go back to my pipe. It isn't easy to tell when I've smoked all the tobacco mixture. When I have, I'm still not through with prayers. Suddenly I notice the man and his dog again in front of me, not far away, but I am invisible and protected. I realize then that the trail loops around the circle I've chosen. I carry on with my prayers, holding the wooden pipe. Now I fully focus on prayer, not the pipe but I miss the heat that touched me before. Prayers finally over, I clean the pipestone pipe, continuing to give heartfelt thanks for Isabel and all my friends.

My Power Place had been such an important base in my Bear Tribe adventure. One of the staff there suggested that we find such a place not far from home. "Befriend that spot, visit it regularly, like a good friend." Mer Bleue offered itself and pointed the way and so I'd found my Power Place. I had taken a step in re-entry, bringing the magic of the adventure out west to my own doorstep. I responded as well to some inner understanding of its importance to my whole being and I used it for prayer with my pipe.

The value to me of this new spiritual tool is hard to overestimate. Not only is a Power Place a source of healing energy in and of itself, it undoubtedly adds to the power of any prayer or ceremony carried out there. Why not find such a place for yourself, close enough to home that you can readily visit it?

What else did I bring back that I incorporated into my day-to-day life? Most significant, which I have not mentioned anywhere in the adventure, was my new appreciation for water. Vision Mountain had a spring well but water had to be conserved with care, given the numbers of people using it. Showers were reduced to twice a week and ever since I give thanks for water whenever I shower.

So far so good. Yet I also needed time on my own, no contacting friends too soon. I grounded myself with finances and grocery shopping. Yet that nagging question remained. *What now?*

Dream time faced the issue too. In one dream, I was nearing the end of my present employment. When someone went by I felt vaguely uncomfortable about not doing anything. I went off in search of a machine and some cards to see how much I could finish off. A friend offered her pass card hesitantly, not supposed to do so. I said "No thanks," not even knowing what floor I needed, planning to ask for help at the building.

As I wrote down the dream, noting its searching, its uncertainty, my eyes fell on *The Book of Runes*. I drew a stone, focusing on this period of time I was entering. The Rune I drew was Thurisaz, "Gateway, Place of Non-Action, The God Thor." The book offered this guidance:

> "This Rune indicates that there is work to be done both inside and outside yourself. The gateway is the frontier between Heaven and the mundane. Arriving here is a recognition of your readiness to contact the luminous, the Divine, to illuminate your experience so that its meaning shines through its form.
>
> Thurisaz is a Rune of non-action. The gateway is not to be approached and passed through without contemplation. Here you are being confronted with a true reflection of what is hidden in yourself, what must be exposed and examined before successful action

can be undertaken. This Rune strengthens your ability to wait. Now is not a time to make decisions. Deep transformational forces are at work in this next-to-last of the Cycle Runes.

Visualize yourself standing before a gateway on a hilltop. Your entire life lies out behind you and below. Before you step through, pause and review the past: the learning and the joys, the victories and the sorrows – everything it took to bring you here. Observe it all, bless it all, release it all. For in letting go of the past you reclaim your power.

Step through the gateway now." (pp.125-126)

As I wrote the advice in my journal, I realized that even the timing of Isabel's death was symbolic, since she was the last significant tie to my past employment.

Another step in re-entry. I made no conscious effort to do the review *The Book of Runes* advised, yet I was led along that path in the events that followed.

It's a sunny fall day, some leaves on the ground but still some yellows, and reds on maples and browns on oaks. I set out for my Power Place for a ceremony. I crackle my way through the newly fallen leaves, smelling their soft decay scent in the air.

I think back to a week earlier when I visited my Power Place. That day I was drawn to hug the hemlock in the circle. It has numerous thin small dead snags low down and its bark is rough and jagged. Nevertheless I wanted to hug it and gingerly avoided the snags to reach its all of six-inch diameter trunk. I wrapped my arms around it, placed my cheek on its bark. Tears and tenderness soon flooded over me. I sat down close to the tree. The open flow turned to memories of Dad, who died two years before at Thanksgiving. I revisited a number of the good times we shared, heart aching, yet a tender smile on hand too. I decided then to return for a ceremony in which I would read aloud the eulogy that I had given at his memorial service. I would bury something in the ground to represent giving away my sadness and sense of loss. Then I would focus on one of his qualities that was both his greatest strength and his greatest weakness, one that I share – over reliance on reason and logic.

I reach my Power Place and prepare myself, facing the hemlock. I stand and read the appreciation aloud slowly, my voice capturing my deep respect and love for him. In places my voice breaks and I am in tears as I read. Fortunately, I hadn't had that problem when I read it at the service. I finish and sit for a moment and listen to the hymn of a flock of chickadees working their way by, deeing at one another and me.

Hymn over, I get to my knees and scoop a hole in the soft rich black earth for a very small grave. In deference to the environment, I bury leaves to symbolize my sadness and loss. The first half of the ceremony is over.

I sit again and begin to voice out loud my feelings about reason and logic. It's easy to acknowledge their advantages but I squirm where I sit as I push beyond to how I have depended on them for a sense of control in my life. My chest is tight. I recognize that I've used these qualities to shut out my emotions, put down any sparks of trusting intuition. I want this to change but I'm scared to let go. You can trust reason and logic, not intuition. My brain is alive with that thought. But my heart pushes for more, wants release. The policewoman and prisoner wrestle.

I whittle away at a dead branch with my Swiss army knife. The stack of chips attests to my inner struggle. Finally I vow to let go, seek to nurture emotions and intuition in the future. That spoken,

I add my chips to the leaves in the hole and cover it over. Calmness, peace and sturdy energy as well take their place. The chickadees pass by again, accompanying the music I feel inside.

I sit for a while, basking in this glow of contentment, and then refill my backpack, don it, and walk back through the softly crackling leaves to the trail to continue the circuit. Very shortly, I flush a grouse. I thank it. The last paragraph of Grouse in *Medicine Cards* is the most relevant: "Back in touch with Earth and your body, Grouse may then teach you how to notice the energy flows that put you in harmony and balance with body, mind, and spirit." (p.175)

Soon I notice a garter snake, loosely curled at the edge of the trail about nine feet ahead. I stop, sure this is important. Snake raises its head and turns towards me, its tongue darting out. Quite a tongue. Most of it is a bright red but the last half-inch is black. It makes no effort to leave. I wait, then move forward and crouch. Snake twists itself into considerably tighter coils, continues facing me and still makes no effort to leave. I'm with it for close to an hour, ending up not more than a foot away and sticking out my hand, only three inches from Snake. Snake charmer, except we have the roles reversed. Snake stays right there, mostly guarded, flicking out its tongue, at times relaxed enough to quit the flicking. It gradually shifts its coil to the centre of the path. Once, as I simply have to stand up and stretch, it makes a quick dart of its head in my direction as though to strike. *If it does it again suddenly when I am fully crouched, a fear reaction will come out of me too.*

Sometimes it moves almost imperceptibly closer. My legs give out before I determine if it will ever touch my hand. I've never been so close to a snake other than touching one that someone had grabbed. They always slither off before I am anywhere nearly as close.

The message?

Snake is Transmutation. I see it as a recognition of the ceremony that I have just completed. A transmutation is taking place. I am now allowing it and Great Spirit is acknowledging my effort in a way I can't miss. How exciting!

The quote in *Medicine Cards* that feels most appropriate is:

"Move through the dreamlike illusion that has insisted on static continuity, and find a new rhythm as your body glides across the sands of consciousness, like a river winding its way toward the great waters of the sea. Immerse yourself in that water, and know that the single droplet which you represent is being accepted by the whole." (p.62)

The following Saturday my new vow was tested. I accompanied Louise to a weekend workshop. The leader had been trained to use Tibetan bells and that drew me. But the program was for the group to be a healing circle focusing on bringing out very early childhood memories of our relationships with our parents, going back to the time in the womb as well as after birth. Listening to the music the leader played did not elicit any memories for me. We broke into groups. He moved from group to group, offering suggestions if someone was stuck.

He instructed my group to push me around as I lay on my back in order to loosen me up. The harder I tried to let go, the tenser I became. We shifted to breathing techniques. No better. Finally, one of the women caressed my head and hand. Gentleness brought tears but no memories.

It was a long day; it went on until nine p.m. I thought it would never end, like a nightmare where you try to move and can't. I was exhausted, a wrung-out dishrag. My back and legs ached from all the sitting on the floor without support. My head and shoulders drooped with disappointment and discouragement: the old blocks were still in control. I couldn't handle the thought of a second day.

By morning it occurred to me that my totem animal, Opossum, had been in play and that in some of their techniques to open my feelings, my body had simply played dead. I accepted that I hadn't felt the warmth and caring there that allows me to trust and grow. I began to realize that it wasn't negative old blocks that had stopped me but rather an inner recognition that this wasn't the right environment for me. Not all situations are appropriate for trust and growth. I needed to trust my instincts and be guided by them.

After breakfast, I opt for a visit to my Power Place instead of the workshop. I check with my inner self through my fingers. I can let them guide me completely.

The leaves are mostly down now. The leaf smell in the air is stronger. I arrive at my Power Place and follow instructions to sit, lean against the central maple and face the sun. Soon I am too warm and remove my Taiga jacket, leaving it under me. *What next?* Nothing in particular - just be here. I settle back comfortably. Dragonfly lands close by. I watch it intently and can even see it turning its head occasionally. *Don't think I've ever noticed that before.* I watch it land in a couple of more distant spots. Once the light catches it, making its wings iridescent. *Medicine Cards* says:

> "Look within and feel the sense-of-self energy within ourselves. Notice if it is ebbing. . .The *illusion* was that we would be happier if we did it their way. In forfeiting what we know is right and true for us personally, we give away our power. It is time for us to take it back." (p.146)

And then the incredible happens. I suddenly notice a 14-inch green and yellow garter snake about half way between me and the rim of my circle. It is gliding almost noiselessly toward me. I beg it to keep coming and it does. It is soon inches from my left hiking boot. After a little indecision, it climbs on and curls itself there in the sun. I can't believe it, struggle with difficulty to watch it since my knees are bent and I don't dare move. Old fear of snakes nibbles at me. *I don't want it wandering up inside my pant leg.*

I fold the pant and hold it close! After some time Snake descends to the ground again, looks around and then glides towards me between my two legs. I stay frozen with awe and delight, not fear. Snake swings a little to its left, undulates past under my right knee, slips up onto my jacket, curling itself there, head aloft and alert, all of an inch from my hip. I put a finger down slowly toward it; I prefer to have Snake on my hand if it chooses to come up. It opens its mouth wide a couple of times but no darting its tongue.

It doesn't want my finger there. I raise my hand to my lap again and remain spellbound. Snake keeps me company for some time and then leaves.

My emotions explode. I sob, the sobs wrenched up from deep within. As my sobbing subsides, I struggle to identify the feeling. Gratitude seems likely but not quite right. Gradually it dawns on me. It is the sobbing of a hurt child, who needs company, reassurance, and encouragement that she can do it. That is what Snake has just done. Until Snake's gesture, I hadn't recovered from Saturday's feeling of failure: I had already broken my vow to open myself to emotions. I had even started questioning whether I had misinterpreted the meaning of my previous encounter with Snake. *Snake has come and reassured me and offered me its company, releasing my emotion ever more strongly than occurred on Saturday. This was the right environment!*

Now tears of gratitude flow warmly down my cheeks. I'm bathed in glorious warmth, joy and peace. I hate to leave but it's growing cooler. I slip into my jacket, put on my backpack, and return leisurely to my car, thanking Dee for her call that I hear en route.

These months thus marked strong confirmation that I was on my path, in fact gliding to the centre of my path as the first snake had done and I was flying with Eagle as well. What clear signs I was receiving. There was yet another.

Louise requested that we play a game of Transformation, another tool to guide us in understanding a personal current issue or resolve a problem. This is a board game in which you pass through physical, emotional, mental and spiritual levels before the game is completed. Your progress around the board is determined by rolling dice. According to where you land, you face setbacks, receive insights and so on.

To begin the game, the players choose the topic for which they seek help. My pipe was foremost in my mind and my focus became how to be worthy of using a pipe. The smoking of a pipe is a sacred form of prayer to natives. They consider that the smoke carries the prayers directly to the Creator. My visit to Pipestone, Minnesota further reinforced how special it was. To move towards this sacred tradition was something I wanted to honour fully.

The insights that came in the course of the game were relevant. One word, however, that I received while I was working at the emotional level in the game was "surprise." That puzzled me. It didn't appear to fit and I cast it aside. Louise was convinced that I would have a significant surprise on the emotional level within the next few days.

A few fall colours are still lingering. The morning following playing the Transformation game I set off for the Gatineau Hills, across the Ottawa River and into Quebec, less than an hour from home. I drive to Black Lake, a small lake with a circular trail climbing behind it, offering glorious views of the Ottawa valley and river. In the fall it catches the hawk migration.

It is misty at first and remains somewhat hazy but Grandfather Sun is in evidence. I peel off my sweatshirt and push up my sleeves. There is even a new supply of black flies, or their relatives, having a last fall fling too. I stride on up the hill toward my favourite viewpoint on a big rock outcropping, stopping here and there to seek out the owner of bird chirps. I reach the outcropping. Looking out from here, the colours that remain on the hillside are muted reds and yellows mixed with the gray of leafless trees. I have brought my little wood pipe. I sit cross-legged, pipe stem in my right palm. Given the game the night before, the theme of my prayer on the rock is my desire to be worthy of the pipe. A blue jay shrieks raucously now and then. After I finish my prayer, I am enveloped in a glow of peace and warmth.

Finally, I return to the trail, an apple in hand to carry on with the day's celebration. I crunch into the apple. The bite is so large that I have trouble shifting it in my mouth to suck out the juice. My favourite Empires have just appeared in the stores, so gorgeously crisp that this one matches the beauty of the trees and the day.

It suddenly occurs to me that I haven't thanked my wood pipe for its coming to me at Vision Mountain or for its help this particular day. I no sooner voice my appreciation than a large raptor sails over, twenty feet above and ahead of me. I stop dead in my tracks, neck upturned. I can't believe my eyes – a mature bald eagle, white head and tail, brown-black body. *The eagle of my pipe. What an incredible confirmation that I am meant to have the pipe that Mary is making for me!*

I watch it gliding, seldom flapping, mastering the thermal currents, sailing with the flow. When it is finally beyond my sight, I turn, light-hearted, light-footed, and glide on my way too. What an emotional surprise the game had forecast!

The year-end brought another ending. I finished writing *The Bird Tribe Gathers*. I had mixed feelings when Crane, the great blue heron, rounded off her turn and the group decided to break for the summer. I smudged my thanks while printing the last bit. Then flicked off the power bar without getting out of the program first. Panic! But I only lost the punctuation changes for the last chapter and a page of the story.

My chest swelled with pride at completing it. At the same time there was a tinge of sadness in my heart: I had greatly enjoyed the writing and each of the birds. Also anxious about what came next and wanting to start soon. Writing was my major "career" output and had become an anchor for me.

Critiques of my work, editing and changes still lay ahead but the first draft was completed. I had taken my first tentative step toward sharing the path I was on with those beyond my immediate circle of friends.

Part IV *1991*

18

Day-to-Day Life

SO FAR I HAVE described the major events soon after my return from the Bear Tribe that were each a reflection of changes in my approach, mostly as a result of my experiences out there. In a sense they were part of my day-to-day life, but highlights.

Now it's time to wander more quietly through my life. How were all my adventures of 1989 and 1990 weaving themselves into my day by day life by 1991? How was I using my spiritual tools?

I find it hard to pinpoint now when I first started to wean myself off red meat and to cut back on chicken and fish as well. Reducing cheese came later. Certainly, Louise introduced me to Ballantine's book, *Diet and Nutrition*, well before the spring of 1990.

As I moved to vegetarianism, I recognized the need to learn more about nutrition and during the fall of 1990 I bought or borrowed a number of books on the subject. I tried to improve my diet, introducing tofu and tempeh into my repertoire.

This interest also opened my mind to herbal medicine. Louise and another friend guided me. I used garlic pills to fight a virus and bought preparations to help balance my system. I went to evening classes on herbs. In keeping with what I was learning, I gathered mullein and made oil from it, which I used to loosen wax in my ears.

Both the emphasis on nutrition and the interest in herbs were directions that challenged my previous reliance on the medical profession when it came to health care. As I gained more respect for alternative methods of dealing with illness, I realized how culturally bound I had been to relying on a traditional doctor.

Communication with my body and my higher self through my fingers was now solidly entrenched in my daily living. I used it routinely for guidance about food but often, also, about what my activities were to be, day by day and week by week. They told me when it was time for automatic writing and, of course, were crucial in the timing of the writing of *The Bird Tribe Gathers*. I relied on them to check out aspects of ceremonies that I was devising. One new direction emerged this year after I obtained Machaelle Small Wright's book, *Perelandra Garden Workbook*. She describes how to contact the plant Devas and the Nature Spirits of a garden, exactly what I'd been doing working with my jade plant.

While nothing in 1991 matched the Snake Medicine experience of 1990, much happened at my Power Place over the course of the year. I smoked my pipe and carried out ceremonies there. Small Winged Ones frequently came by at appropriate moments; Pileated Woodpecker visited once; Porcupine rested in trees nearby; Chipmunk visited; Great Horned Owl nested in sight of it, and Moose crossed it.

The trees were constant and I began recognizing different personalities among them. Maple was always there to assist me and hugging it brought a warm, supportive, strong feeling. Beech was more aloof and much colder but sometimes open to hugs. It welcomed my friend, Sue, several times. Hemlock, which I thought might be somewhat prickly, was the most tender and drew out emotion most readily. It was under her that I did ceremonies.

Sue was welcomed there by the Place and I also took Louise. But it was very much a private space and I was very selective about who went with me.

In May I attended a women's healing circle run by Lynne. One of the topics that she raised was anger. I found myself unable to get in touch with examples in my past and became uptight. The next afternoon, at my fingers' instigation, I took my problem out to my Power Place and there I had the opportunity to look at my ingrained belief in not expressing anger. I was becoming able to accept anger more readily in others and even in myself if it was related to work, but still had difficulty identifying it in my relationships with good friends, let alone expressing it. I recognized a recent example with Lynne. "You are going all the way out there to plant turnips?" was her way of envisioning my upcoming summer at Vision Mountain. I was hurt by her disdain. After recognizing my hurt and anger out on my Power Place, I was able to bring it up to her after the session that night. She acknowledged how her flippant response had affected me and I was at peace for having raised how I felt.

I continued to expand my reliance on intuition. My fingers pushed me at times to "know" without consulting them and so more frequently I tried to get in touch with my inner knowing and then just confirm with my fingers.

Seeking guidance from my Inner Self through my fingers was part of my day-to-day life. I also found myself using the Runes, Medicine Cards, Sacred Path Cards and I Ching as tools to help me at certain times, but never in the sense of "It would be fun to draw such and such today." I was now drawing a Medicine Card to guide me every three months but I wasn't always tuned in to the animal as consistently as I wanted to be.

The importance of my dreams and my ability to recall them varied a great deal. My ability to decipher them increased as I made more of an effort to apply various techniques and was learning my own personal symbols.

At Louise's suggestion, I went on to take my level two reiki. This enabled me to do long distance reiki, which I used infrequently. Louise and I did a 21-day reiki exchange. No miracles ensued, but by the end there was some improvement in my lower back as well as in Louise's abdomen. It was useful in making us both aware of variation day to day in how it felt both to receive and to channel the energy. I became very comfortable in using it and in improvising according to the needs at the time.

How much I had learned became more evident at the Bear Tribe in the summer of 1991. During an evening reiki exchange I felt that I would have been more able to "lead" the evening than the two masters who were present. I found myself willing to offer reiki to others and I used it on my own stomach, in particular, on a regular basis.

As for my writing, I asked for comments on *The Bird Tribe Gathers* from a poet/writer whom I knew. He suggested a drastic change. I could see why but it implied undoing the entire concept of the gathering of the birds. Fairly quickly, I came upon a solution that partially addressed his ideas and brought in a new element – the entire book became written from Dee's perspective.

Since July of 1989, I had been completing annual progress reviews of my spiritual path. By 1991 I was discovering how helpful they were in recognizing how much I had accomplished in the course of the year. I was integrating my reading and new experiences into my day-to-day life and my belief systems were gradually evolving to incorporate all this new learning. Recording my path and undertaking annual reviews of my progress were in and of themselves additional tools in my tool kit.

If you haven't already done so, maybe now is the time to consider which of my many spiritual tools belong in your own kit. And beyond that, see how you can put one to use in the coming week.

19

Vision Quest: Preparations

ALTHOUGH MY NEW PATH was clearly influencing my day-to-day life in a variety of ways, I was far from satisfied. Leading a spiritual life truly meant daily, in fact, moment to moment to me. I was far from that. I honoured the plants and animals that gave of themselves for my food. That was daily all right, but the rest came and went. Nor did I have a spiritual purpose that was constantly guiding my life. That's why I applied for the Vision Quest program.

Could I also discover more about day-to-day living by being out there on Vision Mountain with the Bear Tribe for the better part of the summer? That's what I set my sights on–see and experience how they incorporated this spiritual path into their day-to-day lives. There was even the question of whether, after a summer, I would feel that I needed to live as a full-time resident for a while. Now I didn't allow that thought to surface very often; it would mean leaving behind my life back here, my friends, Sue in particular, and most of my belongings as well. My stomach churned at all of that and I pushed it out of my thoughts whenever it popped up. In fact, my energy turned primarily to preparing for the Vision Quest.

Several times now I've mentioned Vision Quests. What exactly is a Vision Quest? I had already done a mini Vision Quest during my first weekend at Manitoulin Island. At that time, I had fasted all day and stayed all night in the circle I had chosen, following ceremony instructions and seeking a "vision." The Bear Tribe program outline talked of up to four days and nights out on Vision Mountain, minimal belongings, plenty of water, staying in a circle of a radius of 10-15 feet. Out there alone. Not true, Nature was with us. We had a notebook and pen and yarn to hang out each day to signal that all was well. Four days and nights to seek vision, seek answers to our questions. No food, just water. The deprivation was to signal our strong intent, giving up comfort and food to make way to receive.

I had applied in the fall for the Vision Quest program as well as to work in the Bear Tribe garden. I was quickly accepted for the Vision Quest program and in April was sent *Vision Quest* by Steven Foster with Meredith Little, to read.

I began reading right away. The book speaks of stages in which preparation, giving away, and letting go are step one. Then comes crossing the threshold and starting the quest itself. The journey of the quest is the mighty third step. And then on to the final step, re-entering the world from which we came. The book suggests keeping a journal to record the preparation, finding the focus, and building intent. The journal can begin as soon as you form the intent of going on a vision quest. *Well, that date is already well past. Never mind, now is another starting point.*

I bought a journal that day, the cover divided into four triangles, yellow to the right, blue below, orange to the left, pink above. All pastel shades separated by black designs like fish lures and flowers outlined in black in each of the triangles. It resembled a Medicine Wheel, light and full of promise and became my journal, a prayer added later on the inside front cover. I found this prayer in a book in the Spokane museum, just before my quest:

> "Oh Great Spirit: whose voice I hear in the winds, and whose breath gives life to all the world, hear me. I am woman/man before you, one of your many children – I am small and weak. I need your strength and wisdom. Let me walk in beauty and make my eyes ever behold the red and purple sunset. Make my hands respect the things you have made, my ears sharp to hear your voice. Make me wise so that I may know the things you have taught my people – the lesson you have hidden in every leaf and rock. I seek strength not to be superior to my brothers or my sisters but to be able to fight my greatest enemy – myself. Make me ever ready to come to you with clean hands and straight eyes, so when life fades as a fading sunset, my spirit may come to you without shame."

I was ready to start the day after *Vision Quest* arrived, but, oh so true to my patterns, I stalled. *O.K. Now I've got the journal, what goes in it?*

My fear of not being eloquent enough to match the journal, match the journey that lay ahead – my need for perfection. What better way to scare myself off and hold back?

Two days later I thought back to my first ceremony at Manitoulin Island where I so badly wanted to get it "right," and how the rain cleansed me long enough for the ceremony to unfold. This memory was enough to free me again. The first entry reported that I went to my Power Place in Mer Bleue, anxious to tell it of my intent. I checked Great Horned Owl's nest, which is visible from there and looked straight into the eyes of two young owlets, eight inches tall. My heart thumped with delight. More than just the owlets. I saw a porcupine and a fox on that outing. *Not sure how to interpret all this more than that it feels auspicious.*

There were messages there. The owlets symbolized the beginning of new learning and wisdom while Porcupine was stating that all I required was my trust and innocence. Fox, the master of camouflage and adaptability, signaled tools I would also put to use on this voyage.

The next journal entry is about a Medicine Walk that same week. I visit out to my Power Place mid-morning with just water for my lunch, as practice for the fast of the quest. On my way into the woods a broad-winged hawk calls and later I see it soaring. *Be aware, attentive.*

I sit with my back against the beech tree in my circle, not my usual resting place. *I shall have a new Power Place for my quest.* I examine the fist-size black rock that I have brought with me. It has flecks of rainbow colours scattered here and there. *The dark I'll explore through the Vision Quest will divulge its own new colours.*

I take off my hiking boots and socks. Warm enough for that. The leafy earth is cool, almost spongy under foot. There's a smell of new growth in the air. I settle in for several hours – no three-or four-day quest, but a starter. I struggle to express my focus for the quest. *What am I giving up? What is dying through the Vision Quest?*

I don't know what I'm giving up. I've already quit my job and I'm already changing my life style. I want to confirm these changes. I want a clearer picture of "who my people are" and "how I am to serve." This is going to be relinquishing control and, in the process, taking control. Strange, but that's what it's about.

So I'm giving up control. What else am I seeking?

Well, I brought along this black rock. I'm looking into myself, want to become more aware of my emotions. How do I overcome obstacles? How come I lost the close connection with Spirit I had as a child? How come I lost much of my imagination? So uncovering some of the past is part of what I seek. I also yearn to hear Nature better, not have to go through all this active "analyzing."

I voice all this to the Nature Spirits. Now I sit back and wait. Even as I voice my questions, my purpose as I see it now, I notice the flies. Not biting black flies but just curious, exploring house flies, country flies here. They light on my feet, tickling me. Next it's my arms and hands, checking me out. One is unique, part of its body a shiny green. It stays with me more than the others, then flies off but soon returns. *Flies are not supposed to be easy to communicate with. What is your purpose? How insignificant you are. Me too. You've brought me this message. You are showing me we all have something to share with all our relations. Wow, that's close to communication with me. That's like what Michael Roads describes in* <u>Talking with Nature</u>.

I listen to brown creepers singing. It's not often I hear their clear melody. Chickadees come close. Dee of my book makes them welcome friends.

My legs cramp: I've got to stretch. I can't stay still any longer. Up I get, can't resist going over to the fallen log near the Owl nest tree. *Wouldn't it be neat to find a feather for the Medicine pouch I made at the Bear Tribe last summer?*

I move to the other end of the log. *What's this? A feather, but something else, too. Why it's part of an egg shell from Owl's nest. There's a little feather fluff inside. Oh my, symbol of wisdom emerging, birthing. What a gift for my pouch. That sure beats <u>my</u> expectations.*

I examine the trough of water that runs through between this log and my Power Place. *How can it be? There's a two-inch long fish in there. Mystery, that's all I can say.*

When the fish has left, I step into the water but quickly retreat. It's cold! Next I note a furled young plant determinedly piercing its way through two dead leaves to reach the sun. *Strong enough intent and it's amazing what you can achieve. And dead materials don't stop new growth.* I go down on one knee and pull off the brittle, curled maple leaf, crumbling it in my fingers.

Time to go. Back on the trail, my thoughts return to the vision quest book. *What will I be leaving behind during my Vision Quest "death"?*

A garter snake startles me and it slithers off. I watch and in the process notice a heap of leaves trembling on the ground. I approach closer. There's at least one more snake there. The one I have been watching returns and enters the leaves as though trying to rouse the others into coming out, too. It enters and exits a couple of times. *Snake. Transmutation and change. Am I that Snake, trying to encourage my friends, who are not ready yet to emerge, breathe in Spring?*

I sum it all up. *Lots of inspiration from just a few hours. And, surprisingly, no hunger pangs.*

Next step to my summer Vision Quest comes in May with an overnight ceremony at Lynne's in the Gatineau. Friday I draw an Animal Medicine card for guidance. It's Badger, one of my totems. *Aggressiveness. I wonder what the ceremony will be. Will it be the one where I die, like the beginning of my first ceremony at Manitoulin Island? Bet it is, links in with the quest this summer.*

I am in my circle before dark and lay out everything and wait until it seems dark enough to begin. In no time the candle is spluttering. *What's new!!* I look for my small flashlight and can't find it. I search through my pack three times. *I really am back to Manitoulin. How compulsive. Get on with the ceremony.*

Later, as the first candle comes to its end, I reach for another and pull out the flashlight. *In synch now.*

It is the death ceremony, where I invite friends and relatives to my funeral. So many with me. I choose to talk to my brother, Jon, first. Quickly I'm in tears. I talk and talk. Voice my confusion at his having left me when I was so young, my sadness at his loss. *Time to move on.*

Next I turn to Mom and finally Dad. I talk of the positives and the negatives. This takes time. On to more relatives and then I turn to friends. *I sure am making up for missing this part at Manitoulin!*

Funeral over, I turn to the rest of the ceremony. First, as part of my dying, I am to cut the cord of attachment to all places and things. *This is tough. It's going to be hard to leave Nature as it is on this planet. Material things won't bother me nearly as much.*

I think of giving away other possessions right now. *It's not so much any specific material item that gives me a problem in letting go. But I am dependent on a car, this summer my tent. . . and most of all my financial security. I couldn't give up all that too, as did Irena Tweedie in* Daughter of Fire.

I have my sleeping bag with me but not my foam. I lie on the ground in my bag. The ground feels soft at first but as time goes on my hips and back get sorer and sorer, dull toothache pain. Finally I have to leave during the false dawn. A call of White-throated Sparrow lets me know it's O.K. *This is a teaching from Nature. I'll need my foam for the August Vision Quest. I wonder if this means that the path ahead will be hard and even that I may have to quit early?* I return to my tent and fall asleep.

In the morning I talk with one of my friends. She spoke <u>with</u> her relatives and friends, conversations back and forth. I stiffen. *How one-sided my dialogue was. Did I do it wrong?*

No, I was voicing my opinions and feelings, an important step for me. This is the Badger quality of aggressiveness. Thank you, Badger.

I speak with another friend. She is disappointed. It has all seemed less significant than the experiences of others. I reassure her.

Back home, I think about how different this ceremony has been for me, so much more "doing" than "receiving." *I guess that was what Badger was all about.* I feel cheated though. There was so much less involvement of the universe this time.

Remember what I said to my friend: "It's different for everyone. We get what we need."

Vision Quest spoke of the quest as beginning with preparation. I have applied my focus and intent well. As a result I'm clearer on what I seek and I've realized that I need to respect my body's limitations.

20

Departure Jitters

IT'S THE SECOND HALF of May with June 1st my departure date and I'm getting the jitters. May 17 I admit in my Vision Quest journal that a variety of emotions are enveloping me–fear of failure in not completing the Vision Quest, or, on the other hand, fear that this big adventure won't answer the questions I've set. I manage to acknowledge these feelings in my journal and commend myself for doing so.

On May 20 when I awake I recall a dream. I was at the edge of a fast flowing river, holding the rope of a canoe. I thought of swimming across holding the rope. The canoe went to where I wanted to go but the current quickly pulled it away from there. I wasn't sure I was strong enough to fight the current swimming, particularly if the canoe, too, was pulling me downstream. I couldn't see a paddle and was hesitant to try crossing in the canoe for fear of overturning. At that point of indecision, I woke. *The canoe represents my present attachments and possessions both materially and otherwise. This sure catches my fear vividly!*

It didn't occur to me then that the canoe could also represent me. I could complete the Vision Quest but the current would then pull me much farther than I anticipated. And I was afraid of that current.

Later that day I finish reading *Vision Quest* and turn to another book on questing by the same authors, *The Roaring of the Sacred River*. As I start Part 2 on Severance, there is a quote from *I Ching*:

"Waiting. if you are sincere, You have light and success. Perseverance brings good fortune. It furthers one to cross the great water."

I think back to my dream. *This certainly tells me what I needed to do in the dream. Maybe it's time to do an I Ching reading of my own for my Vision Quest.*

Out come my coins and my book. My reading is the hexagram "Chin/Progress." I have no moving lines in the reading, which disappoints me. I start to read:

"The hexagram represents the sun rising over the earth. It is therefore the symbol of rapid, easy progress, which at the same time means ever widening expansion and clarity.

"The Judgment

Progress. The powerful prince is honored with horses in large numbers. In a single day he is granted audience three times.

"This pictures a time when a powerful feudal lord rallies the other lords around the sovereign and pledges fealty and peace. Sovereign rewards him richly and invites him to a closer intimacy. . .

"This leader has enough clarity of vision not to

abuse his great influence but to use it rather for the benefit of his ruler. His ruler in turn is free of all jealousy, showers presents on the great man and invites him continually to his court. An enlightened ruler and an obedient servant – this is the condition on which great progress depends.

"The Image

"The light of the sun as it rises over the earth is by nature clear. The higher the sun rises, the more it emerges from the dark mists, spreading the pristine purity of its rays over an ever widening area. The real nature of man is likewise originally good, but it becomes clouded by contact with earthly things and therefore needs purification before it can shine forth in its native clarity." (pp. 136-7)

I go on to read the moving lines, which do not apply to me. They refer to possible obstacles of one sort or another – uncertainty; kept from getting in touch with the man in authority; might reproach himself for lack of energy to make the most of the propitiousness of the time.

How pure the hexagram is for me and what a wonderful message to make sure I have the courage to cross over the roaring river! I feel more confident.

That doesn't last long. Two days later my closest friend, Sue, is home sick. I feel guilty about leaving her in the lurch. There's a lump in my throat. *Should I ask her if she wants me to put off going out?*

My fingers say "no."

This quest really does involve separation. This sure makes it more real and worrying. I'm close to tears. I take a deep breath: *but I've got to do it and Sue does have to face her own challenges. I haven't thought about this aspect before. I guess it's not up to me to determine where all the lessons are. Help me Great Spirit to accept and to face what I must face.*

The next day Sue asks me to devise a ceremony for us before I leave. We start by thanking Great Spirit for the ceremony and call in our totem animals and other guides. Our voices ring out clearly. Next we voice our respective fears to Rabbit and then let "Thumper" take them away. We're more hesitant, less loud in how we voice them, and far more serious. Sue cries. Fears out of the way, we take each direction in turn and talk of what lies ahead and the help we need and draw an Animal Medicine card. When the four directions are completed, we thank the animals who have volunteered themselves. As part of a release from attachments, I ask Sue to choose something of mine that she would like. She chooses an ashtray from New Zealand and later I give it to her. To close we hug each other. For each of the four directions, while hugging, we take a deep breath and exhale, three times in a row, and then let go of each other and step back. This is a separation exercise I've learned from Lynne.

The ceremony has required an incredible amount of Kleenex for Sue and some for me too. The animals that volunteer to aid me are Rabbit in the South, Dragonfly in the West, Dolphin in the North and Armadillo in the East. To have Rabbit with me, particularly in the South, is very reassuring since I always view Rabbit as someone to whom I can turn over my fears, as we have already done in the ceremony.

June 1 arrives. I depart in a well-packed car for Birch Island and an overnight stay with Lillian. Next morning we are up at 5:30 for a Pipe Ceremony at the foot of the path to Dreamers' Rock. My journey has truly begun.

Three days later in the late afternoon as I approach Sturgis, near Bear Butte, it is dark, almost black. It is pouring as I enter town. *Going to Bear Butte right now in this storm would be crazy.* Nevertheless, I check with my fingers. No hesitation on their part – go. So I check into a motel and go.

To my surprise, as I drive the short distance to Bear Butte, the rain dwindles to a spatter. As I get my first view of Bear Butte, my solar plexus does a somersault and I am close to tears; the return to a long-lost friend. *What a contrast to my blasé crossing of the country to date.*

The same ranger I had met the previous summer, Chuck, recognizes me and gives me his map for the trail. I don my rain pants and set off. The Thunder Beings greet me but from the other side of Bear Butte. At times I need my pancho as well as my rain pants but it never rains hard. I see lightning in the distance but the thunder is closer at hand and continues on and off throughout my visit. *No Eagle this time but friendly Thunder Beings instead!*

The evening is transformed into a glorious outing and my fingers encourage me to go to the top. I have the mountain to myself and the Thunder Beings, although a number of natives are camped below. *Sure am glad I followed my fingers' advice to come.*

That isn't the end of my visit. The next morning dawns sunny and clear. My fingers say to return: so back I go. I am at the Visitor Center at 7:50, 10 minutes before it opens. While it seems unnecessary, my fingers say to wait. Chuck arrives to open the Center and we talk. I discover that the entry fee does not apply to persons coming for religious purposes. Anyone there for religious purposes may also go off the trails. *I am cleared to go anywhere on the mountain!* I am in tears.

My fingers opt for the ceremonial trail route, to search for a spot with my back in the East facing West. Shortly after I start, I come upon an ideal walking stick. I proceed up to the saddle between the two peaks, leave the trail and scramble up to my right. I reach a rock outcrop with two small pines on either side of me. As I sit with my back to the rock, I face across to the main peak and also have a view North to the plains below. Violet-green swallows swoop around.

I call out that I want help to hear Nature clearly through this quest on which I am heading. The cries of the swallows answer mine. Then they go back to chattering. The wind comes and goes, blowing coolly on my face. There is quiet as I, too, settle down. I pull the remaining bark off my new walking stick. *Will I keep the bark? No, no need to hang on to dead parts.*

Grass blowing in the wind catches my attention as I sit and "listen." *Flow freely like the grass so that Nature just permeates my being.*

Time to go. Before leaving, I tie a tiny red flannel bag, filled with tobacco, a hair and some spit, to a branch of the Pine I considered the female. I then slide my way down to the main trail and on down to the parking lot. As I am about to leave, Mountain Bluebird, who also greeted my arrival, flies by very close. Chuck suggests that perhaps it is my Spirit Guide.

Winged Ones certainly often are guides for me. I think back to the pigeons I saw the day before. I viewed them with disgust. *Domestic Pigeons don't belong here in the wild.* Today I see a link. *The pigeons represent "civilization." Their being here on this sacred mountain is like my being here. I'm one of the Rainbow People. Maybe pigeons are the Winged equivalent!*

The way I have been drawn to Bear Butte and the well-being it has brought strike me forcefully as I leave. *On my way back home, here is the place to smoke a pipe of gratitude, using my new pipe.*

With that thought, it is easier to break away and depart. I don't head immediately for Vision Mountain and the Bear Tribe. Carol, my friend from the introductory program the previous summer, is now living in northern Idaho. I have arranged to spend two days with her before carrying on to Vision Mountain. As I draw close, I get cold feet, literally and figuratively. *We hit it off well last summer but two days together with no program?*

In answer, I see a partial rainbow ahead. As I round a turn in the road, a horse is galloping along ahead of me. *That's a funny shape for a horse. . .It's a MOOSE!* I slow down. Moose does not and disappears around another turn. *Perfect symbols, the joy and beauty of a rainbow and self esteem of Moose.*

I always think of myself as a non-talker. Well, in two days of non-stop talking with Carol, time lost totally in absorbed conversation, I discover a me I'd never heard before.

June 14, the momentous day, arrives. I am on the road by 8:00, destination Vision Mountain. I start up the dirt road to the Bear Tribe at 1:30 p.m. I see someone in the garden, pull in and ask for Ave, whom I believe is in charge of the garden. A man in his late 30s with unkempt hair haltingly says she isn't here. He points up the mountain towards the Bear Tribe longhouse. *That makes sense.*

So I drive on up. I meet Beth, the Bear Tribe resident who will be my boss. We chat briefly but she's busy. I go to my last year's Power Place. Tears fill my eyes as I hug the central Pine. Here I feel truly welcomed. I sit on my ledge, drinking it all in. The wind whispers to me in the pines and the day's warmth brings out their sweet smell. My tension evaporates like steam from a kettle.

It's time to return to the garden. The wiry German is Werner and he's in charge. As I reach the garden area, I see Matt, one of last year's program teachers. I ask him where I am supposed to camp. He points out a general area across the field, behind the foundation of Sun Bear's home, to be built this summer. The area has a stand of small pines. *So there will be some shelter.*

I spend considerable time selecting a site. I put up my tent and dig a trench around it. This is serious camping: I'm here for most of a month.

Settled in, I return to the "mud" kitchen (with rain, the floor always gets muddy?). It's a one-room screened building, wood painted deep red. There are several chairs, a small sofa, a large rectangular table, and lots of counters and shelves. A few shelves hold personal belongings, some seeds for the garden and the rest pots and pans and cooking supplies. We have a fridge and stove. This is where I'll eat, not up at the longhouse with the Bear Tribe residents.

It's nearly 6:00. No sign of anyone. I'm hungry. So I make myself a toasted cheese and tomato sandwich. Later I meet Ave and we chat. I learn she is here with her two children and her new boyfriend. It is she who told Werner about the Bear Tribe. They all are Germans, except Ave's boyfriend, who is Austrian. The children speak no English, Werner next to none.

It is almost dark as I return to my tent and it's cold. I undress, get into my sleeping bag and spread Sue's over mine. She's going to join me for a holiday mid-July and I've brought her gear out with mine. I quickly discover that I'm on enough of a slope that I need to hoist myself back up from time to time. My mind is an alarm clock wound up and ringing. I take a long time getting to sleep.

The gardening stage of the adventure is about to begin. I'll return to that stage later. Getting to Vision Mountain is part of my Vision Quest. Now we're here, I'll skip to when the program begins.

21

The Program Begins

AUG. 16. This morning I feel that my preparations have all been completed. I'm tranquil. *The lull before the storm?* I am verging on diarrhea but I attribute that to drinking water out of the tap at the longhouse. I'm uncomfortable with all these new people arriving. *Sure hope most things are done in smaller groups.*

We have three days to prepare. The main feature of this first day is an afternoon Medicine Walk, an opportunity for us to start listening to Nature and for our leaders to get to know us better as we tell our tales afterwards.

I choose the question: "How do I learn to better 'hear' the messages of my own inner self and of all my relations?" As I set off, my attention is caught by an upended stump up the hill. I climb up to it. I have forgotten that it lies behind Evelyn Eaton's sweat lodge. Having been drawn here, I call on her for help during my Vision Quest. The stump points me on to her Medicine Wheel.

On my way to the Medicine Wheel, I come upon a foot-high pine in the shelter of two mature pines. I am drawn to Tiny Pine. I run my fingers over its long, rough needles and then I sit down on the path across from it in the shade of the larger trees. I ask its help. *Even in your youth you can teach me.* One of the participants comes up the trail and I move off. *I'm not allowing Tiny Pine to answer.*

Back I go and sit for some time. Others come up the trail and pass between me and Tiny Pine. Only one participant circles around us. I feel tears and tenderness for Tiny Pine. I'm also frustrated at not being open to its message. I nevertheless thank it and leave tobacco and water.

It was only years later as I wrote that I was properly centred for Tiny Pine's message. Tiny Pine represented my Child within. By sitting there with it, I was recognizing at some level my need to search wisdom from my Child within. I didn't hear that day. I needed the centering of the quest itself to hear that Child.

Back to the Medicine Walk. *I'm not sure about going on to the Wheel.*

Red-Breasted Nuthatch cries "Yank, yank."

"*Yes, yes,*" it's saying. I proceed up to the wheel, a circle comprised of large stones in the four directions and smaller ones around the circumference. I sit on the large stone near the east tree. Sensing that I'm seeking a new, deeper way to connect now, I close my eyes. Images come. Horse, then Deer, then *Is it Wolf?*

I ask for a repeat but see Owl with a very open eye. I interpret. *I have the power, need to be gentle with myself about this quest and a teacher will be there if my "eyes" are open.*

A big black ant visits, reminding me to be patient. I check my fingers to see if I have completed the assigned Medicine Walk and get a "yes."

I stop to watch a grasshopper and ask it what direction I should go now. It isn't hopping anywhere. It walks a short space and puts its long pointed end into the earth. It repeats this several times. Meanwhile, I hear a scraping noise coming from a nearby Pepsi can inside the fence near a deserted house. I reach for the can and shake it. Several grasshoppers drop out, one dead. I return to my other grasshopper, who is still engaged in the same activity. I struggle for the meaning of all this. *The direction I am to go is towards a sexual or life energy connection with the Earth and I am to help "the children," All my Relations.*

In hindsight now, knowing what lay ahead, Grasshopper was more specific. "Go find your Power Place for your Vision Quest. Get connected with the Earth where you are going to be."

In any event, I hear Red-Breasted Nuthatch cry "Yank, yank" again.

O.K. I follow its general direction. Then Dee, Mountain Chickadee, takes over and I follow her up the mountain. I reach an area where I have expansive views both east and west. *I'd like my quest location to offer me a view in both directions.*

As I stroll on up, I come upon a rocky area, large boulders together in a clump, with a couple of trees right by them. From here I have views both ways. I halt, attentive now to this as a potential site. *Is there enough shade? A reasonable place to lie?*

Yes.

I'll keep this site in mind.

There is a somewhat similar cluster of boulders close by on the other side of the path, but no trees. I carry on, almost as far as we are to go, but it becomes impossible to see both East and West at once. I turn and walk back.

As I near my potential Vision Quest sites, I hear a noise in the grass not far from the road, on the side of my preferred site. A smallish snake slithers away and it's quickly out of sight. A golf ball is in my throat. *Bull snake or rattler?* Considerable stomach and inner turmoil, too. *Have I the courage to take one of these sites? You encourage me Snake but you also represent one of my greatest fears on this Quest. Can I handle a rattler?*

Yet somehow, right from the start, I "know" that this is a good sign and that this is where I'll go.

After supper we meet in our small circle and take turns describing our Medicine Walks. Our leaders ask questions. They ask us to look at what happens and our reactions and search the link with our life situation. Our whole life situation and how we react to our lives is a broader perspective than I've used before.

The evening closes with a pipe ceremony and I ask for a dream to confirm whether or not I have found my site.

Aug. 17. Not one dream, but two. In the first I am about to return home but it is raining and I have a distance to go without a car. One of my work colleagues, who is black, offers to go with me. After initially questioning why he should get wet too, I realize that at least I can drive him back after. I accept.

The second is longer. The Chairman of the Board for which I worked, a former university professor, gave me a dinner coupon for two to a very posh restaurant. I get to the entrance stairway. I find the Chairman is there to accompany me, which surprises and pleases me. We go up to the small restaurant. Near the top, the Chairman has me stand on a landing. He pushes a lever which raises the landing and I am swung around 180 degrees to enter the dining room. There are windows around three sides, looking out over water. I choose a table by the window on the centre side so as to have a view in all three directions. This is a really posh place. The Chairman says that a waiter will soon take over and bring more drinks and our meal.

What extraordinary dreams. I never dreamed about my previous work place even when I was working there. It is signaling that this quest is work. The first one suggests some emotional struggle. My dark within will become a colleague. That particular colleague never worked too hard and so I guess I won't find this all that difficult. And then there's this posh restaurant. It does have the expansive view of the site I chose. A posh restaurant with one of my favourite teachers taking me.

I smile, stretch out in my sleeping bag, (not quite as posh as the restaurant) and gratefully bask in the warmth of my bag and the memory of my dreams.

That afternoon, we set off to find our Vision Quest sites. I return immediately to the location I'd found the day before. Ross has chosen a site not far away. My body tenses as I spot him. Bad moment. *I don't want to leave.*

As I expect, my fingers agree that there is no problem for me if Ross stays too. We get together twice to talk it over. Ross really likes his spot. He's willing to accept my presence. Next discussion he mentions that he may be nude much of the time. I indicate that I may be too. We still prefer to tolerate each other rather than move. After my experience with Carol's and my Power Place sites the previous summer, I realize I'm far more concerned about disturbing Ross than about his disturbing me.

I become more acquainted with my site. The pine on the edge of my circle has branches low to the ground and offers shade all day. There are a great many ants there, who wander all over me and tickle. The eating area for our group is infested with yellow-jackets and several participants have been stung. Up here I am pleased to discover that there are none. *Thank goodness!*

There are two possible sleeping places. The main one with the view, which is right beside one of the large boulders, won't get much shade during the day. So I search for and find a number of suitable sitting spots, back rests included. *With my foam along as well, I should be fine. A sheet of plastic, some plastic bags and my pancho should take care of rain.*

I sit crosslegged and soon meet ants galore and various other insects. One large grasshopper demonstrates how much they walk rather than jump. Chattering red-breasted nuthatches, a turkey vulture and a Townshend's solitaire all make appearances. So does Chipmunk. My eyes feel heavy and the heat drains the energy out of me. I want to snooze, close my eyes several times, but don't fall asleep. Or do I? The conch sounds at 5:30. *It can't be 5:30 already.*

That evening, the staff mentions that rattlesnakes sleep at night. I somehow feel lighter. There is a fire in the centre of the teepee and we are to throw our fears into the fire. Mine has already vanished. I can't think of anything else. Twice during the session Grasshopper jumps up on me. The significance doesn't hit me. Should I have put my fear of making leaps into the fire?

Aug. 18. We take it easy on this final day before the quest. We meet individually with our leaders for final tips, carry water up to our sites and pack. My orange-red backpack isn't big and my load should be reasonable, albeit clumsy with my sleeping bag and foam attached outside.

There is a final pipe ceremony. It's dark when we finish. I've packed my flashlight and struggle back to my tent.

* * *

Over the two days after the Quest, we meet in our small groups. Each in turn shares what feels appropriate and the others bear witness. Our leader takes notes as each talks. When one finishes, he repeats back what he has heard in a third-person tale of a hero or heroine. He explains that when we hear our tale spoken impersonally in the third person we can step back and truly recognize our own journey as that of a hero or heroine. I ask him not to tell my tale. I want to write it myself as part of this quest. And so, back home, weeks later, my tale is written in the third person that enables me to see the heroine clearly.

22

Vision Quest of a Heroine

SHE STOOD THERE after breakfast the day before her Vision Quest began, she who was to become a heroine. Her left hand on her hip, she reflected on how much pleasure she had felt having the honour to give the prayer before breakfast. Suddenly she felt something moving in her hand. YELLOW-JACKET. The fear of being stung jarred her to full attention. Her back straightened and she held her breath. Carefully she brought her hand forward, hoping to release the creature without harm to herself nor to it. She slowly opened her hand and was amazed to see not harm but sheer beauty. Moth, in Fire shades of brown and orange remained in her hand. She released her breath and body tension both at once and simply stared at Moth in wonder. Soon though, it was so stunning that she hastened to show it to those around her. Moth stayed for several minutes before flying off.

She knew Moth's presence was significant and that it was important that it was Moth and not Butterfly, with whom she was more familiar. "The dark has its own beauty," she thought and then she remembered that Moth played a significant part in one of the books by Carlos Castaneda. For the life of her, she couldn't recall the significance. So, as was often her way, she was attentive to the Universe around her and its signals but she had to wait until later to unravel the message.

Next morning, following a Sweat Lodge ceremony, a warm hug from her friend, Carol, and blessings from the threshold circle of leaders and helpers, she swung the pack to her back, gently and respectfully lifted her Pipe bag, took a deep breath, and started off up the mountain. In recognition of the seriousness of her mission, she walked slowly, like a bride up the aisle, to her Sacred Spot, without any pauses, as symbol of the determination that filled her.

Our heroine-to-be had two primary objectives. She was seeking a Vision of the long-term goal on her path and the shorter-term theme for a book. She was, however, also seeking Adventure, which would bring her closer to All her Relations, including herself. She knew that this was work and not just play. The dream she had had two days before confirmed that it was work, and that, while the dark was a part of the quest, the pleasures of a posh restaurant also awaited her.

Arriving at her Sacred Spot delighted our heroine-to-be. Her first task was to determine which colour of yarn she would post. It would set the agenda for each of her days on the Mountain since she would proceed around the Medicine Wheel. She opted for yellow and the East, the place of Light, Illumination and Vision as the most suitable beginning for her quest. The yarn posted, our heroine-to-be outlined her circle lightly with cornmeal. The "circle" was flexible, with bulges where need be, to include or exclude Relations, such as Trees and Rocks, according to what felt "right." Thus protected, she entered her Sacred Spot, closing her imaginary door behind her.

She began by making herself at home, taking her time to decide how to lay out her "rooms" and her belongings. This was her first teaching, for it had never occurred to her that she had a true Taurus need for a "home," wherever she might be. The settling-in completed, she laid out her pipe carrying bag as her altar and gazed approvingly at its brightly coloured Mayan pattern. Next she performed the ceremony of bringing the bowl and stem of her Pipe together, running her finger lovingly over the etched eagle carving of the white quartz stone. Solemnly, she got to her knees, gazed out at the Universe audience in front of her, and explained fully and clearly to All her Relations her purposes for being there. She welcomed all those who would come to her Sacred Spot with teachings for her benefit.

She spent the remainder of her day in the East, meeting a number of her Relations. Ant, Grasshopper, Nuthatch, Chickadee, Butterfly, Chipmunk, all made early appearances to say "hello." She was open to the Universe, literally and figuratively. She explored the freedom of air skinny-dipping. She discovered how Air could caress her as tenderly as Water and she felt the same currents of warm and cold spots. Apart from the sheer bodily pleasure, she recognized the teaching of letting go of inhibitions. To cap the experience, Red-tailed Hawk, Mahad'Yuni[1] appeared just then to support her in breaking this inhibition that had stemmed from an important female in her life, her Mother.

More freedom came as ants made love to her; as a black-and-white butterfly, in the colours of her truth line, marked the outline of her ethereal Self about her; and as she experienced the sacredness of sexuality. Nuthatch came in and yanked "yes-yes" and in the distance Red-tailed Hawk cried out her support. So the pleasures of the posh restaurant of her earlier dream were much in evidence that day in the East.

There also were hints of what lay ahead. In the late afternoon, she retired to her bed-sitter, underneath the Rocks that held her plastic rain shelter in place. She had a niggling feeling that one might fall and hit her but pooh-poohed the idea. Moments later, Breeze jiggled Rock and it did fall, hitting our-heroine-to-be on the arm. She noted in her journal, "PAY ATTENTION TO INNER VOICE."

Her fears of being invaded in her sleeping bag by unwelcome Relations, such as ants, and her lack of attention to the potential comfort her foam could offer if properly used, all contributed to a night of poor sleep. Her hips hurt and she tossed and turned in her search for comfort.

So far in our tale, our heroine has done nothing to merit that title apart from providing the central character for our story. As day two unveiled itself and she turned to the South, the home of the Child, of Water and of Emotion, the drama began.

The evening before she had had some gas and felt a mite queasy. By morning her stomach felt much queasier. One-day fasts had never fazed her at all and she was not prepared for this turn of events. Fear took hold and increased by leaps and bounds, an enormous entity just out sight. If she was sick, could she complete her Quest? Would it get worse? Could she stick it out? Would it harm

---

[1] Mahad'Yuni is the Medicine name of Evelyn Eaton, who had lived on Vision Mountain. Before her death, she had said that she would always be present there in the form of the Red-tailed Hawk.

her? What could she do? She felt sorry for herself. She knew that it would be foolish to stick it out solely out of pride and stubbornness. She didn't want to have to go back to camp for the green magma they had said could help. In fact, she didn't want to ask for help in any way: she was never good at that. The least unsatisfactory approach of which she could think was to write a message to leave out with her yarn, asking for some green magma to be brought on the rounds the next day. She took that step and then prayed for understanding of the teaching.

As she snuggled back into her sleeping bag, still feeling sorry for herself, even crying a little, it occurred to her that if Great Spirit could visit this discomfort upon her, Great Spirit could also take it away. So she prayed again for help, if that wouldn't undermine the teaching.

Let her journal notes tell what happened:

"Had barely finished voicing it (her prayer) when two Red-breasted Nuthatches came in, one to the tree behind me, not six feet from me. They chattered away and what a sense of caring and concern they brought me. In tears a bit before, tears now burst forth in gratefulness at their arrival, an immediate response of the Universe. They went off and very shortly four arrived, this time even closer. One big black ant, the kind I like best, came and stayed still on my leg. Can't express how grateful I feel for such a strong, quick response.

* * *

"Heard tapping in Grandfather Pine – rapid, several times, probably Flicker. Looked over to see if my message was gone and could see something there. Was completely overwhelmed by quick response with the green magma and the thoughtfulness of leaving the container to use as a cup. Tears streaming this a.m. on Emotion Day! Writing the previous sentence, a white-breasted nuthatch flew low into Grandfather Pine and chattered away to catch my attention. I assured her I was feeling a whole lot better and she flew off."

So our Heroine learned to acknowledge her weaknesses and ask for help, readily accepted the help that immediately came, and was ever so grateful besides. She was starting to wear the mantle of her title.

She sat up with renewed energy and started considerable exploring of her Inner Knowing as a child and how it was discouraged by well-meaning adults until, still young, she stowed it away and accepted the "truths" of the grownups. Now she realized that she could purposely unlock that Inner Knowing, which had been poking through, particularly in the last couple of years, and which she had been trying to rediscover. The enormity of the revelation, only glimpsed dimly before, struck her. She ended that session by standing and using some of her precious Water for a cleansing ceremony. Everyone was present as witness as she vowed to rely on her Inner Knowing from then on.

To help her through that hot, hot day of much discomfort, she turned again in the afternoon to the magic of All her Relations. Seven Ravens heralded a breath of cooler air, a pair of red-tailed Hawks gave a demonstration of illusion as they appeared and disappeared in a cloud-free sky. Butterfly landed in her ear, tickling it, and nine turkey vultures soared above. She went to bed before sunset, hoping sleep would make her feel better, not yet having succumbed to her green magma. Grasshopper plunked down on her hat, alerting her that the Sun was about to set. Startled, she opened her eyes to the soft golden light on Grandfather Pine and, while doing so, the light was turned off. She marvelled at the magic and beauty and was dimly aware of singing jumbled up chants in her head as she drifted off.

Day 3 was the day in the West. Our heroine was a little confused about the significance for her of the West since teachings she had received were not always the same. So for her it was to be the day of Death, Change, Introspection and Vision. She woke before sunrise, and feeling some better, she awaited the Sun in order to give thanks for its light and its warmth (other than in the afternoon!). She prayed for vision and for a return to the posh restaurant of her dream.

It was a day of new beginnings, heralded early on by appearances of a Cassin's finch and noisy Stellar's jays. A Cooper's hawk sailed by just above the path as yet more evidence of the delicacies of her posh restaurant. Turkey Vulture cruised low over her and then returned to fly a figure eight directly in front of her. Suddenly, perhaps the infinity symbol alerted her, she realized the message of Turkey Vulture. Eagle couldn't make it at this time of year and so Turkey Vulture was here, standing in for Eagle. Since Eagle is her special protector and guide on her path, this was a revelation that overwhelmed her and she cried. Two staff came by on their daily check. Our heroine smiled, noted such tenderness in her heart toward them. Then she was forcefully struck with a wallop by the recognition that they, too, were part of the marvel and mystery of Nature, as was she, herself.

The rock across the way was shaped like an enormous frog, head downward as though ready to dive into cleansing water. The image was fitting to hold in her mind on this day in the West.

Her thoughts turned to how she might give something back to the mountain and to the Bear Tribe. She thought of where she might be living and how she might turn into reality her earlier dream of a healing centre where people could learn to be more in tune with Nature and themselves.

By afternoon, she was feeling queasy again. She still hadn't stooped to using the green magma. She realized that she was playing Coyote Medicine on herself as she tricked herself, part day by part day, to staying on. She reasoned that she couldn't make it down in the heat of the afternoon; it was too late in the evening before she started feeling better; she didn't want to go down by Moonlight and besides the nights were enjoyable; the mornings were the best part of the day and she couldn't go down then. So she grinned and stayed on, allowing a stunning green beetle with a Tibetan mask on its back to entertain her, along with noisy gray jays as evening drew on.

As the day of the North of Clarity, Reason and Vision dawned, (see how she emphasizes Vision) our heroine awoke with an inner sureness that she would complete her quest. When she went to her morning shady porch of the West, she discovered that Frog had left the rock across from her and now the rocks formed an unmistakable outline of Owl, with the head and mane of Horse leaning on Owl. A chipmunk came and sat on Owl's head, busily preening herself. The significance was not lost on our heroine. For her Owl was wisdom and Horse was power. She was coming through her quest, having discovered new wisdom and power within. Chipmunk was a gatherer and that she, too, was doing. Later she appreciated the action of preening and grooming as the stage that she, too, was reaching.

During the day she thought more of the healing centre she envisioned. She was unsure whether this day of reason was putting her too much into her mind and what Great Spirit felt about her musings. So she turned to attentive watching of grasshoppers, since she had already discovered that Grasshopper was one of her Vision Quest teachers. She still didn't know its significance and message for her and how it reflected her life. So she watched and she watched, shifting her position once or twice as time passed. She watched how they jumped, or rather how seldom they jumped. They stayed still interminably, moved slowly, explored, ate, copulated, occasionally took a short hop. She was impressed by how seldom such talented jumpers actually used that power, and it wasn't necessarily out of fright that they leapt far. She thought of her own life and the leaps she had taken. She was more like Grasshopper than she had realized. She had taken a number of big leaps in her life, sometimes by choice and sometimes nudged soundly by circumstances. Often, she preferred to be still or liked quiet exploring. Grasshopper was exploring her Pipe and her sacred walking stick from Bear Butte. It seemed interested in spirituality as was she.

In the evening she took down her plastic and a dead grasshopper fell out. She decided that it was not a giveaway for her Medicine pouch and placed it in the abalone shell on her altar. Ant soon found it. It tried dismembering it and carrying the pieces away. Away where? Up the sheer cliff of the rock beside her. The enormity of the task awed our heroine. As she slipped into her sleeping bag, she felt sure that the grasshopper would be gone by the morning. She realized that if she could have that kind of trust in what an ant could achieve, she had best have the same kind of trust in herself.

Here she was on the last night, still not sure of her vision - neither of the healing centre nor of what book she should be writing. While watching Grasshopper, the title, *Grasshopper's Path to Spirituality* had come to her, but was it time for that book? She went with her Inner Knowing that she was not meant to stay up all night crying for a vision. How else could she find the answers to her questions? She decided to rise during the night when Grandmother Moon was no longer so bright as to block out the Stars. She would ask for a shooting Star to signal "yes" to her vision and another for "yes" to her book. If either answer was "no," Great Spirit would have to find some way to show her what was intended.

For the first time, it became cloudy. As she turned over from time to time, she noticed the clouds, frowned, and realized that her plan might fail. She knew the time had not yet come. And then the dreams came. The first was about compromise, with which she wasn't satisfied even in the dream. It was not till much later that she realized the dream was advising her that her plan was compromised by the clouds and she would have to settle for an alternate way of confirming her vision. The second was the confirmation. In it, she searched all over for writing material on which to put the telegram message that was being relayed to her again. She scrambled up some scaffolding trying to reach paper, couldn't get to it and was bitten by Donkey on her way back down. The bite was in the shape of an asterisk and blood trickled down in a long streamer from it. As she lay awake thinking about the dreams, she gradually came to understand the miracle of the second dream. The Don, or Lord, held the "key" in the form of the bite, which was the star. The blood signified by its path that this was a shooting star. Our heroine's vision of a healing centre was confirmed and she knew it. She was so excited that she couldn't fall back to sleep, even though she now felt confident that what was to be written would also be shown in a dream.

Dawn broke without her falling back to sleep. What a magnificent dawn to crown the Vision Quest. For the first time there were clouds near

NATURE SPEAKS: I LISTEN   101

Grandfather Sun to catch the colours that only sunrise and sunset can bring. Off a little to the South the clouds were black and thunder and lightning cracked out their greeting to the day. The quest was over and our heroine stood tall. In the course of her adventure, she had conquered her dark, had revelled in a posh restaurant and was coming back with her Vision as well.

Her knees were wobbly as she slung her backpack onto her back. She moved gently and lightly down the path, welcomed her neighbour questor, Ross, but in very few words. The importance of speech had diminished.

Our heroine returned to the threshold circle, eager for her welcoming back and especially the warm embrace from her friend, Carol. There was bitter yarrow tea to drink and then a bowl of broth. She lingered over each exquisite sip, appreciating it as the finest wine. No, as a far greater gift than that. Then she turned to her first task – she needed to settle back in to her home, her snug tent!

The second dream came a night later. In it she learned that she was to bring together the spirituality of Mahad'Yuni with Joseph Campbell's grasp of the meaning of myths. Out of this will flow her next writing. This myth is a beginning. (This book is the rest.)

When she returned east to her home, once again she took time to settle back in. Then she turned to the task of reviewing her quest. The Moth who visited her prior to her quest begged clarification. She searched for its role for Carlos Castaneda and found his and her message in his *Tales of Power*:

> "You had an appointment with a moth. Knowledge is a moth. . .
>
> "The moths are the heralds or, better yet, the guardians of eternity. . . Knowledge comes floating like specks of gold dust, the same dust that covers the wings of moths. So, for a warrior, knowledge is like taking a shower, or being rained on by specks of dark gold dust . . .
>
> "Don't waste your power on trifles," he said. "You are dealing with that immensity out there. . .To turn that magnificence out there into reasonableness doesn't do anything for you. Here, surrounding us, is eternity itself. To engage in reducing it to a manageable nonsense is petty and outright disastrous." (pp.35-40)

I continue to carry the myth with me as I walk my path. To try to scientifically explain what happened would be petty and outright disastrous. The richness of the Vision Quest experience was awesome. There were layers and layers of messages brought to me in such varied ways. There were lessons for me to learn from it. Some I learned very quickly, such as the significance of Moth. But new insights continue to emerge over the years. Vision Quests are like that if we choose to keep learning from them. More insights come as I write.

After the Medicine Walk that we took before the quest, our leader had urged that we look for the links between the Medicine Walk and our life as a whole.

What have I learned about who I am through my rich quest? The answer came in many forms. Before I even set out, Moth captured key elements. I felt fear at the unknown in my hand, imagining the worst. I held my breath but cautiously brought my hand around and opened it, my curiosity mixed with the fear. And then I was awestruck by the beauty I held. Wonder and gratitude supplanted my fear. I showed Moth to everyone with childlike delight. But I had difficulty interpreting what it all meant right away. So often this pattern of fear, worry, caution, curiosity, awe, gratitude and finally sharing is how I respond to unknowns in my life.

There were a number of habits that surfaced or I abandoned out there that hold me back from being the person I'd like to become. On day one I basked in the freedom of letting go of inhibitions that have restricted me most of my life. Day two I realized how hard it is to pay attention to my own inner voice and knowing. Again I found myself imagining the worst when I felt queasy. What a struggle it was to ask for help.

I balanced off these dark side aspects of me with the tenacity with which I stuck with the obstacles and found solutions, even if I needed to trick myself in the process. Right at the beginning, I learned how much a personalized home base meant to me. I also underscored for myself how readily Nature, from hawks and nuthatches to ants and grasshoppers, could be company for me, whatever my mood. I could allow Nature to change that mood, and how enriching and absorbing I found her to be.

Day three brought me another big lesson. I discovered the degree to which I had put myself and other humans down as lesser than the rest of Nature, which is not so entangled with mind games as us. In fact, the helpers were just as rich a part of Nature, and, more importantly, so was I.

On day four, I uncovered the sureness and strength that lay within, unleashed it to feel and hold close. Horse was part of me. I was filled with such a strong inner knowing then that I would complete the quest. I am a survivor. But as I sought my vision, I faced my clinging to control, and to getting things just right. Compromise wasn't satisfying, I thought, until I surrendered and discovered that the way to my dreams might come in ways that were well beyond my tunnel vision.

Just as Moth summed me up at the beginning, on Day four it was Grasshopper's turn.

Grasshopper's mirror was of someone who likes to be quiet, sometimes still, and often curiously exploring. Grasshopper registered a keen interest in spirituality and the tools that helped bring me there by wandering over them at length. Spirituality is central to my life and path now. But most of all, Grasshopper helped me see that even skilled leapers don't leap much of the time. They choose where they leap and fear is seldom the key factor. He helped me to see that I am like that too. He showed me that there was much I could admire in myself.

In fact, that summer I was taking other Grasshopper leaps. In the light of what I learned about myself through the quest, let's turn back to the rest of the adventure.

23

Diary of a Summer

THE VISION QUEST was only one mirror of the theatre of my life. Other productions were on my life stage, several more Grasshopper leaps. Firstly, I donned a new costume as gardener. The second, however, was the bigger leap. A human being, brought up as an only child, who had lived the past 20 years on her own, chose to live and work as part of a community. That culture shock was a quest of its own. I also responded to the opportunity to create ceremony once again and I finally obtained and awakened my eagle pipe. And so now I take you with me on these other facets of the summer quest.

This part begins back on March 25. I had sent in my application to work in the garden the previous fall. No word in January, not even acknowledgement of my request. Nothing in February. *When should I hear? Do I show my impatience and write again?* In March still no word. Third week of March I phone my friend, Carol, in Idaho. "They should be taking their decisions any time now," she says. "Phone Beth early morning Pacific time. She's in charge of selection."

Mar. 25. At 12:30 my time, I call the Bear Tribe. Beth answers the phone. She doesn't have my application in her folder and they are meeting in the afternoon to make the selections. She takes my data over the phone. Late afternoon, my phone rings; I'm accepted. Ave, from last year's program, will be working in the garden. Dates will be firmed up after she arrives. My heart is bursting with excitement. I want to jump for joy but restrain myself. *Couldn't be a clearer message that Great Spirit is looking after me and I'm supposed to work in the garden this summer.*

Time to return to Vision Mountain and the Bear Tribe. You've already gone there with me, pitched the tent, had dinner alone and gone to bed. The next step in the adventure is tomorrow.

June 15. Apparently, we don't normally do much work on the weekends. I'm full of energy, need action to settle me down. *I came here to help in the garden. Why get me to arrive just before a weekend if we don't work on weekends?*

I get some hot herbal tea and toast at the mud kitchen and then Werner shows me the garden. Many of the vegetables I don't recognize. He knows the names in German. Tour finished, he tells me what I can do. All this takes a German-English dictionary.

Werner has suggested that I collect comfrey and stinging nettles from the edges of a wooded area for a brew to discourage the insects eating the plants. *Now is the time to put Machaelle Small Wright's <u>Garden Workbook</u> ideas into practice.* Carol introduced me to this book the previous summer. That was where Carol had learned finger testing. The book found me back home and I devoured it during the winter. Use the Nature Spirits and the plant Devas to guide your work in a garden, where to plant things, what to plant, what fertilizers to use, mulch, everything.

Here at the Bear Tribe, I want to combine the native way of honouring with tobacco and seeking guidance through my fingers. I offer tobacco and ask the Devas to help me in my choice of particular plants. I take my time gathering the stinging nettles and comfrey and add them to a barrel of water. Then I turn to weeding carrots, one vegetable I can identify. *It feels good to make a start and to familiarize myself with the garden, too.*

I return to the mud kitchen to find a stack of dirty dishes. I launch in but realize that Armadillo, who is a good model for setting boundaries, has got to be sure not to clean up for others regularly.

Beth has told me that there will be a barbecue for supper. Around 5:30 I walk up to the longhouse. That's not where it is. It's back down the hill a way at the closest neighbours' home. The woman who tells me this assumes that those who are going have already left.

I backtrack and wind my way past magpies to the proper cabin but no sounds and only two cars. By now it's after 6:00 p.m., yet I'm the first to arrive. The two women had decided no one was coming. After half an hour, Ave, Herbert and the two children arrive and we are the Bear Tribe. Two other neighbours drop in much later but refuse to eat because they haven't brought anything to this potluck supper. Our Bear Tribe group have come empty-handed, hadn't been told it is a potluck supper. By this time we've eaten everything in sight. *How embarrassing.* I don't know what to say and become quiet. I'm embarrassed for the Bear Tribe, but irritated as well.

I'm the first to leave. I notice I'm pulling and biting at my fingers. *Haven't been doing much of this lately. Seems to be related to my irritation and displeasure with the Bear Tribe casualness and rudeness about this invitation, and my personal embarrassment too.*

June 16. After breakfast, Beth arrives at the mud kitchen. She listens well, easy-going, yet practical. As long as there is enough for me to do in the garden, that can be my full-time work placement. Just keep her posted. *That sounds great. I want to work in the garden full time.* Beth says she will call last night's hostesses. I'm pleased with how she has responded to what I have said.

From my perspective, cooking here remains to be worked out. It's not overly pleasant being with the others all together because, out of necessity, it's all in German. I'm the outsider. *I realize I'm a foreigner here in the U.S., but not speaking the language hadn't occurred to me! Apart from that, they are not vegetarian and I suspect the kids won't like the spices I often use. I may prefer to cook my own meals separately. They aren't very good about washing and cleaning up either. So I shall be tested in learning how to deal with these situations.*

Mosha, one of the former Bear Tribe residents, who has just graduated from university, is holding a Giveaway up at the longhouse to celebrate. The celebration begins with awakening the drum and singing chants. My heart sings as well as my voice. *How glad I am to have a ceremony like this so early on. This is what I am looking for in this community.*

Mosha gives gifts to all the Bear Tribe residents. Mary presents her with a mortarboard with branch antlers on it. We circle around and thank Mosha, then devour ice cream, cookies and a cake.

And now a big moment. Mary takes me over to her work cabin and shows me how my pipe is progressing. The eagle's head bowl cries out as Eagle and my heart soars. I caress the bowl, its smooth, almost oily surface in sharp contrast to the energy of the beak and eyes. Mary says that I can do some work on the stem myself. Mary will show me how later in the month. *That's better yet. Help to make my own pipe.*

I speak to Moon Deer, another resident, and ask if she will awaken my pipe in a ceremony. With no hesitation, she accepts.

Now that you have experienced the initial days in detail, let me take you through the weeks that follow without having you weed each bed I weed, plant each seed I plant, day by day. I'll have you join me for some of the moments - gardening, ceremony, whatever - but otherwise I'll summarize week by week. After all, you may not love gardening as much as I discovered I do.

June 17 – 23. My week in the garden begins with weeding. In fact, weeding is part of each day, the strawberry patch, banana peppers, kohlrabi and spinach. My knees, back and one hip ache. I am constantly shifting position. But how I enjoy it. *Wonder if this enjoyment will wear off. Somehow I don't think so.* Freeing the plants brings not just aesthetic pleasure. I breathe more freely with them, feel a connection that soothes me.

On Tuesday I help Werner put up chicken wire for sugar peas and on Wednesday I plant them. A female hummingbird flies in close and lands. I stop to tell her about the feeder closer to the mud kitchen. Just then a male zips in and does his courtship diving display in front of both of us. He enthralls me, her too. Later a raven circles several times, lands at the top of a pine and croaks and croaks harshly. I laugh. *I can't understand you any better than this German crew.*

What else transpires this week? On Monday Ave and Werner have an argument in German. After Werner leaves, Ave fills me in on the situation. Werner is a loner which has made it next to impossible to do things as a community, the way Ave would like. She says that they are comfortable with a mostly vegetarian diet. *Good lesson in not jumping to my own conclusions without discussion with others. Sure read that one wrong.*

Monday I give a tobacco prayer to Great Spirit in the morning on the way to the mud kitchen and another prayer in the evening. *I suspect this can readily become a habit here. Now this is day-to-day spirituality in practice.*

Tuesday, after lunch they bring us down a "new" fridge. Was it ever dirty! I clean it inside and out. *That's my fridge duty for a while!* Steve, a carpenter, arrives as a member of the crew to build a home for Sun Bear and I show him around.

By Wednesday evening a second Steve is eating with us. Having others who speak English is a relief for me. Afterwards there is a weekly meeting for part-timers, led by one of the residents. She uses a Talking Stick and offers advice on how to deal with problems between people. Then we have a pipe ceremony. *Glad we'll be having pipe ceremonies regularly.*

Thursday I don't sleep well, tossing and turning, worrying about cooking for my second turn this week, not knowing how many will show up. *Not sure why this is bothering me since I was inventive on Tuesday in preparing a salad dressing and I obviously can do OK.*

It's a showery day. My back aches and my knees creak whenever I stand. I collapse in a deep armchair in the mud kitchen for quite some time, feeling guilty at taking a lengthy break.

By Friday I'm noting the sharp contrast between our two Steves. One is a doer, on the go all the time. I like him. The other talks a good line but I have a suspicion that not much has been accomplished. He says he doesn't want to talk about his lost tent and clothes but frequently does. I grit my teeth. The other Steve catches him on it politely, asking if he isn't the one who has raised the topic. *Maybe he is as irked by him as I am becoming. I'm not sorry that he will be eating at the longhouse.*

Doer Steve fixes a mini rototiller for me, which I then use. Later, when Werner returns, he says it isn't good to use it in our cultivated rows. Steve is surprised and obviously wouldn't want to be working for Werner but I'm content to do things Werner's way, learn what I can, simply enjoy the garden, the birds, the day.

At supper with Werner and Steve on Saturday, Steve talks about communities. He is convinced the ideal size is about 60 adults and up to 30 children. I'm learning a lot from him. He has just graduated as a naturopath, eager to share what he's learned. *I guess this is one thing a community like this offers me – access to a variety of people with differing interests and skills.*

Sunday afternoon there is a sweat and I decide to fast until it is over. I pack for it and don my bathing suit. *Oh bother. I forgot that they don't allow women in the sweat if they're on their "moon time"* (native term for menstruating). Since I am on mine, off comes the bathing suit. Steve helps me prepare a salad and I drive up.

Moon Deer asks me to be the door keeper. That makes me responsible for opening and closing the door flaps between rounds and bringing them more water when it is needed. Busy time, as I protect clothes and a drum from a shower and Moon Deer asks me to give the prayer to call in the Spirit Keeper of the South. Between rounds Tom notices a pure white moth. When I get it on my finger to move it out of the way, it doesn't want to leave. The white cat, Friday, is with me most of the time and tries to enter the sweat. I keep her out. The white of the moth and of Friday makes me think of Grandmother Twylah and the colours. *White, part of my truth line, is for serving. This is an occasion to do so.* No wonder my heart is so open and soft.

Sweat over, there is dinner at the longhouse. Sherry has made delicious pumpkin bread and someone else a curry. *Am I ever hungry.*

June 24 – 30. One morning I work hard weeding two beds of corn while Werner weeds the other four. He doesn't remove the grass or weeds, leaving them as mulch. I dub myself "Speedy Gonzalez" but that is hard to explain to Werner.

Wednesday afternoon I discover that the peas I planted are poking their wee sprouts through the ground. I am elated and as I put mulch around them in the late afternoon, I chat away to them, simply delighted at watching them break through.

Later in the week Werner and I work on two beds close to one another to prepare them for new seeding. Mine had onions that haven't done well. Werner removes sorrel roots. I am actually ahead of him for a while since the roots of sorrel turn out to be demons. Speedy Gonzalez grins, much amused.

Thursday, when I finish my garden work, I walk along up the dusty dirt road, sweating with the heat of the day, to find Mary. She gets out my pipe stem and a file and shows me how to work on it. I return back down and, while awaiting Werner's dinner, continue filing the stem. Very quickly I have a sense of what I want. I'm fully absorbed, each stroke undertaken with care and pleasure.

This is the day that I note my reaction to the constant changes in who is eating here. The entire construction crew lands in for lunch – a noisy crew and messy. One of them sounds almost as though he'd like to eat all his meals here and talks about chicken and meat. My whole body tenses. My jaws clamp shut. Before I leave, I speak to Ave. Lunch is reasonable since they work so close by, but I'm <u>not</u> enthusiastic about them being here for dinner. I somehow don't think they'll pitch in to cooking, shopping and washing up. By suppertime I am more accepting. *What's happening here? Is it adaptation that is good for me or is it not wanting to be stepped on. Maybe both. I don't know what's reasonable and what isn't.*

The weekend comes and a visit with Carol in Idaho. Sunday is a cloudy, drizzly day. We stay inside and cook and chat. I mention the noisy construction crew. Carol says she is very sensitive to noise and often doesn't want music playing. I jerk to attention, pulling the string to a lightbulb. This is the first time I've realized that it isn't just too many people that gets to me, it's often too much noise. *No wonder I find it so stressful in the mud kitchen at noontime.*

I realize how accepted and contented I am in Carol's company. Such contrast with the mud kitchen at noontime helps me acknowledge how much stress I have been under – new surroundings, concern for keeping dry, learning how to garden, knowing that I am slow, cooking without recipes for unknown and changing numbers, different people around all the time, no one I can confide in, poor weather for the Vision Questers arousing fear of my not being able to complete mine. All those at least. Then, on top of that, when I become tense, irritated by changes, and wanting to avoid them, I'm hard on myself for my reaction. *How unfair.* I am able to talk about all this with Carol so openly and what a floodgate release that brings.

July 1 – 7. The garden time includes clearing new beds with Werner and two new Germans, Veronica and Wally. One morning, we need short stakes for the new beds and I am breaking sticks to make them. One pops up and cracks me on the nose. *Good lesson about breaking sticks and fortunately it misses my eyes.*

Wally prepares two herbal remedies to put on my nose. I go back to work, cutting more chicken mesh for the rows of peas. They now have tendrils and are growing by leaps and bounds. *I really like having primary responsibility for them.*

Ironically, I plant turnips today, just after mailing a letter to Lynne. Her reaction to my coming to work in the garden here had been, "What! You're going to go all the way out there to plant turnips?"

And I can't stand turnips. Now it strikes me funny and I have a good laugh.

We are all making a big effort to prepare the garden to look its best for a garden ceremony on Sunday evening. I go back to the strawberry bed, one of my first thorough efforts. You wouldn't guess that, based on the quantity of weeds there now. *So much for my theory that if you do a thorough job they won't grow back as much.*

Tuesday I have an unusual dream. I am at the edge of a woods and a black bear ambles past me, close. I reach out to tap someone ahead of me and it is a moose, who turns and walks toward and past me. Then an antelope charges and like a matador, I eventually bring it to the ground. *Bear's introspection has helped me touch Moose's self esteem and that is enabling me to be in control of Antelope's action. That's encouraging: I'm truly learning from all my experiences here.*

As it turns out, it is also foretelling what lies just ahead. That day, Ave talks to me of the ceremony for the garden on Sunday, seeking advice on how to do it. Before I rise on Wednesday, I mull it over. *I think we should enact the planting of the garden with Ave and Werner as the gardeners, giving prayers or whatever in English and German respectively. The rest of us can provide the props such as bringing compost, etc. Peas can represent the past, present and future of the garden. Maybe Veronica and I can act as narrators in German and English respectively.* As I leave the tent, there is a daddy-long-legs on the door. *Communication was the weak part of the ceremony of our group last year, not getting everyone involved. Have to see if I can do better this time.*

Our garden ceremony is Sunday evening. By then I am boasting two black eyes from my Friday stick encounter, but with no mirrors around I'm not upset by my odd appearance, just on edge about my role.

At first it looks like very few are coming. I keep looking anxiously up the road. Eventually most show up. I am mistress of ceremonies and Veronica translates for the Germans. Ave's prayers are forceful, Werner's very short: he's uncomfortable. The kids are great, eager to pass the seeds the gathering will plant and the water for them. They hand out produce too. Not much yet but enough to fill the bill. Then they act out the garden hazards. Willi is Raymond the goose and can't stop quacking. That is all for the better since Ronya's puppies aren't ready on cue and Herbert has to go off for one. I ad-lib in the interim, highlighting the persistence of Willi's goose.

As the ceremony comes to an end, I am ready to take a well-earned bow. Not just my black eyes are glowing. Moon Deer and Beth, both very good at preparing ceremonies, tell me that there has been a good mix to this one. My chest and heart expand yet more. Sun Bear says nothing. *Maybe that is a lesson in itself – I don't need his recognition to know I've engineered a good ceremony.*

Besides, he doesn't need to. I've been moved by his presence during the ceremony, for he stayed on his knees throughout. Deep acknowledgement of ceremony and prayer.

Next morning I awake, aware of a powerful dream. I was playing ball and hit a really solid one that sailed over to a row of buildings with glass windows, breaking one. I went over to take responsibility for it. The buildings were storage units and I had broken the one for the royal yacht, Britannia. *I've had dreams about the Queen before. She is my Higher Self. This time I've broken into a storage unit, opened something new. The yacht spells a voyage. I've touched into one of my important creative abilities.*

I don't fall back to sleep. I'm far too energized by the dream and its focusing on what I accomplished yesterday. After all, it is the first group ceremony, other than the exercise the previous summer, that I have brought to fruition.

July 8 – 14. On Tuesday I want time alone. Doer Steve needs assistance and calls on Veronica, which leaves me alone. I work slowly, indigestion bothering me. My stomach feels like it has sharp nails piercing it when I stay bent over for any length of time, but it's time to think. *I'm searching for a place where my beliefs and life style are totally in synch with others. I still seem to expect too much from a native setting. My religion is eclectic and will inevitably be my own version.*

That evening I meet with Moon Deer to go over the pipe awakening ceremony. I'm more uptight about this than the garden ceremony. My pipe is a personal connection for me with Great Spirit. *Wonder if I'll remember all of the ceremony. Will I really know whether I have permission to smoke the pipe or not? I can't use my fingers when my hands are up in the air holding my pipe bowl and stem! Am I worthy enough?*

After we're through, I continue up to the Evelyn Eaton Medicine Wheel where we'll hold the ceremony. It looks so cared for. Jackie has tidied it up and mine will be the first ceremony there since she has done so.

Wednesday, I ponder my lack of a feather to use with my smudge bowl at my pipe ceremony. *Great Spirit I would really like to have one. Please gift me one either today or Thursday.*

The next day three of us drive to a fruit farm to pick strawberries for jam for the longhouse residents. As I am working my way along a row of berries, I happen to turn and look back. Under a plant not far off lies a hawk feather, Great Spirit's answer to my prayer. I'm in tears and become even more excited about the upcoming ceremony.

Late that afternoon, I bring my pipe to the Sweat Lodge behind the mud kitchen. I sit with my back to the Lodge entrance with its altar to my right and attempt a "dry run." I struggle. It's hard to tell where to put the match I light because I can't see the hole with the pipe in my mouth. It's hard to feel the smoke. *Is the tiny hole partially clogged?*

I forget one part, as well as the song at the end. Then I discover I haven't smoked all the kinick-kinick (a mixture of dried sweet clover and bearberry). As I move to put the pipe away, Ronya, Ave's dog, arrives and wants to play on my cloth altar. She rolls over. I struggle to keep her off but she can't roll over the other way to get on her feet because the sweat altar creates too high a hill. *Am I demonstrating my loyalty to my pipe or fighting off such loyalty?* In any event I'm glad of this dry run.

The pipe awakening ceremony is that evening. At 8:15 we go up to the Medicine Wheel. I ask where we should sit. The Wheel, with a diameter of 20 feet, is obviously too large for seven of us to sit around and pass a pipe. Moon Deer's response is for me to be on the third limb of the tall ponderosa pine that borders the Wheel. We settle for sitting around the South-west quadrant.

Moon Deer passes my pipe around, asking everyone to voice gifts to go in the pipe. A deer bounds gracefully past us. (Moon Deer later claims to have been training the deer for a year.) Coco, Mary's dog, chases after the deer and then comes to the circle just as the pipe has gone its rounds. *May I hand my pipe to Coco also?* Later, yet another dog joins us. *So loyalty to the pipe is a strong message.*

Moon Deer now calls on everyone to voice a prayer aloud. Carol's prayer and her tears move me. I, too, have tears in my eyes. It's time to begin smoking. I have trouble getting my pipe lit and then forget the puffs in the six directions. Gradually my shoulders relax. I draw the smoke in slowly, enjoy the aftertaste in my mouth and savour the symbol of blowing it out to Great Spirit. It lasts for a long, long time. *Sure keeps me busy blessing all my relations, totems, friends and on and on.*

A bat flies over as the end approaches and the setting sun horizon is breathtaking in its hues of orange and red. My heart is full, almost hurting. I am moved and grateful for all that has taken place and particularly that I could have this awakening ceremony with just my invited guests.

Friday Veronica and I finish my gardening stint by tidying the sage plants with all their prickly stems from last year's growth. I can't get it completed before it is time for me to have lunch and head to Spokane. *Fine way to end my work in the garden, a task not completed.* But by then I'd learned that gardening is never completed.

My work at the Bear Tribe drew to a close. On the way home, I smoked my pipe at Bear Butte as I had planned. Just as I finished smoking, I heard a cry and two golden eagles soared over me. Eagle, itself, acknowledging my decision to take my pipe apart there, final symbol of the end of my Vision Quest.

Looking back on it all, the summer was a form of personal retreat, a Grasshopper leap made not for the way of the hermit but more of a monastic experience. What did I learn through it all?

There was the magic of ceremony, bringing a group together, pouring out prayer and gratitude in a way that had been foreign to me. I discovered I had a feeling for ceremony. It was in me, like the seed of the pea just waiting to sprout when watered and given the warmth of the sun.

I learned that community living, even of a spiritual group, still had its ups and downs. Ceremony was not woven in to each moment but drew the group together only from time to time. The spiritual theme supplied a motive for working out problems when they arose, but problems there were.

I learned the importance of Armadillo's medicine of setting boundaries to help me form the space I needed, giving others theirs. I recognized the need to flow more with the constant changes and adapted better as the month went on. But I came to realize that community was not for me, not idyllic as I had imagined, not an automatic entry to bringing Spirit into my moment by moment, day by day life.

And yet I had found the community I was seeking. It was Nature. I found it in the plants, the trees, the Winged Ones. I had come with the heart space I'd felt the previous year during my garden visit. That heart space and caring opened my being to the magic of the life and growth of a seed to a pea or carrot or the root of the sorrel. No longer were they plants just taken for granted but instead they became living beings as unique as I. They thrived on nourishment and caring and were ever so giving. I, who have always enjoyed being a team player, had found a new team. There was a purity and simplicity in the plants that I realized we only struggled to match as humans.

I connected with Nature in new and deeper ways than ever before and discovered the joy of caring, nurturing, working together with All my Relations. In Nature, I discovered "family," there for me, for us, wherever we may be.

So I sought to bring the magic and caring I'd experienced there back to my life on my own, back in a way that through me would touch my friends and now you, my readers, as well.

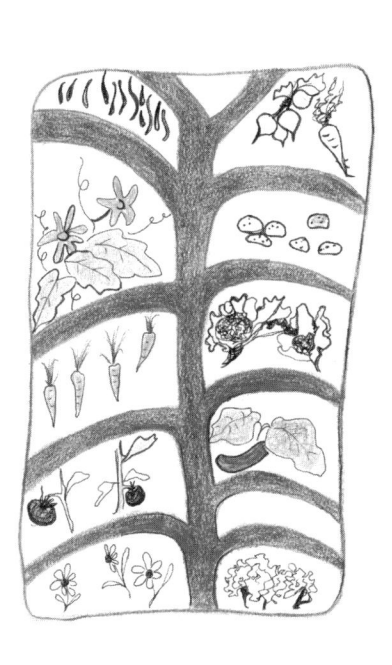

Part V *1992*

24

The Year of Searching

I KNEW NOW that my spiritual home was in Nature, not with the Bear Tribe. Furthermore, the Vision Quest had reconfirmed my purpose: creating a healing centre of some kind. That goal still seemed a long way off, not something I was ready to launch into right away. So, in some respects, what I came back with from my summer at the Bear Tribe was vague, not nearly concrete enough for a Taurus such as I. So 1992 became the year of searching in all aspects of my life: purpose, writing, ways to help others, relationships. The themes from 1991's Vision Quest played their part in 1992, steering the search if you will. So Grasshopper was with me. Some leaps, little steps as well, exploring her environment. That's how 1992 was woven.

Like me, you're trying to recall the more specific purposes of that quest of 1991. After the quest when I wrote it up, they stood out clearly:

To see a clearer picture of "who my people are" and "how I am to serve;"

To learn to be better able to hear what Nature has to say to me, without so much active "analyzing" on my part;

To become more aware of my emotions and how I overcome obstacles; and

To discover why I hadn't been "allowed" to keep my close connection with Spirit and imagination that I had had as a child.

The last, so specific, was fully answered in the quest itself. My Inner Knowing was not respected by Mother: she knew what was best for me. And so I pushed my "knowing" aside.

Before we turn to each of the other three issues, let's get a feel for why searching is how best to describe the year. "Writing practice," a variation on automatic writing, picked up on some of my inner searching twice in October. The first starts with a phrase from Natalie Goldberg's *Writing Down the Bones*.

Writing Practice Embraces your Whole Life

"Writing practice embraces your whole life." That sounds right. Yet Natalie talks of practice as practice for a game, practice for a novel or whatever. That sells it short. She never compares it with a "medical practice," where, let's hope, the doctor isn't just practicing on us. Writing practice is both practice for, and the practice of writing itself. An added chapter heading may mark the only difference or the writing practice on a given occasion may turn out to be the end product itself. So hard to feel the distinction. Practice isn't there if we don't write. I wrote *The Bird Tribe Gathers* over a long period of time, only when so directed. In between, from time to time, there was unconscious writing, what Natalie calls writing practice. Letters, too, have always been my writing practice. So I was doing it but infrequently. Is writing part of my path? I feel deep, deep down it is: I create, I share, I breathe in writing. So if it is, then I want to breathe more often. I wrote "want" instead of "need," felt "need" was a "should" word, a word of guilt and duty but need is also the word of survival, the word of growth and development. Plants need water, need sun. They can't live without them. I "should" water them makes a distinction between me and them and imposes a duty on me. If we are truly one, watering them is my need too and needs must be fulfilled if we are to live fully in the moment.

So easy not to recognize something in us as a need, a need to honour, cherish, nurture. Writing is such a need for me. Caring for my body is another. My arm. What is it telling me? It speaks loud and clear. It hurts when I push too hard, try to be too strong, hurts when I bend over in the yoga mudra position - the position of surrender.

Fighting surrender? Stopped up short, my mind coming in. Getting too close to a truth? Mind, we don't need that trick anymore. You and I can work together, protecting ourselves in other more open ways. Or do I fool myself? Am I still unprepared to accept myself, my needs, to let myself surrender to myself and the Divine? For I am divine. Divine is not perfection. It is part of the all, a tiny speck, unique. The aloe plant's spikes droop over, go straight up willy-nilly. No thing of beauty, a function of its environment, and its dependence on me to meet its needs. So too Jade, gangly, curling around in crazy curves to have a moment in the sun. Its essence, Japanese delicate beauty, strangled by an environment that offers inadequate sun and my lack of courage to prune it, aid it to rediscover its centre. So it goes with me. No environment is perfect but like Aloe and Jade, I am unique and I offer healing and growth and beauty in my own way too. Accept myself, learn who I am, stretch my limits gently, caringly, lovingly and see how I can grow.

Day by day struggles, writing practice and the practice of writing wrapped in one. So it must be for me. Creator, help me find my ways to create, create in all I do but give room for writing, nourish it with frequent watering and sun - using it, finding ways to let its growth be shared along the way, coming to fruition when the time is ripe.

Purpose

A purpose to all things. Plants. An inner knowing as a seed somehow develops a particular species of plant that finds a nook where it can survive – or it comes to a more abrupt halt. I planted sunflower seeds under the garage overhang this spring. I have always wanted to grow sunflowers and have them close at hand - not just grow them, because I planted them out in my garden plot, too, but still needed them in my own back yard. Why? I don't know why. Their bursting vitality, so startlingly golden, so large, so defiant. Short-lived despite the strength of the stalk. Their daring, their defiance, their confident thrust out into the world, on vivid display for all to see. But back to my seeds planted in the back yard.

Several had better situations than the one in the corner, driest place of all. But someone nibbled the others off at a tender age and only the one in the corner survived. Leaf after leaf, a gigantic effort for a couple of inches of leaf. The stalk was slender but it kept on pushing up. By

August the seeds in the garden plot were plants three feet tall, large leaves 6 inches long, broad, solid. The stalk was strong. Too crowded there, a foot apart. So I brought one home, transplanted it beside the fence. Meanwhile the fragile cousin in the corner, one foot tall, got trampled by a squirrel. Its stalk bent over, crippled, it refused to die. It had its purpose - bloom. By late August I discovered a small bud, impossible as it seemed. Before I left mid-September, black squirrel returned and nipped the bud. I returned early October. First frosts had come but had not deterred most of my garden plants. I glanced at cousin sunflower. The transplant's bloom long since come and gone, offered food for someone and all the seeds were gone. But cousin, all bent over, 18 inches of crippled stalk at best, had a wee golden flower. It knew its purpose and it persevered. What determination in the face of such bleak odds! I'll offer tobacco to that flower today. How else to honour its courage, its fulfillment of its purpose?

So sunflowers and their purpose met. But here am I at 52, seeking my purpose still. I vision quested and sensed a purpose - writing and a healing centre, bringing the healing power of nature to others. It is deep in me and yet I, who pride myself on my perseverance, my determination, am little farther ahead this year than last.

Writing? I honoured *The Bird Tribe Gathers* and printed 100 copies, feel good about that. This fall, a writing course and yes, a step towards my writing goals. New ideas, new commitment, awareness of how to plant my seeds in the fertile environment of the garden plot and not leave them struggling under an overhanging garage roof.

Yet the healing centre remains seeds in a package. What holds me back? With the garden I needed someone else to be partners with, or so I thought. It turned out to be a garden on my own and much work, much pleasure and I give great thanks that I took the plunge. No fear next time. I look forward to another round. Yet with the healing centre and Medicine Walks, I hold back. I want a partner, want Sue. But my dream of a healing centre is not hers or not yet. And now she says five more years until she retires. Too long. I need to start. Not just the writing, though maybe a year focused on writing and the garden will allow composting time and better growth in both those gardens. But somehow, the seeds of the other need to get out of the package before they are no longer capable of germination.

Medicine Walks. I know their power. I speak of their power to friends from time to time but no one has tried it. Maybe I need to get one or two friends together and make an outing of one. See what happens and enjoy ourselves. Do I dare try? No partner. Why am I loathe to start out anyway?

Purpose. Something in my core, in my being. Nature is that to me. Yet if it is so central to my being, why am I struggling like the sunflower in the corner rather than like the ones in the garden plot or even the transplanted one? Crippled sunflower wasn't in the right place, wasn't getting the right nourishment in spite of my best intentions? Planting myself in different environments, providing different nourishment. I don't feel as captive as the crippled sunflower but somehow I am not reaching my sunflower potential either.

Commitment

Committed. Interesting to see me using that word since I flee away from it, time after time.

It does come in more often now. I stayed with yoga for a good part of the summer. I kept my commitment to my garden plot week in and week out, the only break being the three-week vacation in September to which I was also "committed." Commitment to three weeks with Timba, my neighbour's dog, while Carmen was away. That was a joyful lesson in the potential pleasure of commitment. How I enjoyed Timba's barking, rushing around in circles, jumping up on me. If that's what commitment is about, bring me more.

I have steered away from it in writing. My experience with *The Bird Tribe Gathers* was that when the time was right according to my fingers, then that was the time to write. That was a stage I needed for discovering intuition and free flow of writing without mind and reason control. Now I feel it is time to move on to stage two and here discipline and commitment have centre stage. Only I wrote "hear" discipline and commitment, and yes, suddenly I was ready to hear those words.

I have a goal now too. I feel *Grasshopper's Path to Spirituality* is ready to commence. I came upon a collection of nature snippets in a bookstore in Northampton in September and I knew it was giving me a format. I didn't pick it up but wandered round the aisles. Then when I had a sense of its importance as a guide for me, I searched it out again but never did find it. Idea hatched but not to become too attached to someone else's style, I dare say.

Commitment, fear. Fear of responsibility, fear of losing control. Responsibility, the ability to respond. So much more comfortable with it when phrased that way and yet also uneasy about my ability to respond, lack of confidence about ever getting a book published by a publishing house. Yet knowing writing is a way that I can share with others my love of Nature, my discovery of her role as Guide. How that has changed my life, what exciting risk experiences it brings. Eagles, not a one-night stand but a love affair that endures, a fling here, a fling there, stretched out from Mill Village, Nova Scotia to Bear Butte to the sea wall at Stanley Park. The first encounter the morning of Sharon's death, November 12, 1987, the most recent in Maryland in September 1992. The eagles are committed to being with me as inspiration. Why am I so honoured? I feel so unworthy, so insignificant and yet they keep coming back and coincidence won't do, synchronicity it is. I don't doubt. Each time, I acknowledge a power far greater than me, a power I am powerless over. It is inescapably there. So I am committed too, since it is clear that eagles have this tie with me. If they keep on maintaining their contact, as five years show, then I am at the other end of that tie and I am attached, committed, unknowing though I may have been.

That's like me and responsibility. I worked hard as a Parole Board Member, taking decisions that affected individuals and the community every day. Yet suggest what a responsibility it was and I inwardly backed away. Goes back a long way. Something about a public school report card that said I didn't like taking responsibility.

Commitment, fear of responsibility, fear of loss of control. Loss of control because tied down and can't escape. The garden this summer kept me here in Ottawa all summer. And yet I choose to do the same again next year. I feel a choice at the same time. Choosing. That is the key, wanting something enough to make that choice. That ties in with the whole question of purpose and goals where again I block.

Spiritual guide. I want one, yet I fear the commitment. What would I have to do, give up? Not wanting it enough yet? And yet eagle is a symbol of that very commitment and is a spiritual guide. Do I fear recognizing that I already have made that commitment? No, I know I'm on a path. I have chosen to start along it and know I shall walk it from now until I die. Choice. Purposes, goals. I feel directionless, no specific goals. Yet the broad one, walking my spiritual path is clear and welcome. How funny I am. That big universe rattling goal, I am comfortable with, rely on, am bringing into my life daily in meditation, in prayer, in honouring the food I eat, in developing ceremonies of gratitude or seeking help or letting go. But I fear lesser goals, commitments, for fear of losing control, losing my freedom. How absurd.

Why are small things harder than big ones? Why such fear? Or is it a vestige of past fears that have had their day and are being thrust out, trying not to relinquish their power as they feel it slipping away, so slippery they can't hold on. A pleasant thought that only habit gives them credence today.

Want to write, want to publish a book. If this kind of writing practice is the way. . .Not if. Inwardly I know it's my way. I see I have made a commitment I hadn't realized I'd already made and the key words are "Inwardly, I know it's my way." Inner knowing. Get in touch with that, let it burst out of its seed covering and I'll be there to help it free itself from the pod and water it, weed it and wonder at its magic. Commitment with a full heart when commitment is no commitment, when ability to respond is merely doing what I really want to do.

My dreams also speak to my search for purpose. In one I was asked what my purpose is and I replied, "self-fulfillment that also offers something to others." In another, I viewed a large area of concentric circles. I "saw" energy at various places that represented parts of my path. They were scattered in the area, including two near the centre. I went back to examine each and found, to my surprise, that tiny plants with flowers were now blooming in each spot. I couldn't relocate the exact spot of one of the two central ones and no plants were in sight there.

The first dream, with the need for self-fulfillment and pleasure as the core to involvement and energy, fits well with the writing practice discoveries. The second points out that one of my central goals is still missing. Is this the healing centre of my Vision Quest? But I also need to look at and acknowledge the energies that are already flowering so that I can promote them as well as look at other parts of the wheel to develop more balance.

My writing practices and my dreams captured the reality that, even when we are on our path, there are times of doubt and of searching. That's part of the path. Through those ebbs we open ourselves once again and then we're ready to flow on once more. Without these cycles we'd grow complacent, fail to reach out, become attached to where we're at. It's hard to remember that when we're caught in the ebb but remember the certainty of the ebb and flow of the tides and of the continuous cycle of seasons. What's important is finding our personal tools that bring us through those ebbs and open us up for what lies ahead.

For me writing practice is one of those tools. Medicine Walks are another. And the big one was the Vision Quest itself. Yet my goals were broad and so were the answers and that left me searching for how best to bring those answers into my life and my path right then. Time for me to remember, too, that Grasshopper's big leaps were few. More often he was still or took small steps.

25

How to Serve

SEARCHING was permeating my being in '92. How does it tie in with the themes of the Vision Quest? Let's turn with Grasshopper and observe how they appeared.

The first theme was how I am to serve. Good concrete way to begin after all that search for purpose. Early in the year I began with the tangible seeking out of volunteer work, wanting to start to serve. Literacy and the Humane Society were two of the volunteer projects that called to me.

One program in particular at the Humane Society appealed to me. It was taking puppies, kittens, cats or dogs from the shelter to nursing homes for seniors. Two-fold this volunteering. Getting the animals out of their cages if only for an hour or two and bringing their spontaneity, their unpredictability, their companionship, into the lives of seniors, captive as much as the pets. Choosing the pets that would respond to the settings was part of the fun. A cat that ran and hid was little use for this. Which liked to be stroked and handled, roughly sometimes by muscles that were out of control? I liked that role, bringing these groups together, having the time with the pets.

A second reaching out in "how to serve" brought me to a literacy organization, People, Words & Change. It offered training sessions to help us tutors get started, support from the staff, and the books required as we tutored the match they arranged for us.

Were these endeavours part of my path or merely diversions? One brought me to Timba, my neighbour's dog, and she's part of my path, part of my listening to Nature. The literacy was less obvious, yet there were signs it was meant to be. I selected *A Promise is a Promise* as a book that one young mother might read to her children. On the first outing I showed it to her. The day before her children had brought the same book home from their library. Synchronicity. Later I worked with someone who said at first he wouldn't spell. It's hard to learn to write if you refuse to spell. That quickly changed but oh how tough it was for him. Then, when a friend asked whether I'd turned to Spirit for help, I put out a prayer right away. Within a week as I read Tony Robbin's *Unlimited Power*, I was told of a way that eases the woes of spelling. I tried it. A breakthrough. Not instant success but it broke the old image of "I can't spell" and allowed for some progress. No clear connection with my path but learning along the way and in future years the link with People, Words & Change has played a clearer role.

Small beginnings but a start just the same. The other direction was writing. As you have already discovered, *The Bird Tribe Gathers* got into print in '92. The summer before, at Vision

Mountain, Wabun, a book publishing agent, suggested its size was not likely to meet most publishers' standards. Lack of courage also played its part in my choice to self-publish. A small printing outfit offered a reasonable price. It was July when the big moment came. I went in to collect my 100 copies in black and white and two in colour. I had no idea how thrilling that moment would be. I was in print with a professional-looking book. I stood taller. The woman who had collated it said she enjoyed it and had made a copy to read to her children. That first review was just what I needed to spur me on to send out notice of the book's availability to friends.

In September, I read Pic's chapter at the annual meeting of People, Words & Change, another debut out of the way. My voice was stiff at first, but all went well.

By the time of my progress review in November, I was noting that I had missed having *The Bird Tribe Gathers* to write. Where was my writing to head? In a channelling back in December '91, Kristine had suggested that I might write on birds in mythology, creating a story about them. The idea interested me and over the winter and spring I searched for the meaning of birds for Native Americans in myths, legends, whatever I could find. It wasn't easy and how to decide what was recent fiction and what were myths or legends long handed down was often puzzling. I bogged down and so did my computer, not up to transferring material from one program to another as I now wanted it to do.

Fall came and I attended a course at the Omega Institute in New York state, where I learned about writing practice. Why was it a big step? Because it validated the automatic writing I already was doing as being central to a method Natalie Goldberg calls "writing practice." It introduced the discipline of timed writing practice on a frequent basis. This pushed me to write more regularly and brought practice that I hadn't provided myself previously. So writing practice replaced automatic writing. The approach remained writing first thoughts without editing, just keeping the pen moving. My style changed with the onset of writing practice. The day after the referendum on the proposed constitutional changes, I wrote for two hours on the topic, "My Canada." I liked what I wrote but had difficulty knowing how to deal with my lack of complete sentences as a writing style. The flow lost some of its effect when I shifted to more grammatically correct English. I didn't solve the dilemma but it certainly wasn't a poem. And as you have discovered, I've learned to stay with that style.

Less frequently, I also wrote poems that year, one to honour the sunflowers of the garden plot:

The Little Sunflower

It was at the base of a once proud sunflower stalk
whose days were cut short:
someone broke off the large head
before it could turn its golden splendour
to seeds for waiting birds.
Now at the head of a small, drooping branch,
it defied its assailant
and burst forth once more.

I touched its delicate head,
anxious to capture its petals on film.
As I turned it to face its mirror the sun,
it snapped off at its base.
This assailant was stunned at her act.

The little sunflower came home,
entered a vase and found its place
in the sun,
in the sun of awe and respect
at its beauty.

>   Van Gogh came alive
>   as it bent its small head -
>   its yellow so piercing
>   it tingled my spine;
>   its centre of ochre enriched
>   by a circle of gold.
>
>   Transformed -
>   the little sunflower a Goddess,
>   the assailant its Saviour.

As you saw in the previous chapter, I began having a strong feeling that it was time to start writing *Grasshopper's Path to Spirituality*, the original name for this book. At first I thought it would be a volume of Nature snippets. It wasn't until mid-December my writing practice brought a new thrust, the one this book has taken:

Grasshopper's Path to Spirituality

I want to start moving on *Grasshopper's Path to Spirituality*. I search a framework that catches interest, brings a flow and variety, like Dee's role in *The Bird Tribe Gathers*. Is it <u>my</u> story that carries the flow this time or will Spirit direct some other way? When will I know? What will help make it all happen? How do I go from events recorded long before writing practice came into my life to this new style? So many questions. But I want to start, need to start. It's like this writing practice. I could have wasted time searching the title this morning and not got down to writing. No excuses. Time to end that.

And as you can see, I did start.

26

The Garden Power Place

TIME NOW to turn to the listening to nature theme. I'm eager to tell you about one of the beginnings, my garden plot. It was a whole new way in my relating to Nature, that had begun in the Bear Tribe garden the summer before, but which blossomed more fully in '92. My search for hearing Nature better was not restricted to the garden experience. Medicine Walks again played a role. But first on to the garden plot.

It didn't occur to me until late August of 1992 that my summer garden plot had become my Power Place. I tended to think of the Winged Ones, the Four-Leggeds and even trees, the Standing People, as the Nature to which I was listening. Yet the garden plot was a co-creation of the Nature Spirits and me. Learning to listen to Nature. So that's why I turn first to the garden.

How did I come to have a garden plot? Spirit at work in mysterious ways. The City of Gloucester, where I lived at the time, published a monthly pamphlet, *The Gloucester Leader*. I never looked at it. Each month it arrived in the mail, I picked it out and put it in the recycling bin in the kitchen. No interest in Council minutes and such. But in March, for the very first time, I flipped through it before I reached the bin. And there it was, an advertisement for garden plots, two locations, both 10 minutes by car from home. Annual Meeting of the Garden Association in March, the time to sign up for a plot. Plots 25' x 50'. That's big to a condo owner, this condo owner, single at that. Couldn't possibly look after a garden that size. Mentioned it to Liz, my next door neighbour. "I'll join you," she said.

Liz, a gardener? Quite a surprise to me. So there was the partner I thought I would need.

March 11, night of the annual meeting, a blizzard. I left the People, Words & Change training session early and drove to Blackburn Hamlet. New territory for me and I lost my way in the storm. Doubled back and arrived late at the school. People coming out, meeting speeded up because of the storm. I ask someone if he was at the Garden Association meeting and is it too late to sign up for a plot? "Come to our car." He was a member of the Executive. I sat in the back behind him and his wife, discussed the merits of each of the areas. Taps at one close to each plot, not so close at the other. That's what decided me. No water carrying to add to the task. Blackburn Hamlet plot it was and I signed up, paid my $15.00 by cheque right then, and became a garden plot renter. Synchronicity – Spirit ensuring I was not in a crowd while I made an important decision.

May. We were eager to start. Liz and I drove out to find the garden plot on a Tuesday. The road in was hard to locate even when we could see the plots from the back of the nearby school. We found

123

the road, drove in and watched the plowing begin. Plots not yet staked, we had only a general sense of where our own would be.

The garden staking took place the next night and by Friday I could contain myself no longer and went over in the evening. With Machaelle Small Wright's experiences in *Perelandra Garden Workbook* guiding me, I began consulting with the Nature Spirits through my fingers with yes/no questions. The Nature Spirits asked for four quadrants with a square for them in the corner of one, near the centre of the plot. I decided to go with that without checking with Liz and started digging in the farthest quadrants. *Feels good to get started*, I noted.

Next the Nature Spirits offered a design with seven rows in each quadrant. One pair, diagonally opposite each other, was straight rows. The other pair's rows were curved.

I worked alone on the weekend, exhausted myself but got the garden all dug.

Wednesday of the following week was the red-letter day: the first planting of seeds. Here is the journal entry:

> Turned out peas were the first thing we planted - appropriate for me. Got Liz and her mother over and gave a tobacco prayer. Found I didn't have any hesitation doing it since it was not even at a particularly "thinking" level, just the only way to proceed, "had to be done," by choice, not duty.

By the end of that week I had planted most of the garden and I had driven to a road construction site in the Gatineau to search for four pink granite stones for the Nature Spirit plot. I asked permission to take the stones and give them new purpose in life and offered tobacco in thanks. A few days later a friend and I took the stones, sage plants and marigolds over to the garden one evening and placed them carefully in the Nature Spirit plot, offering a prayer and tobacco to the Nature Spirits.

On May 27 my journal notes:

> The Chinese cabbage is up!! Not sure of anything else, although leeks or beets may be coming. No sign of peas.

During this week I began some "companion" planting by putting radishes in with the cucumbers to help drive cucumber beetles away and marigolds among the potatoes, broccoli and the yellow beans. Sue visited that weekend and I was delighted to show the garden to her and discovered in the process that more plants were now up. She encouraged my delight and quickly found her niche in watering, her way to support and nurture both me and the garden.

June. I was out to the garden almost daily and my journal notes that it felt funny if I didn't go over, even when it rained. By now I was already well beyond my level of gardening expertise. I had planted leek seeds only to re-read their section in my gardening book and discover that their growing time was six to seven months while here they would be lucky to get five. I had bought plants as well but had put them in clumps in the manner of chives. My garden neighbours came to the rescue and I replanted my leeks individually like onions. Later on they told me of the need to build up the soil around them to aid with their blanching.

Colorado potato beetles had arrived on the scene. At least their orange eggs were easy to spot. Something was affecting the lower leaves of the tomato plants. The local garden centre thought it might be spider mites and only soap and water might work, otherwise a garden pesticide spray. No spray for me and I settled for soap and water without much success. I found it upsetting to see "pests" hurting the plants.

By mid-June I had given up on my parsnip seeds ever coming up. My journal noted:

> I was all set to hoe the parsnip row, since it still seemed to be all weeds. Then the dog's paw prints that so upset me a few weeks earlier performed their role for the garden. Isolated in one of them were two parsnip seedlings. So they are coming after all.
>
> Weeding the parsnips was really fun. Weeds were ones that pulled out easily. Once I got them out of an area, parsnips emerged and it was more effective than looking for the parsnips first.

Now what isn't evident so far is the degree of obsession I had about weeding. My garden plot was to be tended carefully and that meant getting all the weeds out. I was still the Speedy Gonzalez of the previous summer and the weeds reappeared far faster than I could pull them out. What pleasure I got when I finished a section of weeding. How often I was stunned at the time it was when I decided to quit and head home. And even more amazing to me was how Great Spirit would nudge me to call it a day just at the right time whenever I had other places I had to be. How I loved it. One day my journal noted:

> Having Quad 4 weeded makes the garden look great since Quad 4 is the interesting shape and the spacing of the plants makes it even more evident than in Quad 2 in the distance.

July. As you have probably gathered, Liz wasn't out all that often to help. It turned out that she got a contract out of town and was mostly away. A new helper in the form of my other next door neighbour, Carmen, came to the rescue. She joined me about once a week in July. My journal noted:

> Carmen obviously enjoys weeding but goes a little faster than me. Net result of two of us and her enthusiasm was a lot accomplished.

By now I had an overabundance of Chinese cabbage and Swiss chard, the kale was getting big enough to pick its leaves and zucchini and peas were in flower. My over-enthusiasm for fertilizing the cauliflower led to several wilting and my learning how easy it is to hurt their roots. I had placed wire cages around the tomato plants when I first put them in. I woke one night with the feeling these plants felt caged in by their supports. Next day I asked the plants. They answered "yes" but they didn't want me trying to take the supports off at this late stage.

By late in the month when Sue was visiting, we were picking beans, carrots, Swiss chard, zucchini, green peppers, lettuce and the first broccoli. At home I prepared a zucchini, onion, carrot and green pepper dish very lovingly and gave a prayer at dinner honouring the vegetables and Mother, whose recipe I followed.

August. The first week in August, the row of sunflowers reached their spectacular best. Sue and I were over for produce daily and finally one day my journal noted:

> Over for produce in the morning. Got Sue to take me back to the garden and leave me there while she went for her massage. I weeded Quad 3 and half of Quad 4. In the morning I had felt like a plunderer. Recently I seem to have been coming and only taking from it, not working with it. Granted it takes a while to pick the produce now! But just the same, I really wanted to return and work with it. I was tired but felt much better when Sue returned.

The pleasure of working in the garden and the beauty I saw in it led me to thoughts about doing it again the next year. The idea of giving it the pattern of a tree or flowering plant popped into my head. I checked with the Nature Spirits, who liked the idea. I even found myself excited thinking about it. One day as I was taking pictures, another gardener passed by and I could sense he thought I was nuts. My journal caught my reaction:

> I just feel sorry for him, not enjoying his garden for the wonder and beauty it is.

Later in August on one occasion I was feeling angry at Sue for postponing her arrival. I headed off to the garden and explained to the Nature Spirits I was still feeling angry or irritated with Sue and wanted help to release that. Took out a number of the broccoli plants and tidied up the nasturtiums, which were now truly on display. I removed a red potato plant and discovered more potatoes. Then I dug up some yellow and green bean plants, thanking them for all their efforts on my behalf. This opened up the marigolds better. It felt good putting some of the garden to rest.

The anger was fully released. It wasn't until the next week, however, that in a question and answer period with my fingers, I came to realize that the garden plot had become my Power Place for the summer. No wonder the Nature Spirits had so readily helped me release my anger.

Sept. I was away much of September but my journal recorded my continuing appreciation:

> Took Timba for a walk and surveyed some of the other gardens in the plot. One or two stand out as being well cared for. Some are jungles.
>
> Dug up the rest of the potatoes. Had a sixth sense for avoiding putting the spade down on any of them and so no injured ones this time. I'm going to miss working in the garden. I feel sadness as I gradually bring it to rest.

Oct. As soon as I returned home in early October, I was back over to the garden plot. My journal noted:

> Looks ever so different, all flowers dead, tomatoes and green pepper plants too, and beans all up. Lots remaining however. Brought home onions, two enormous zucchini and three cucumbers and Carmen has two large bags in my fridge - green peppers, beans, zucchini.

It was now time for the final putting to bed of the garden. Mid-October Carmen came over with me. She dug up most of the parsnips, the last crop to be harvested, while I turned soil. I dug the last half dozen parsnips to honour them. Completed all the digging except the central path from the Nature Spirit area to the foot of the plot.

Finally October 16 brought the gardening season to an end. Here is what I wrote in my journal:

> Looking like rain any time. So I went to the garden before I had intended for a final garden ceremony. Took tobacco, my wood pipe and the tape recorder and a Tibetan flute tape. A woman was working in her garden across from mine. I felt self-conscious. So I crouched down at the Nature Spirit plot, sprinkled tobacco all around its outer edge and brought the rocks out in front. Was given permission to cut some of the sage, offering more tobacco and thanks in exchange. Prayed my gratitude with my little pipe, then moved stones and sage to the foot of the garden. Started the tape and had it playing the whole time I dug up the path from the Nature Spirit plot to the foot of the garden. I felt content with that sacred touch. It started to sprinkle as I turned the last shovels of soil and not much later was raining hard. Feels funny to know my garden plot days are over for the season.

Now, in 1995, I'm flying out west, with notes in my pocket for summing up what the garden plot meant to me.

One word for the garden adventure: pleasure, overriding pleasure for 20 weeks that year. The pleasure came in many forms. Creativity in the form of the garden itself, the part marked off for Nature Spirits with stones, and sage and marigolds. What pleasure creativity with those Nature Spirits brought me.

Then there was the learning that took place out there. There was the help from neighbours. The leeks stand out for that. But book learning too and guidance from the Nature Spirits. Asking advice, yet voicing my choices as well, and so much aware of the guidance given. Team work has always brought pleasure to me.

Then as the garden sprung up and wrought its magic of growth, blossoms, and food for the table, I was awed by the beauty and the wonder of growth. This garden my flower garden, comprised primarily of things I could eat, but pleasing the eye as well.

And two other facets of pleasure were there. The pleasure of caring I'd never felt so deeply before. I was part of the magic created. My caring helped nurture the growth that took place. What pleasure in that and in sharing its beauty with others. And no less a part of it all was the miracle of mindfulness, lost in the moment of caring out there. Sense of time vanished, other realities put aside as I puttered, weeded, nurtured. All pleasure. New dimensions of that word surfacing for me in that garden plot.

At the start, so leery of taking it on all alone. Yet Liz was away for much of the summer and I was at peace, caring for the garden, watching it all unfold. Taking responsibility, sharing it with the Nature Spirits, learning as I went along, no fear of failure, just joy in all that transpired. Struggles with weeds, with "pests," with lack of experience, too.

Yet that was part of the mosaic, part of the challenge I met with such openness and eagerness. A new approach to living all part of the message that the garden plot offered to me. Not all taken in as a message right then, but there to draw on when needed. Another Grasshopper leap taken.

27

Listening to Nature and Ceremony

AS I READ BACK through my ceremonies and Medicine Walks of the year, I realize how much more closely they are linked together than previously. And so I shall take you with me in this other aspect of my listening to Nature in 1992. One of the ceremonies was the Seawall ceremony in Vancouver with which this book opens. Another is a combination of Medicine Walk and ceremony.

Oct. 31. Lynne was having a bonfire for a giveaway on Hallows' Eve at her new property where she was going to rebuild a home. *What was I to give away?*

I turned to my fingers for help. They were clear about having something definite in mind, but "no's" I kept getting to a long list of possible giveaways. Then finally I hit it: my fear of asking for a spiritual advisor. So clear my fingers were. No room for hesitation on my part. I began with a Medicine Walk.

I set out late morning for a rendezvous with my Power Place in Mer Bleue, off on a mission. *Tonight I am to give away something to Spirit to make way for the new year that follows Hallows' Eve. It is the time to let go of my fear of asking Spirit to bring me my Spiritual Guide. I want that guide and the clarity of purpose that will likely ensue and yet I have been unable to take that plunge. Today my Higher Self has told me it's time. No more tomorrows on this one. Funny, I accepted this fate without question, acknowledging my fear, not knowing what it really is.*

I launch into the next step. *To give it away I'll need to identify it, flesh it out, give it body to be thrown into the fire. That spells seeking help from the Nature Spirits to pinpoint that fear. Fear is there all right, fear of my unknown fears.*

My chest tightens and my belly becomes taut too. I arrive at the parking lot, take a deep breath, put on my sky blue backpack. Tobacco pouch in hand, armed with peanuts and sunflower seeds for the jays, chickadees, black squirrels and chipmunks, I stop at the entry to the woods. I take out tobacco, offer it to the Nature Spirits and tell them my intent, my request that they help me label my fears. No sooner done than a flock of small Winged Ones, giving soft calls, arrive in the trees around me. Juncos and chickadees respond to my "pishes" and, always hoping they'll come to my hand, I hurriedly take off my pack and get out some sunflower seeds. I "pish" some more, my offering held out but no one dares come. *Lack of trust* flashes through my mind. Already stopped in my tracks, now I am stopped in more than a physical way. Within seconds of my request, Nature has replied. *The core of my fears lie in hiding because I, like the birds, lack adequate trust in the Provider.*

I wander along the path, ready to muse over the meaning of lack of trust. *Why my lack of trust?*

Childhood experience of my older brother taken suddenly away when I was only three? Why did Spirit do that?

The leaves rustle under foot as I walk. A jay calls in the distance but it is quiet here now. No chatter from squirrels, no twitter from birds, no wind rustling the leaves of the few trees holding on still to their autumn dress. I can't hold on to the fear in my chest and tummy in the face of this peace. I relax. I'm at home. I near my Power Place and leave the trail to enter it.

The sun is shining on the lower trunk of the central maple. I remove my pancho from my backpack to sit on and place it on the fallen tree that lies close to the sun-lit maple. The sun's warmth hits my face, although my rear end is none too warm.

I ponder my lack of trust. It is just that, not sufficient trust in Spirit to take the plunge. Fear of lack of control, of trusting someone who lets me down. After all, Sun Bear is clear that we remain responsible. "You can't blame flat tires for failure, if it was poor prevention through use of too worn tires," he said.

As I sit here thinking back to the opening message brought so quickly to focus me, I think how many times and how well Spirit, through Nature, has answered my searches. A new thought strikes me. *How can I not trust, confronted by Snake, by Eagle, by Red-breasted and White-breasted Nuthatches? How can I possibly not trust?*

I sit back to take that in. I notice a small beige moth darting about. *What on earth is it doing still alive on a cold day like this following a night of sharp frost?*

I see another and then another. The quiet woods aren't quiet after all. Silent yes, but life is moving, darting here and there. *Moth is knowledge. Knowledge is all about me if I just notice it. That's clear, I've heard that one before. I accept it, too. But if my teacher, my guide is like that, how will I know it's there for me? Will it come to me? Will one of these moths come to me, land on me?*

One approaches at the side but passes by. Another, straight ahead starts in a bee line toward me but then meanders off in another direction. *What knowledge is really for me? Will I know it or will I meet someone, have I already met someone, Lillian perhaps, who is that Spiritual Guide waiting for me? Have I not been centered enough to see her clearly, or, like the moths, are the number meandering here and there on the outskirts of my life leaving me confused as to which is for me?*

A maple blocks the sun and I shiver. *Am I to stay longer?*

Yes, a bit. I wait, hear voices, try hard to blend into the environment and not be seen. These two seem to have disturbed a bird. It gives strange calls. *Pileated woodpecker perhaps?*

The two pass by talking, immersed in their world, leaving me undisturbed in mine. I rise to leave, face the opposite direction, scan my home here. A flash of red not far away and there, near the base of a maple, is the pileated woodpecker, long black body, bright red crest, white face markings. I burst into a big smile. *What dignity. What determination and single-mindedness as it works away, pecking, not drumming. My day is made. The queen of the woods at this time of year, challenged only perhaps by the great horned owl, but certainly queen today.*

My heart bursts with gratitude and I salute the woodpecker. It flies off low, the flash of white in its wings visible. It's time for me to walk farther and see if other messages lie in wait.

Back on the trail, I think I see a large bird flying low. I follow. A jay moves off. *I don't think that was it.* But I see nothing else. *I'll cut back to the main trail.*

I turn and then, not far ahead, I see Pileated once again, working on a tree at the edge of the trail. I approach slowly, quietly. It ignores me, works around the base of the tree, then up the trunk 5-10 feet. Then it gazes about, spots another candidate and flies to a tree on the other side of the trail a little farther ahead. I follow slowly, captivated, drinking in its beauty, pleased at its preference for the bases of the trees. At this height, it looks even bigger than usual. The sun hits it, magnifying its spendour and I gasp. It works its way along the path.

Suddenly it strikes me. *Nature heard my question about how I'd know my Spiritual Guide. Would I recognize that person? Clearly I shall have no doubt at all. I've been following without the slightest hesitation for some time now and Pileated is leading me right along my path.*

I continue to follow, with new cause for amazement. At the main path the bird turns right, along it, toward my car. I trail along behind. Finally it flies a little farther off the path now that I am clearly on my homeward way. It settles in. I'm cold, throw tobacco in honour of it and stride more quickly now, trying to warm my hands.

I sum up the lessons. *Give away my lack of trust. How can I not trust? My Guide will appear to me and I'll follow without hesitation along my path as I am led along until I am close enough to home that my Guide can leave me.*

End of thought and a loud chattering call from Pileated behind me, *hand clapping perhaps, or cheering.* I prefer cheering, offer more tobacco as I leave the woods and re-enter my car.

That evening the ceremony didn't get under way until almost 11. People came and went. Most were there for partying. Just two of us came prepared. Phyllis had a dark mask she'd made in September and was ready now to release. I had a box, my giveaway written along one side: "lack of trust in Great Spirit to ask for a Spiritual Guide." In a group like this, I hesitated to voice my prayer, and particularly this giveaway of mine, so serious for such a gathering. That led me to give away my hesitation as well as my lack of trust. In the round for requests, I asked for my Spiritual Guide, as well as for *Grasshopper's Path to Spirituality* and its format.

Later, as I fell into bed, I was aware of an easy letting go of the giveaway and the calling in too, not lack of investment, but rather full commitment, ceremony completed.

I have taken you with me now on another Medicine Walk and ceremony. I want you to see how they play a role in my life, not every day, but from time to time as I need them. Ceremony commenced for me as something provided by someone else. There was ritual and instructions to be followed. When I immersed myself fully into them, they became mine and my focus and intent brought answers from Nature and from within. As you can see, however, I have shifted to creating my own ceremonies, incorporating ritual I have learned from others or adding my own. It is a powerful way to centre my focus and intent and open myself for recognizing the response of Spirit and Nature, thus helping me to find the wisdom within. Neither ceremonies nor Medicine Walks need be complex. What counts is that they come from the heart. You find what is comfortable for you, what allows you to open your wisdom within. For me the response has always been generous. I want to say also that what I receive is proportional to the intent and focus that I have put out, yet that sells the response short, so generous it always is.

28

Emotions and Obstacles

WHAT LEARNING took place over the year that tied in with my Vision Quest purpose of becoming more aware of my emotions and how I overcome obstacles? Let me pull together the threads of that journey.

The searching for purpose came from the heart, an emotional crying out as I sought my path and I've shown you that. The issue of a Spiritual Guide shows up in the Medicine Walk and ceremony you've read about.

I also let intuition play a role in my life. *The Gloucester Leader* led me to my garden plot, so often my teacher for my living that year. Intuition also guided me to Medicine Walks and ceremony. How else to describe how the Seawall ceremony came to be?

Let's turn now to my relationship with Sue and to yoga.

My relationship with Sue was an emotional learning that ran through the year. This was Sue's year to take a leave from work, give herself time for her personal life, including me. I saw it as the chance for us to begin to discover how life, more often together, would fall into place. We'd shared an apartment back in the early '70s but ever since then we have each lived alone. I had high hopes. *How to adapt to more time together? What new possibilities would it bring to each of us?*

First obstacle to face was that her year's leave was cut in half, due to a job opportunity that Sue couldn't pass up.

You ran across hints of the pleasure and frustration over the course of this leave in the tale of my garden plot. Let's turn now to two of my writing practices that touch more on this theme:

Shuffling Feet

I awake at the crack of dawn, 6:00 a.m. in July. I do my breathing exercise as I lie on my back on my double bed, my window, to my right alerting me to the break of day. Breathing in to a count of 7, hold for 28, out for 14. Ten times in all and I feel alert, ready to sit up, launch back in to Tony Robbin's *Unlimited Power*.

I read how to lessen fear. I'm excited, want to practice, but can't read the exercise and get into visualization all at the same time. I need Sue to try it with, each instructing the other. I'm impatient, eager to tell her about it, try it out.

Noise from her room. *Good, she's awake.* I hear her shuffle into the bathroom. The toilet flushes and I know she'll head here. She enters, one foot scuffing the carpet, then the other, head bowed. She crawls in beside me.

"Good morning," I ring out.

"Mornin'," she grunts in reply.

With noble patience I wait what seems an eon before I launch in again. "Reading something really good in this book," I say. "There's an exercise I want us to try."

Can't she even give me a second to wake up, groans Sue to herself. "What kind of work? I don't want work," she voices to me.

"Oh," I say deflated. "It's not important. I'll just go on reading." My body sags back on the pillows behind me. Disappointed, can't understand why Sue turns it into work. Inwardly I pout: *She's the one who likes playing with concepts.*

A little peace, thinks Sue. Then, guiltily, *Maybe I should hear her out.*

But the moment is gone. It finds a new breath that evening as we eat at Rose's Cafe with a friend. I dare to start into this tale as an example of the woes of a night person living with a day person. I start off with my side. Sue rejoins from hers. Our friend laughs, so do we. The recounting draws more and more stitches and now we relish this moment, laughing at the past with detachment and the clarity it brings.

Now I listen to the shuffle and respect its message. Now Sue tries breathing exercises too. Distance, allowing distance to soften a tension, seek its meaning, its raison d'être so that it retains its strength as a joke and nothing more. My pen stopped. Fear, is that what stops me short? Fear of our differences driving us apart? Fear of loneliness? And yet our sharing the tale brought us closer together, the deep companionship of laughing together, not at one another but with one another. Don't take life too seriously: a bottom line I need to learn. Laugh at my foibles. Let me learn of them in this way. It takes such closeness to draw them out and someone special like Sue to stay with the snags and untangle them.

Sue and I: a Relationship of Nurturance Only? Surely not!

This week has been one of looking at Sue's and my relationship from a somewhat new perspective. Before she left, Sue put a card beneath my pillow. One of the two spotted animals on the front says: "I know sometimes I'm not easy to get along with. . .(and inside). . .and I just want to thank you for loving me when I'm not very lovable." Sue added, "for giving me your best when I'm at my worst. You really are very special."

I wrote my reaction in my journal:

> I recognize that this visit has been her usual beginning of recovery, then off elsewhere but somehow the card jarred me and I need to look at it. Certainly I'm not at my best. Breaking my routines is hard for me and sorting out the ones that matter is a challenge that I haven't yet worked out.
>
> I continued to be puzzled by my reaction, which I couldn't define. I've asked Great Spirit to make this time with Sue a time for growth. This past Monday Great Spirit brought it to my attention again. Sue called. When I asked her how she was, she burst into tears, admitting that the weekend with a friend had been tiring because she was always trying to anticipate what the friend might need. Later on, I asked if she had decided when

she was coming back. Sue replied the following Monday night. Now the original plan was that she would be back on the weekend. I gritted my teeth, stomach tensing, but said nothing, recognizing the still fragile nature of her emotional state.

After I hung up, I cursed out loud and struck my pillow with my fist. Talk about a repeat of the old pattern. Not only had she left when she was just starting to show some signs of returning energy, now she was staying an extra weekend doing something that tired her last weekend. A good formula for returning here as exhausted as when she arrived in July. Gradually the focus shifted and my anger turned to why I always let this pattern unfold this way. I've never looked at my behaviour in all this before. I offer Sue the support and nurturing that she doesn't get elsewhere. I help her to recharge herself. It has never occurred to me to suggest that she recharge herself before visiting me. And yet I frequently feel frustrated because I am raring to pursue new ideas about relationships, about patterning of behaviour, about longer term goals for the two of us and she is too tired to focus on such energy-requiring objectives. It all seems like work to her when she needs a vacation. Or is it the manner in which I present such challenges? I like them to be structured and is it structure that Sue can't face at the moment?

When I went for my massage on Wednesday, I was prepared to talk. As Joy finished the hour-long massage, I was close to tears, grateful for the nurturing and loving her hands had brought to my body. I told her briefly about my anger, aware from my tears that I was still upset.

Back home, I had a really good cry, not from anger but sadness. Surely our relationship has more to it than just the basic, granted important, nurturing. And yet that has been the major focus for some time and it is usually somewhat lopsided; Sue being in a more critical state of need than I. She is attentive to my exuberant sharing of what I have done - such as the Vision Quest last year and the publishing of *The Bird Tribe Gathers*. But I want and need more than that. Sue's inability to focus on her own needs rather than meeting the needs of others hinders our getting on to other things. My acquiescence, not allowing my different but also substantial needs to be strongly enough voiced, compounds the problem.

There are valid "reasons" for Sue to assume the nurturing role for others rather than attend to her own needs or my less apparently urgent ones. But are we going to permit her leave to be frittered away in this manner? If so, would that not symbolize our inability to break this pattern? Am I going to put off my need for more than nurturing indefinitely?

Now is the time, for the programs we are attending together over the next little while have the potential for offering us both new opportunities for growth and adventure, individually and jointly.

Our pattern is an opportunity for growth.

For several years, I have searched for ways to attain more physical flexibility. I tried massage, went to chiropractors, and joined a Tai Chi group. The latter focused on movements, never brought us to its spiritual, meditative side. And I pushed too hard, stiffer at the end than when I began. I tried a stint of Hatha yoga, far too hard for me. Meditation was part of that class and I realized then that yoga could be a blend of spirit and body. I didn't pursue it farther until 1992. At the end of April Mercedes told me of a workshop in May. Gurudev, spiritual leader of the Kripalu Yoga Centre, was coming. Started his own form of yoga with flow experience a part of it, linked closely to spirituality. Flow experience was allowing the body not the mind to choose the moves through an altered state of consciousness. Now that sounded like what I was after.

I went to the weekend. Gurudev gave a demonstration. One hundred and fifty or more in the room. Not a sound. Never would have believed a human form could bend as he did. And the flow was "a thing of beauty." My jaw trembled and tears flowed.

The blessing ceremony, where most of the group went up to be touched by him, was not for me. Not that kind of spiritual guide for me. And yet his comparison of failure to seek a spiritual teacher to trying to learn medicine or law on one's own rang true.

I bought a tape of beginner yoga and practised in preparation for a weekend workshop by Joy in June and then a week for "Women in Yoga" at Gurudev's Kripalu Center in September with Sue.

The week at Kripalu showed me again how inflexible my body still was. I learned more of the postures and how a partner can help. Something Gurudev said in a tape we watched struck home to me:

"Your body is the most sacred place of pilgrimage you'll ever come to. It is the dwelling place of Divine Spirit; it is the true temple of God."

I sure have built myself a pretty uncomfortable temple! Writing practice after Day 1 catches my frustration:

The Pain of Yoga

I tried to be gentle. I tried to listen but this afternoon after the meditation, as I regained my seat on my pillows, twice a cry came out of me. My lower back screamed. At the end of the session, I was close to tears, feel them welling up now as I write. I want to get in touch with my body, honour it, understand this pain. I thought I released it as I lay there and yet I felt worse afterwards. I am discouraged, tired, frustrated, wanting to nurture myself and not knowing how. What do I want? That ice cream, chocolate-covered on a stick, looked so good. The sauna eased my body while I was in it.

Later the heavy evening breathed moisture on my body as I sat on the steps of the centre. Hints of moisture, just as it was at the beginning of the sauna. I'm not ready to really let go: not like the weather's thunder, lightning, the whole bit.

At the end of the week, I wrote of the last flow exercise:

The Joy of Yoga

Flow, sweet flow, gentle flow. My back wants to bend, to arch. My arm floats up and back. I note and let go. I go with it, glad to follow, surprised but willing. More arches. More surprises. But gentleness and flow. Let go.

Where now? My body knows. Child pose and peace and calm. Then moon salutation, arch again. New joy, new flow.

I note inward calm and trust. The tree with eyes closed? No. Was that me or my body? Second thoughts of one or other. Half moons. The stretch, the opening and up, up and opening once again. Flow, stretch, gentleness. Slowing down.

What a contrast that was. My progress review summed up where I was at the end of the year:

Yoga is strengthening and straightening my lower back and gradually bringing strength and flexibility into my upper torso and arms. I am still hindered by a sore arm and shoulder. Nevertheless, commencing with the moon salutation and then moving into my own posture flow all to the accompaniment of Tibetan flute music is satisfying.

Even by the end of the year, I was still searching. A writing practice catches my feelings and thoughts:

Energy Leaks

I know I have a purpose here, a message to put forth. As I grow and help others grow, a little compost trickles out here and there to Sue and other friends, and in *The Bird Tribe Gathers*. But it feels more like energy leaking than opening a tap deliberately and pouring forth what I have to offer. Leaks in the hose prevent a good strong spray reaching the whole garden, drenching it thoroughly enough to allow the roots of the plants to sink down, secure in their nourishment, secure for the plant they support.

I sense that potential. Why are my roots not that well nourished, supported, to allow that growth and flowering in me? Where do I turn for that watering? Within? Without? Am I missing certain nutrients? How do I know?

Great Spirit, when I write like this I see the questions and then I realize where I turn. To you, with ceremony and pipe. I ask for your help, your guidance, that Spiritual Guide I seek.

Spider appears in my vision, climbing back up to the ceiling from an invisible thread. Like me, Spider was dangling in mid-air but unlike me, he knew his connection, his link with the heavens, the Universe, and he went straight up and is now marching across the ceiling. Did he hear my questions, my cry for help and suspend himself there before my eyes to show me the route? *Kinship With all Life* says it's possible. Thank you, Spider for catching my eye and confirming my answers.

Emotions and obstacles, the final Vision Quest theme. So what did I learn about facing obstacles through my relationship with Sue and her leave? Writing practices captured frustration and laughter, hindsight bringing clarity then and now. In the fall Sue and I had three weeks together. It started with the program at the Omega Institute. We launched into writing there. Jogging and meditation were the other ingredients. We both were surprised and pleased with moments of jogging. Neither of us went there for that. Each of the activities was highly individual and personal. Yet being together, supporting each other and sharing our adventures allowed the experience to be fuller.

We had travel time then to explore, relax and enjoy before the yoga program began. Again our experiences varied, though sharing the pain in stretching beyond the limits our bodies could stand. And again the walking alone yet sharing.

But my lingering impression of the leave was frustration. It was as though I couldn't let go of the first big obstacle, the loss of half of the time. And that coloured how I viewed it. I held on to the perspective of how short it was, highlighting the frustrations. It is now much later, that I see how I failed to accept that obstacle and stay in the moment. The leave was life. The unexpected steps in and we can go with the flow or fight it. At the time I fought it and lessened the pleasure.

And what did I learn through my searching this year? I learned to ask for help and guidance through prayer, dreams and ceremony, and then let go of control and simply trust. Even the yoga showed the need to let go of control and trust. That's what the messages were. They are not easy for me to sustain. Often in the leave time I slipped. Same message time and again. Be patient and trust. Teachers surround me and are eager to help when I ask. All I need do is open my heart to receive, the message that is there for us all.

29

Brooke Medicine Eagle

AS THE END OF THE YEAR was approaching, one answer to my searching appeared. The next teacher that Pileated Woodpecker symbolized, arrived in November. I went to a workshop in Toronto run by Brooke Medicine Eagle. I was reading her *White Buffalo Woman Comes Singing* and I was taken with what I read.

When I got to the hotel room for the two-day workshop, I wondered if Brooke would appear before the workshop began. Somehow I thought that would be indicative of her style. My journal notes:

> Well, she came out just as I was registering and my heart turned over. My anticipation level was high, though I was desperately trying not to have expectations.

Brooke is a slender woman of medium height and almost waist-length, long brown hair. Her eyes sparkle and each of her movements is energy unleashed. I knew she had been raised on a Crow reservation in Montana by her parents, whom she described in her book as half-breed. Her spiritual path did not really unfold until her late twenties. But she had made up for lost time since then and was now well grounded in native spiritual ways, melding them into her eclectic upbringing and schooling.

I was drawn to her energy and her care for the earth. The teaching on the second day was on consensus for reaching decisions. Brooke applied it to our developing a ceremony for the afternoon. Seated in a circle, we went around the circle, offering our ideas on what the ceremony should be. Brooke asked me to start and as I had had an image of the yoga mountain posture, I suggested it might be a symbolic model to follow. Not surprisingly, that didn't catch anyone's interest. Most participants were off in concepts with no thought as to how to bring them into a ceremony.

When Brooke's turn came, she suggested that we talk to the drum or the altar and that we listen there too. I did, without much faltering, and what popped into my head was the rounds of a sweat as the basic pattern of rounds for our ceremony of dance and music. This could include a round of what we wanted to release and a round for what we wanted to receive, a round of our prayers for others and a round of silent prayer. So this was the idea that I put forth at the beginning of the second time round the circle. It quickly became the general format on which others built.

My body was tense as I expressed my idea, but my eyes and voice spoke my excitement too. Gradually I realized again how ceremony simply comes to me. It didn't take a dream, just the focusing on the drum. I contributed, stood out in the group in an appropriate way.

The ceremony went well. For me, discovering

again my own power with respect to developing ceremony made the weekend. And getting such good vibes about Brooke made it clear that I wanted more contact with her.

By the end of the workshop, I realized that the only way for me to see more of her was to take a summer program. My journal notes:

> I guess that's the next step. The one I'd like is the first two weeks of August, which isn't great for the garden, but maybe others can help out there.

Part VI   *1993*

30
Creativity Blossoms

NEAR THE END of my Vision Quest at the Bear Tribe in 1991, I watched Ant dismember a dead grasshopper and carry it up the cliff face beside me. Or so that rock seemed to me from Ant's perspective. I had no doubt that Ant would succeed in this task, carrying the spirit of Grasshopper to the top of the mountain. Well, I have chosen 1993 to be the year that brings this book to a close and I feel like Ant wanting to carry Grasshopper's spirit to the top of the cliff.

It has been easy to choose 1993 for closing this book, another eventful year that reached its climax by my moving to the country in November. Was I also carrying Grasshopper's spirit up the cliff in making that move? Yes, and while it signals the end of the book, it also signals a beginning, for my spiritual path did not end, just began a new phase.

But I am back with Ant climbing that cliff as I wind this book down with the events of '93. There are more new beginnings; there are new variations on old themes; and Ant's challenge to me is to use these events to throw more light on Grasshopper's path to spirituality.

January 1 and a new calendar year. Louise suggested a 12-day ceremony. Honour each day and let it speak of the month, one day for each month of the year that lay ahead. And so the first week of January began with outings to our Power Places, alternating whose we visited each day.

At first I assumed solely the ceremony time in the woods would signal the messages for the month that the day represented. Louise saw it differently. Everything that happened throughout the day would be the mirror and messages for her. Once she mentioned this, I saw it that way too. This ceremony and the entire day was very much like a Medicine Walk, with the purpose to throw light on how to proceed in the year ahead. On occasion the outing became its own teaching. Louise followed through for the full 12 days, while I stopped after the 7th, since I left for Toronto on the 8th and a trip to Costa Rica with Sue, the finale of her leave time.

On January 1, Louise and I discovered a porcupine in a tree close to my Power Place. Porcupine, as symbol of trust, innocence and playfulness, was pointing towards Sue's and my trip to Costa Rica as a time for renewal and play. Later in the month that is exactly what happened. It is all captured well by a night on the beach. As we meandered our way back from our dinner, we discovered that some form of algae in the wet sand left a fluorescent outline of our footsteps. We became two kids dancing, making designs with our feet, laughing, enthralled by the magic and mystery that was with us. The sand was cold to our fingers as we touched the mystery and it disappeared. What lightness to my being and what a full heart when I discover and share such moments of magic with Sue.

The most striking pointers of what lay ahead in fact came after I had ended the days of ceremony, or so I thought. The intent remained. The 8th, my drive to Toronto, reflected travelling in August, when I went to Brooke's camp in Montana. We flew to Costa Rica on the 11th and that November was the month I moved to the country, a foreign environment to me.

And yet the day of the ceremony that stands out most in my mind was January 4, a day that brought a lesson in and of itself. The fourth was a day of contrasts, a lesson in how we can see our world in new ways. This was how my writing practice captured the day.

Jan. 4. Gray, foggy day to start, with rain on and off all day, making it possible to chip away the thin layer of ice on the front walk. Out back a skating rink, progressively more dangerous with the water on top of ice too thick to chop.

Well, all is not bleak. Walking in Louise's woods is easier this morning, snow giving way readily with every step. Many boughs are bowed over, struggling under their weight of ice and rain, but the sturdy ones shrug off their ice, a clinking here, a tinkling there. New noises to which to attune. A grouse explodes from close by. We both give thanks. Grouse, spiral dance, personal power. Strong medicine today. My thought, on rising, of a "yucky" day left well behind now. Beauty in these woods, easy travelling, Grouse inspiration.

As we near Grandmother Pine, I sense an inward tug to carry on beyond and say so. Louise agrees and we both walk on. I stop, entranced by straw-like grass, a soft gold in the ice; Louise admires the green of an occasional fern. Then, as we approach the hydro line, something else catches my eye. We both are held, spellbound, by magic. Bushes here look like they carried berries earlier.

The raspberry-like clasp remains and now they are laden with small ice berries, not just drooping down from branches but berries thrust straight out and straight up too. *Impossible* I think but I am absorbed, transfixed by their beauty and magic. I can't resist. I pluck a berry and, like a ripe raspberry, it comes off readily. So real it is, I pop it into my mouth, suck the cold berry of ice. A dreary day? Oh no, a magical day.

I carry on to the doctor's after. As I slowly negotiate a sheet of ice, deliberately sliding now and then, I think of how many extra doctors' visits will ensue from falls. I pause, struck by the contrast between this concern and the hour in the woods earlier on. I am captivated by how we see our world. Yucky, dangerous, if this is all we see. But magic there too. We had walked by "berries," quite a few, until suddenly I perceived anew and awakened a new world and a new day for us both. My lesson was that we all have the power within to turn a "yucky" day or time in our life into a magical one.

So this uncompleted 12-day ceremony reflected once again how readily we can create simple ceremonies or turn short walks into opportunities to connect with our spiritual paths. Put out an intent and be open. Why not take the first day of the next month and prepare for the month ahead using the events of the day or a walk you choose to take as guidelines to help you shape your whole month. Be open and have fun.

I arrived home from Costa Rica on January 26. For Sue and me January felt like the end of the year of her leave. I experienced the emptiness that comes with loss and endings. I filled the hole by planning what lay ahead.

So, on the 31st, I settled in to prepare for February, the beginning month of my year. I began by drawing a Sacred Path card. The Sacred Path cards, along with the book by that name by Jamie

Sams, provide another tool like the Animal Medicine cards. Once again there are 44 cards, a sacred number in native tradition. Sams says that "The purpose of the cards is to show you the steps of your spiritual development in a way that allows you to come to your own personal truths." (p.9). The cards focus on native traditions and teachings and include suggestions on how they may apply to your own situation.

These cards, along with the Animal Medicine cards, runes, and the I Ching, are the tools of this type that seem to suit me best. Tarot cards are a similar tool but one to which I have not been drawn.

I drew East Shield, a card about illumination and clarity. It speaks of a golden door of the East that leads to all other levels of awareness and understanding. As events turned out, in this broad sense it captured the significance of my move to the country near year-end.

Eagle's medicine and protection graces the paths to the East Shield. One path to the wisdom of the East Shield stood out for me: "To use any talent or creativity you have and you will know illumination."

In the section on application, what struck me most forcefully was:

> "Be creative and daring in order to stretch your concept of who you really are and venture into new realms of understanding." (p.92)

How was I to apply it? For starters, inner warmth rolled over me like molten lava at the thought of having Eagle on hand as protector. Turning to the writing of *Grasshopper's Path to Spirituality* would represent using my talent and creativity and take me along one of the paths to illumination and clarity.

Finally, taking the East Shield application to heart, I lined up creative efforts of various kinds for each week of the month. First I would mount a collage of symbols on the staircase wall to complete the ceremony at the Seawall in 1992. Next I would make a necklace for Sue from some of the shells I had gathered in Costa Rica. In the third week I would commence garden planning with the Nature Spirits and to round out the month I would turn my Snow Goose wing into a fan by making a proper holder to encase the end that I grasp.

I was eager for my new year to begin, creativity gurgling inside me.

The first week of the month I launched *Grasshopper's Path to Spirituality*. Six times in the course of the month I sat down and wrote. Not very often, you may think but ever so more often than when I was writing *The Bird Tribe Gathers*. And the book was begun. That's what mattered the most at the time.

There was the Seawall collage to get underway as well. I searched for pictures of the symbols I had chosen to represent each of the family members or friends whom I had honoured: trillium, bald eagle, great blue heron, horse, dragonfly, fuschia, Japanese maple and mountain lion. Photos of four, magazine pictures of another three. Horse stumped me until I turned to the library and and traced a picture I liked. Temporary, until I could get a photo that suited me better. And so right on the first day of the month, I glued all the pictures on the pale blue background sheet that I used for the matting. Then I waited for my next class in Ojibwe to learn how to write "all my relations." Friday, I printed the heading, took down the collage already on the staircase, dismantled it and put the new one in place.

How satisfying to mount it at last. My heart expanded, burst like a bud into flower. I smudged myself and the collage, savoured the sweet aroma of the sage, and prayed aloud, offering thanks to all those relations and the gifts symbolized there. In a quiet but firm voice, I stated my intent to try to live up to the symbols, making them part of me and my path.

The second week was necklace time. Carmen, with far more experience than I with crafts, accompanied me to Lewiscraft to look for supplies. The trick was how to attach the shells since their holes were small. I came back ready to try. That was Monday. Tuesday I set to work, deciding what beads I wanted with the shells. My fingers played on the rough sides of the outer shells and their smooth interiors as I shifted them from one colour of bead to another. Carmen came in the evening and we tinkered with adjustments. Wednesday, all thumbs at something like this, I put it together, enjoying the challenge and allowing patience to make up for too many thumbs. I finally held it out in front of me and smiled. *It looks good.*

I wore it for Carmen, who was genuinely impressed with how well it looked on my green shirt. There's nothing more I could do until after a fitting on Sue in March. Over lunch, I gazed at it and the staircase collage. My shoulders shifted back and my chest pushed outwards, reflecting my pleasure and pride. Two adventures, plunges, that month that stretched me creatively. There was *Grasshopper's Path to Spirituality*, too.

Week 3 was planning the garden. How impatiently and eagerly I looked forward to it over the weekend. (Week 3 didn't start until Monday.) Monday afternoon, with the light of Grandfather Sun streaming in the living room windows, I retrieved the four pink granite rocks and the white crystal centre from last year's Nature Spirit plot from the basement. Then upstairs for my royal purple meditation cushion. Shoes off, abalone shell filled with sage, Perelandra Garden Workbook, ruler, paper, pencil, pen, and I was ready. Smudged myself, breathing in deeply as I gently guided the smoke over my face and then to the rocks. I checked with my fingers to make sure the rocks would stand in for the Nature Spirits, deva of the garden plot. Assured they would, I dove in.

I told the Nature Spirits of my excitement, bounciness, all on edge, eager to begin. I sought their help, eager for their partnership even more this year. Design first. *I know we've been talking generally of a flowering tree but Michaella Small-Wright speaks of circles and the flow of energy. Could we have settled on a flowering tree because I hadn't offered circles as a possibility?* I gave several options - flowering tree, two circles, four circles, other design to be determined. I held my breath and asked out loud, "Flowering tree?"

"Yes."

On the placement of the branches, I jerked up straight in surprise: the branches of the tree were not parallel. *Oh, I see. Allows for rows of different sizes.*

The left side came first. One big row up top, odd shape, as the rows of the side began. The tip of the bottom branch reached almost to the corner.

Right side. Many more rows on this side. *Will it fit?* I wondered, dubiously.

Michaella was right: the Nature Spirits knew their math. It fitted. This side exact. I shook my head and marvelled.

Week 4 was the Snow Goose fan. Got some of the tools more than a year ago, yet couldn't, wouldn't take the plunge. The starter gun fired. I explored on flannelette first, then doe skin, finally a pattern on paper. Proceeded methodically, carefully, experimenting, not daunted when something didn't work, tried something else.

I held my breath when it came to the final cut, the real McCoy. All went well. Then cut the cord with which to sew it together, trusted it would work out, and went with the flow. Exactly right, with just enough left for a loop and a knot. It can hang now, had never thought of that. Going with the flow reaped benefits. And it was finished Friday night. *Why did I put it off for a year? Crazy, wasn't it? Is that what I'm doing about moving to the country? Putting that off, year by year?*

The lesson during the month came home to me one day late in the fourth week. I looked out and saw my neighbour, Carmen out in the field with Timba. Timba was racing through the snow, rolling in it too. Timba, always in the moment, fully engaged, not worrying, living, being. *What I did this month with each of the projects: lost my fears, went with the flow, responded to the challenges. Examples on every side. Why is it so hard to do it all the time?*

These ventures into freeing up my creativity were an important step for me. Working on each of the projects brought joy. I also saw how useful this approach of promoting creativity could be to my life on a regular basis. It didn't hit me then, however, that I was touching in to an extremely important part of myself. In fact it is a part of each of us that we too often fail to allow to flourish fully in our lives.

This exciting adventure would almost certainly not have occurred had I not chosen to seek guidance through one of my spiritual tools. My intuition pointed me to one that worked well in that moment. When I open myself to fully explore how the teaching applies to me, this tool or similar ones become a powerful aid, so well exemplified here.

Let go of skepticism that may hold you back and find such a tool for yourself if you have not already done so. Discover for yourself just how helpful that can be in life. And why not look for some small creative project for this day, or week or month?

A staggering new development in my writing came in March. The writing startled me so, I didn't try more at the time and by the end of the year had completely forgotten it had happened at all. Re-reading my writing practices brought it back and I felt my awe anew. Conversations with Nature. It started in March with another in April. It had dawned on me that maybe I could hold a conversation with an animal through a writing practice. Here is what happened.

Mar. 11.

M.B.:"Oh Spider, I am so excited and so nervous. It's not so much afraid as nervous. Can I really have you speak to me? For so long I have wanted to bridge this chasm, had the feeling that once bridged, communication would move forward by leaps and bounds. Now in the last few days, since I came to Animal Medicine cards in *Grasshopper's Path to Spirituality*, I have a gut feeling about letting the pen write for Nature, speak not my words but hers.

Then this morning I thought of calling on you or Eagle to help me write today. My fingers said yes. Using my sacred Snow Goose fan, I smudged myself, then the cards, then wanted to be sure they were in the upright position and cut them to see. I looked at you, realized I had just made the selection I was preparing to make. Thank you for springing forth so promptly. You've been waiting here in my home these past few days, wandering around my living room, crouched at the join of ceiling and wall over my couch, very much present, waiting, waiting. Now this morning I don't see your physical form but you are forcefully here in the card. I welcome you, seem afraid to take the plunge and let you speak. Please help, please take over."

Spider: "You cause me to smile, the smile of a doting parent or special teacher, aware of your shyness, your nervousness, proud that you are here, asking, wanting new doors opened. Yes, I can speak to you through your pen. Why not? You are I, I am you. All it requires is your openness, your invitation and here I am. Not just me, others can write through your hand, too. But I carry the weaving, the communicating, like to help these first new steps, hesitant at first, eager. Remember when you were a toddler? How you were told they thought you would never walk? Then that day when the new chairs and table just for you, your height, were brought home, placed against the far wall, you took that plunge, got up, walked across the room to them, your first walking on your own?

You have a good description when you speak of a chasm. It's not that wide really but the drop beneath makes it seem so much wider, so much more dangerous, beyond your reach. Yet take the plunge and you wonder what your hesitation was all about. Right?"

M.B.: "I shake my head. You're so right on. Thank you for that encouragement. But part of today goes beyond the pleasure of taking this plunge. I'm eager to hear your message about animal cards, Nature speaking to us humans who seek you out."

Spider: "Whoa, whoa. I'll get on to that. But that's typical of you, you know. Was it Mercedes who pointed it out once before? You can't handle joy, success, bask in it, absorb it, let it fill your being, fill your heart. That's not for you. You must drive on to the next goal somewhere out there, not in your grasp right now. You don't allow yourself to rejoice in the moment. Hummingbird is here for you this month. Welcome him, open your heart to him, bask in his joy. Feel your physical well being, health re-emerging that Dr. Tran and acupuncture is bringing into your physical being. (I went for acupuncture three times a week from March until mid-July.) Stop leaping ahead to what comes next, how complete the overhaul will be. Relish the freedom in turning your neck, no stomach pain at night, ruddy complexion, desire to write, to learn Ojibwe, to ski. Live in the moment and enjoy.

Dee, on your hand, captures your attention, holds you in joy, in love, but she can't be there in your hand all the time. Transfer that gift, hold that teaching in the rest of your life. It's Dee's gift to you this month, yours for the taking. Honour it, learn, bring the teaching into your being. A big lesson for you, not easy, not learned in one day. It undoes all the tapes of the past. Bat is there in the east for you this month, opening the door to rebirth, encouraging you to enter there, avoid a breach birth, go with the flow. They are all there in harmony, part of Dee's message.

Animal Medicine cards or physical beings. We're there to teach you. The teachings are there if you open your heart, your eyes and ask for our help. This is a lot for one go - the first go. Besides, you need to take it all in, stay in the joy of the moment. Be with Hummingbird for a while now. You know me, I'm staying around. I live here. I'm one of your totems. I've been waiting, waiting ever so long for this moment. You've finally found my role, my gift to you, one of them at any rate. Off you go for now."

Apr. 23. My writing practice captures the feel of the month and this time I turn to Grouse.

April. Dreamtime, the Sacred Path card I drew for the month. Yet I have struggled with dreams, failed to write them down, not in tune with messages there. Failed to read the card again until this morning. Have I missed the boat, my appointment with the dreamtime?

January 4 was the ceremony day for this month of April. January 4 was a day of rain, ice, snow. Yet there was incredible beauty in the woods when we saw it anew, ice berries the highlight of our day, changing our day, changing me.

Magic came full flood this week. Not dreamtime or is my bond with Nature, dreamtime too? Monday was not too cold, warm front having collided with cold, petered out into soft drizzle. I needed gloves, rain boots, royal blue rain pants and jacket. It was time to hunt the hermit thrush. Joy upon joy as the birds appeared, white-throated sparrow, my spirit song back to join me again. Grouse, ruff up, catching my attention, not a mate's I fear. Caught mine, dreamtime connection?

I read back today to January 4. That day we flushed a grouse. Signal, dreamtime signal, taking my personal power, finding vision, perspectives that change the world, change me, my world. Spider last month, a new beginning in communication. I've shied away, not tried again. It's frightening, too much power. Is it real? Can I do it again? I'm scared I'll block, lose faith.

M.B.: "Want to speak to Grouse. See if I've read it right. Learn more, venture forth, hear, not just see. Grouse, are you here right now? Will you speak to me?"

Grouse: "I caught your eye, didn't I? No point talking then. You needed to re-read January 4, needed to see the connection that your ceremony and your focus then paid off, registered with us and us with you. You saw with new eyes that morning, transformed by the ice berries. You transformed yourself and them. Dreamtime, yes, the two dimensions wrapped in one. Your dreamtime, a powerful one. You journey that way, you tap our wisdom that way. Writing out in the woods in the future will bring you more, expand your vision farther. You are open out there, more open than now inside. Your pen will flow freely. Take your notebook and your pen. We're ready. You're more ready too.

Fancy way to catch your eye and ear, wasn't it? It's hard to compete with your white-throated sparrow, you know. Not compete, that's just a figure of speech. But it's hard to catch your attention and widen your vision, when you're already captured in delight, in meeting old friends and renewing those ties. I didn't mind. It gave me the chance to strut. It's fun showing off to you, you're so appreciative, so aware of our gifts. Goshawk sends thanks too. You noticed. You notice us all, made us feel your joy and made our day too. Remember that: we give to you, you give to us. We need that support, that encouragement too. Mother Earth, all of us, just like you, like being noticed, like to hear that our presence is special, makes a difference."

So there were important teachings and reminders, such as the importance of voicing our gratitude. In addition, however, through these conversations I learned that my tool of writing could now be channeled in this new direction when I was ready to trust myself and take on the challenge. This brought me a deeper connection with Nature and thus yet closer to what I was coming to see as central to my spiritual path.

31

Preparing the Soil

ACTION TOOK OTHER directions in late spring and early summer. The garden design in my mind sprang into being. Brooke mailed instructions for the August camp program and I plunged into preparation.

It all finally began on Saturday, May 22. By noon on Sunday, I had dug all the rows. The plan was more complex, but the soil was ready and yielding easily. It, too, ready for this new season, acknowledging the caring it had received the preceding year. The flowering tree design made the garden unique and brought me great pleasure. The shape is shown in Part V.

The joy was no less than the preceding year. On July 7 my journal notes:

> Off to the garden to water it, check potatoes and weed some of the parsnips. Lettuce up and possibly another section of raddicio (Carmen's Italian). White-throated sparrow singing this morning and a veery and a black-and-white warbler. I sang too. Lovely morning even if sweat was pouring off me.

The garden plot was clearly my Power Place for another summer. How energizing it is to have such a place in our lives, be it a tree outside a window, a special spot in the woods, or a garden.

In mid-March I was accepted for the Deepening of Spirit camp for women in Montana in August. In April I received instructions on how to prepare. Four fasts to be done before I went: a 1-day and 2-day with as much water as I'd like; a 1-day and 2-day with as little water as possible. We were required to submit notes at camp on how the fasts went. If the fasts were not done, the Vision Quest would be in your tent, not out on the land. Strong incentive that. I turned to exercises, such as stair climbing, to get me fitter.

Fasting. I've been doing it at various times for ceremonies or vision quests. Is it hard? What really is its purpose? As I learned before the 4-day quest at the Bear Tribe, it is a signal of our strong intent, a giving up of food and comfort to make way to receive. It allows our bodies and minds to clear, making our senses more aware. In so doing we increase our opportunities for shifting from the third dimension of this physical reality to the fifth dimension of the dream time and the world of spirit. Once again it is a spiritual tool and, coupled with focus and intent, makes a difference, at some times more markedly than others.

Did I find it hard to fast? I was used to eating meals at regular times, never skipping a meal, and became edgy and hungry if I went much beyond my normal eating times. I expected fasting to be difficult. In fact it was not. Once I had established my intent, it was as though my entire being joined in. I never struggled with hunger pangs on 1-day,

2-day or even the 4-day fast. I become physically weaker and the second or third day may seem ever so long. Finding the best way to come back on food after a 2-day or 4-day fast is more difficult for me than the fast itself. At first anything acidic or hard is painful to swallow. As in all of the path, each of us is unique. And so there is wisdom in Brooke's insistence on having participants practice at home and discover how their body reacts.

If you wish to try a fast for the first time, I suggest you choose a 1-day water fast or even clear broth. Plan ahead for a day that will allow you quiet time for contemplation, indoors or out. Then on the day, pray your intent and purpose. Drink lots of the fluid and be open. Pay attention to your body, thoughts and what takes place in your day. At very least this offers your body an opportunity for cleansing. If you don't still have family meals to prepare, you'll also be amazed at how much more time there is in your day when preparing and eating meals is removed. But more will be there for you to find and explore.

June 26 was one of my 1-day fasts. I find they frequently lead to writing practice, and creativity in the form of ceremony often ensues. This day triggered two ceremonies, both of which I carried out shortly after. Each was important to my path at the time. Writing practice will take us there.

June 26: Fast Day

Breaking away old patterns, old belief systems. Grasshopper taught me big leaps are few and far between. Small steps, the daily path. Yes, yet I'm preparing for a leap right now. I feel it in my bones.

Dreams today spoke of removing layers of clothes, then walking a stretch of shore but the tide coming in, turning me back. See that as only going so far right now.

Sue, I think of her. Wheezing again, her body clogged, symbol of her state of mind, her path. Can she break free, cleanse her body, cleanse her being? Can we break free together and stride our paths together? Or must I walk the path alone as in my dream? Meandering along I was, just being. Glad I can do it easily in my dream. None of the mind games. Discipline, warrior, impatience, guilt about my turtle pace. None of these in the dream. Meandering along, dawning awareness of the tide and the need to turn back. Turned back, no concern, no fear, no regret, noted the route of others, prepared to follow, sensing my body could do it.

I thought the other day of one of Brooke's tapes. Putting incompatible wishes in each hand and clapping the hands together. Is that where I'm at? I want someone in my life, a partner in this path, someone who can co-create our gift to our people. Whether it's part of an organization or not doesn't matter but I don't want to walk my path alone. Hermit though I am in many ways, I'm also a team player and this particular creative, giving Self is the team player. So I search for my team player or players. I've always hoped it's Sue. Maybe later on, not right now. I want a partner on this path now, ready to move on together now, ready to weave our dream together.

So that's in one hand. Vague. Vague because I don't want to restrict too much. Tempted to say woman, Canadian or Brooke. Paint in details, make the dream come alive through detail? Or leave it open for Spirit, for a wiser part of me? Yet centre myself, call it in. If I'm strong enough in focus, can I call it in without the detail? I prepare to act, not alone but together.

The need to act. Is that an issue for this camp?

An issue like knowingly taking responsibility? Partly perhaps. Hard to get in and see myself for who I am and who I can be.

I place a partner building our dream and transforming it into action into my left hand–appropriate for my spiritual path to find its way to my left hand.

I envision this as a clap together. So what's in the right? I'm fighting off the clear image - my relationship with Sue. That's in my right hand. Yes, that's having my cake and eating it too. Partner on my path, co-creating it, all that in my left, but just as solid, just as important, my relationship with Sue in my right. The two can be together. I make the connections, slap them together. Let go fear. Rabbit, come to take it away once more. Nothing will separate Sue and me. Left and right go together, form the church steeple over my head, the yoga steeple, union, left and right together in spiritual harmony, straight and tall, emerging out of the mountain. I like that image. My ceremony for my Power Place before I go, my ritualistic action. Not Brooke's, mine.

And mid-July on the first day of a 2-day fast, I visit my Power Place in Mer Bleue for the ceremony. The mosquitoes are ferocious on the way in. *Will I have to do the ceremony back home instead?*

But when I reach my Power Place the mosquitoes vanish. I stand, arms upstretched in the mountain yoga pose, hands, fingers coming together in a spire. I unite my dream of a partner with whom to co-create our gift to All our Relations, and my relationship with Sue. All there, my head uplifted, carried into the cathedral canopy of the beech and maples of my Power Place, their energy and beauty melded with mine. My heart is so full it showers out warmth like a fireworks display.

But back on June 26, I had turned to a second important issue.

Pileated woodpecker's message last fall showed me following the teacher with no questions, no doubt, then leaving the teacher at the side when it was time to move on. Well Dr. Tran, an acupuncturist to whom I turned, appeared as that teacher in the spring, a Spiritual Guide in a sense. He taught me new realms of healing, the miracle my body is, its yearning for health, its strength to carry me there once energy was returned. Acupuncture brought energy, released my body toxins. Cleansing, key to new growth of the body. Another message of last night's dream. Stripping off old clothes, making way for the new.

Now I'm leaving that teacher aside and it's time to ask for another. Brooke's exercise on a Spiritual Guide. I've started on it, will conclude it today.

Brooke's way. Do hers and mine meet, form companion energy? I like her energy, am drawn to it, trust it, not like Sun Bear, not even like Twylah. Brooke feels right for me. She pushes to limits but emanates support. It's that sense of support bringing me the feeling of safety to draw out the best in me. I feel vibrant, and sense energy.

3:30 now and I have just completed an exercise on calling in a Spiritual Advisor. I stated I am committed, without reservation, to calling in a Spiritual Advisor or Medicine Teacher. Doing so stops me short. The seriousness of my commitment envelops me, overwhelms me. Earlier I called in Dr. Tran. That teaching and healing is drawing to a close. I'm ready for more. Physically I'm ready, but more than that.

Great Spirit has demonstrated that I will be brought what or whom I need regardless of my own expectations. I responded wholeheartedly to the teacher I was brought. It's no longer an exercise in a book. I've done it, experienced it and need only to step into the ceremony and prayer to do so again.

What ceremony this time? Something to honour my past teachers, two-legged and otherwise, then the asking for a new teacher and some offering I leave for that teacher. Where? Black Lake. How about Canada Day, July 1st, up at the lookout? Mix joy, adventure and prayer together. Sounds good.

My journal picks up on the ceremony:

> Up at 4:30 and at Black Lake around sunrise. Bugs aren't bad. As I near my ceremony area, I disturb a large doe. She circles, actually coming a little closer and then grazing. On to the rocks and over to the outer ones. Smudge first, savouring the smell, and then honour all my past and present teachers. That finished I toss two slides, each of past teachers, over the edge.
>
> Next I work through Brooke's exercise for calling in a Spiritual Guide. Offer tobacco at the end and then eat my fruit breakfast, saving the apple for the previous post-prayer place. As I approach that area, I flush a grouse. Ceremony acknowledged.

In each of these instances I once again turned to ceremony to help me prepare for whatever Grasshopper leaps lay ahead. In these instances I followed what Brooke laid out and created around her exercise what was right for me. The key is strong, clear intent and focus, carrying out the ceremony and then letting go, trusting, and allowing Spirit to take over when the time is right. And somewhere in the process Nature brings a symbol of acknowledgment. In the second there were the deer and the grouse, while in the first the absence of the mosquitoes at my Power Place. I couldn't overlook those signs!

32

Grouse Wing and Act of Power

THE DAY finally arrives. I'm off to Montana and Blacktail Ranch. I'm so excited that I'm as bouncy as Tigger in *Winnie-the-Pooh*. I'm also rattled, can't find my keys, worrying about what I may have forgotten. *I know this is big. But in what way?*

I'd read about the part of the program where we seek to discover our power or energy leaks. The thought brings tightness to my chest, just as I had way back at the ceremony of the Night on the Mountain of Fear. I don't realize I am living one of those power leaks right in the moment.

The airport limousine is late in arriving. I'm pacing around the apartment and then back to the window. Finally, a long stretch white limousine pulls up, my limousine for the drive from Sue's to the Lester B. Pearson Toronto International Airport. *A joke of Sue's?*

I laugh. *No, Great Spirit has a sense of humour too. How absurd. Alone, tump sack and back pack in the long "stretched" car, four big bucket seats, tinted glass.*

Reminds me of my dream for my previous Vision Quest, my dream of a posh restaurant. Same message now in a new way. Tension leaves my neck, shoulders, all my body. An outer grin and inner comfort enter.

Reaffirmed the next day as I drew closer to the turnoff for Blacktail Ranch. I spot a "hawk"" in the distance, stop, jump out of the car and quickly focus my binocs. It drifts closer and closer yet. *Big for a hawk. Very big. Golden eagle? Can't be . . . Must be.*

Doubt leaves and my heart opens to warmth and joy. I accept Eagle, welcoming me. Tears are just below the surface. *I'm meant to be here. Spirit is here, my path unfolding before me.*

Later, at the ranch, a vireo rings out its loud, clear notes, welcomes me to the far side of the tenting meadow. I pitch my tent in the long grass. The resilient grass makes the tent floor spring up and down as I unroll my sleeping bag and foams in the living area. It pokes roughly at me directly when I am back outside and placing my extra clothes in their plastic bags in the storage area of the tent back vestibule. Settling in is a form of quietening meditation. I'm ready for the new adventure.

And so it all began. Me eager, such a sense of relief as I viewed the ranch and its trees. I'd feared wide open space with no shelter for vision quest sites. Not wide open Montana hills here, but treed slopes, giant cottonwoods along the chattering river. Open spaces, yes, but ponderosa pines and black spruce and aspens scattered liberally, their leaves and needles offering music for the wind, shelter for animals and questors. I was at home in the setting, even if I took days to fully settle in to the program.

First morning of camp. Day breaks. I arise early and wander back towards the entrance, staying with the familiar. Two deer on the far hillside. Deer are plentiful here I come to know, offering their gentle, playful opening to Spirit. Back to the tenting meadow by 7:00 for morning wake-up. The group leaders arrive with drum and rattles and song and weave their way around the meadow. The song's message is about awakening to our vision. The melody, the words, and the messengers who are singing it all touch my heart and I'm close to tears. Camp has begun.

For orientation we meet in a large, circular teaching tent called a yurt. Chores, hoops (our three small groups), and hoop leaders. Practical business gives way to the opening ceremony led by Brooke. We are to place something on the altar, one by one, calling out a phrase for our intent. The room becomes silent as we each reflect on why we are here. *How to capture it all in a single phrase?*

I settle for "companion energy." Companion energy, only possible when centred well, and thus encompassing a journey into my dark side and my search for an act of power and an act of beauty. Companion energy, connection with All my Relations. My turn comes. I rise to my feet as gracefully as I can muster, move slowly, purposefully, and solemnly to the altar where I gently place down my stones and shells in their red flannel pouch. I straighten and clearly voice my phrase. The last woman takes her turn.

Abruptly the mood shifts as we're on to our names and action symbols for ourselves. "Marg" not "Marje." I have to point that out. I flap my wings, a clear symbol for me but not for them, not yet. We do the rounds repeatedly with much laughter: fun, playful, learning. We change positions. Harder then. More games outside. We learn trust together, creative play. Morning vanishes and the program is launched.

The central core of the program is to determine by the end of camp what an act of empowerment would be that we can undertake in the next six months to a year and similarly what act of beauty we can offer in our world back home. The Acts of Power and Beauty that each participant finally selects are stated in turn at a closing ceremony witnessed by the entire group. To add to the commitment, we each select a stake of something important to us that we will forfeit if we fail to complete the act. Much of the program, including identifying our power leaks, and particularly the vision quest is intended to help us reach our appropriate Acts of Power and Beauty.

Late one evening early in the first week, our hoops meet and we start discussing our power leaks. My body is heavy with fatigue, but I try hard to keep my attention on each speaker. Tension creeps into my shoulders. I can follow the examples that others are sharing, but blank out on mine, a power leak that I fail to recognize. I'm close to tears of frustration. *I can't fail at this.*

Marja, one of my hoop members, helps me see that for me responsibility means nothing less than perfection.

No wonder I shun it! The flash of understanding makes me sit up momentarily but I'm too tired to take it all in and slump back down. The faint glimmer of light is replaced by sharp panic that tightens my stomach. *I don't have enough time to work on this.*

Soon someone else reaches her limit and suggests we call it a night. I'm thankful it's over for now, recognize that there's nothing more I can do that night. Moonlight enables me to easily follow the well-worn path back to my tent, and the cool breeze on my face caresses me, brings me comfort.

Next morning as I lie in my sleeping bag in a semi-dream state, I discover that the left lens of the expensive new sunglasses that I bought for this trip is shattered. At first in my dream I am upset at breaking them, then realize that this is a symbol of shattering some of the dark, creating light on the intuitive side. I fully awaken and grin with delight at the message. As I lie there it is as though a dam has broken inside me, matching the breaking of the lens. I am suddenly open to listing some of my energy leaks. I grab my notebook and write them down then and there.

Another lightbulb comes on. I suddenly know it will help to work with one of my hoop members on our energy leaks. Finger testing leads me to Marja and, on the way back from breakfast, I ask her. My Badger medicine from within is aggressively taking over.

That morning we were taken by school bus to visit a cave. As Marja and I walk back after lunch, we grapple with finding our energy leaks. We laugh, have fun in the process, and finally conclude that while one of our hoop may see herself as "stupid" as one of her energy leaks, we are both "crazy" and that isn't a leak. I am discovering in a very real way Twylah's truth: growth needn't be painful.

Day 1 of the Vision Quest arrived. I walk slowly, with no stops up the wide curving path up the hillside. I'm not sure where I cut off to reach my hillside circle. Gulp. *Oh no, I can't have trouble finding my site.*

I take a deep breath and ask my feet to guide me, am surprised at the angle I set off, but soon see my site directly ahead. Once there, I remove my pack, sling up my ground sheet as I'd figured out earlier in the week and test out how it is lying under it.

Now what? I'm armed with no notebook and no plan for how to proceed. *How naked can I be and yet be fully clothed?*

But, of course, I know I shall start with prayer. I get to my feet and voice my prayers to all the directions, asking for help, stating my intent to seek vision, to search for my Act of Power. Suddenly I'm closing my prayers by singing "Fly like an Eagle, flying so high, circling the universe with wings of pure love." I stand there, facing the vista of hills and valley, and the song pours forth from deep within. As I finish, there is Eagle, flying overhead to my right. Now it's tears that flow. My heart aches and I'm overcome with gratitude for such miraculous spirituality in my life now.

Soon I'm crying too for the pain of having lost all this when Jon died. Anger wells up in my chest and throat. Anger at Jon for dying, leaving me, causing me to lose my spirituality at such a young age. Abruptly, I take a step back. *Me, angry at Jon?*

I'm shocked at myself. I don't cast it off, let it emerge, feel the anger again. Minutes pass. Then I pray, let go of the anger, know it was I who had turned away from Great Spirit and now have turned back. Heart full once again, I thank Eagle, now long gone.

Morning passes quickly but the afternoon drags. My mind wanders to Acts of Power, carving birds, moving out west or to the country, starting a support group, teaching medicine walks, completing this book. *What's happened to the teaching centre? Am I off my path? Will I be put back on it? I don't want limits to this vision. How will Spirit tell me? A dream once again? When? During the quest or a short time after?*

What a lot of mind chatter. So much wanting to trust the Universe, trust Spirit but eager to know, wanting direction, wanting commitment.

Evening comes. My sleeping bag is out ready. I remove my pants, crawl in, burgundy jacket over my blouse, pull my Indian sweater into the bag. I am on a slight slope. The red down bag is slippery. I slide a bit. My back begins to hurt from lying on the hard ground on my back. Turn to one side. Slide some more. Pull myself back up. Slide, slide, a small plant stalk offers a grip for my foot. Hold myself firm. Hard to do when I relax, impossible when I flip to the other side. Deep sighs of frustration. Slide, pull myself up, slide, pull. *Have I dozed, slept? Hardly feels like it, just exercise, slide, pull.*

Something makes me sit up. I must have slept. Night now, stars a million lights, the Milky Way broad, white. I catch myself holding my breath as I gaze in awe. Then a meteorite shoots, broad tail, directly in my view. *Signal. Signal of what?*

No answer.

My thoughts turn back to my sliding. I'm hot to the point of stickiness, even perspiration on my forehead. *Why not get out of the down bag? Place it over me. I'll slip less. Not a problem during the day.*

I try it. Slip a little, far less, much slower. *Good.*

I'm about to drift off when I think back to the shooting star. *Signal. Signal of what? Why am I on a slope? I know better than that (Bear Tribe experience) and even warned by Brooke. Yet here I am. Why?*

My sleeping bag here is my home. That's it. Home on slippery ground, not right for me . . . No, that's not it. It's the home that's sliding, the ground's not bad. So I'm to move, that's clearly my Act of Power.

Out west?

No, the ground here's OK, not perfect, but OK. So near Ottawa, just not where I live now.

No doubt in my mind. Spirit has shown me my Act of Power, made it perfectly clear. I'm to move to the country somewhere near Ottawa. No questioning. No need for an Indian head in the sky. *What a powerful, concrete way to get my vision.*

My heart is so full I have no adequate words to convey the thanks I offer from deep in my soul. I don't struggle for words: I just go with the feeling itself. Ever so wide awake now.

Jitters hit my stomach. *Scary Act of Power . . . Clear sign it's right.*

After a while, I try to sleep. Not easy, caught up now in my Act of Power and Spirit's choice of how to show me. Excited, tired, eager for more.

The rest of the quest was anti-climactic, an easy day in a posh restaurant with a western tanager, dancing insects in late afternoon sun, and the final morning a ruffed grouse on the tree below me to symbolize the spiral dance of my quest and what lay ahead in the months to come.

Light steps and a joyful heart carry me through the long grass, waving in the breeze that cools my cheeks, back down to the hillside trail. The walk is now easy to my feet but how hard to resist the Saskatoon berries that grow at the side of the path. I can taste their juicy tang and sweetness but settle instead for the dazzling beauty of the lazuli buntings that dart quietly among them.

Last evening. Time for the Giveaway Ceremony. We have each brought a gift with us from home for this ceremony of exchanging gifts. I carry my polished abalone shell with me to the yurt. Brooke instructs us to lay our gifts in a circle around the drum where our Medicine Shields had lain that morning as we engaged in the ceremony of stating our Acts of Power and Beauty before the whole group. My thoughts go back to the morning. How solemnly and confidently I'd stood and stated my Act of Power. And then I had received my medicine name. "Winged Ones Invite her Essence" is so beautiful, so inspiring. Back to the moment.

Brooke says, "One gift only. If there are several parts, keep them together in a cluster."

We get up, lay out our gifts. I'm near the door across from Brooke. She puts out her gift. Wing of a medium-sized bird. I stare, totally wrapped up in its beauty. Not sure what it is but struck by it, the gift that stands out for me.

We file slowly and noisily out of the yurt to regroup by age. Eldest, Eliana, is to lead us back in. I'm fifth and not far from her. She leads us slowly around the circle so we can view each gift in the low light from candles. I see only the wing, expect everyone's eye is on it too. My breathing rate quickens.

"Continue," Brooke says to Eliana, "until you reach the gift you want."

Eliana, near the door, keeps moving toward the wing and I hold my breath. She miraculously doesn't stop there, carries on but not far. She stops at woven material. I hardly notice. The wing is near me. *How many gifts, how many of us?*

My heart is starting to pound. I'm fifth. The person next to Eliana picks up the gift next to hers. The third takes hers, the fourth and yes, the wing is mine. I can't believe this synchronicity. Winged Ones Invite her Essence picks up the wing, gently, awed by my good fortune.

My delight is not mine alone. Later, the room is full of it. Joy, pleasure, love springing from each woman around the circle, sharing my joy, adding to it, acknowledging Spirit's way. So clear here. No one can miss it. Brooke comments she knew it would be mine or maybe one or two others. It is I. My joy is overflowing, the smile on my face so broad it hurts.

On the wing is Brooke's card with a message and a tiny purple pouch 1 inch by 3/4 inch, its edges beaded with tiny white beads. Her note tells me she sent a prayer with each bead that I may fulfil my commitment to my Act of Power. I am to add my own symbol to the pouch and leave it on my altar until I have completed my commitment. I am so moved with the thought, the care that has gone into this gift and has come to me, to me for whom it is so special. I'm close to tears. Connected to Brooke now in a strong, personal way. The wing is Grouse. I should have known. Last symbol on my Vision Quest, last symbol of this camp. Grouse and Eagle by me, with me, here at camp and in my life. *Oh Great Spirit, how you honour me, challenge me to reach out, reach for my potential. My commitment is big, a step that leads to other steps, truly an Act of Power, an act of significance for me.*

The evening ends with our dancing around the drummers who beat a strong rhythm on the large drum in the centre of the yurt. A Japanese woman flows gracefully while a black woman tosses herself with sensual vigour. I slip out, gaze up at the stars, so at ease with myself, my heart so full. Then I stroll across the meadow to the ranch house for the last time. My tent is packed and I'll sleep inside.

I had obviously enjoyed the program but was Brooke Medicine Eagle my spiritual guide as I had anticipated and what had I learned? First of all, yes, Brooke guided me to a learning process that works well for me. Not only did I learn much about myself, I was also thrust into my Act of Power. So in these ways she was a teacher or guide for me there.

Do we all need Spiritual Guides and teachers? Who are they? You have seen that I have struggled with this issue. There were many for me over these years. Mine began with Eagle, who first caught my attention and directed me to a spiritual path.

In 1992 Gurudev posed a question that has stuck with me. "Would you try to learn medicine or law without a teacher?" He argued that a spiritual teacher was just as important. Many of the people I read about had been apprentices of one or more teachers. While Nature has been one of my primary guides, I have also needed human teachers to assist me in learning to "listen" to Nature, both without and within. Kristine and Lynne started me on my way but as time went on, I moved farther afield.

Could I have progressed without such an array of teachers and programs? I'm sure I wouldn't have stood still. My intent and focus was far too strong for that. Other teachers closer at hand might have materialized. And many Grasshopper steps took place without the aid of human teachers or programs. Some leaps came alone as well. Yet most of my Grasshopper leaps were propelled by teachers and programs that met my needs of the moment. I urge you to call in a teacher through prayer and intent and treat yourself as best you can when an opportunity presents itself. Spiritual paths are well worth investment of time, energy and money. Why not seek out a leap to further your path?

I came away from the camp with a better understanding of myself through exercises that helped us look at the side of ourselves we hide more successfully from ourselves than from others.

Most important was the path to the learning. Here it was achieved in a setting of warmth and support that reflected what I had seen at Twylah's in 1990: self growth can come about in a joyful way. While it is possible to learn through confrontation as a warrior way, there is also this way of a more peaceful warrior. The latter is clearly my choice of path and how I learn best.

Those aspects of the program were important but they were far from the significance of coming home, having made a commitment to complete a specific act of power within a year. I came back from my Bear Tribe Vision Quest with the vision of a healing centre. It was specific but a large scale vision and there was no time limit attached. Now I had made a commitment, witnessed by the entire group and I had a deadline.

This process of making a commitment with a time limit attached was a powerful new tool. It could be applied to any other program to which I went simply by determining acts of power and beauty afterwards, setting a time limit and holding a ceremony as my own form of witnessing the commitments I might make. I have focused here solely on my Act of Power because it was far more significant for me at this particular camp.

The Deepening of Spirit camp came back home with me, particularly with my Act of Power:

> To move within one year to the country where I have immediate access to Nature.

A commitment, a decision. It felt right there on my Vision Quest spot at Blacktail Ranch. My sleeping bag was so clearly my home and so evident it wasn't in a suitable place. It felt so right that I put my binoculars up as my stake.

Now here I am in Ottawa putting that Act of Power into action. My decision is taken all right. I'm into that same space I've known before when I became committed to something. Decision taken, action follows promptly. I feel that same inner motion, that "get on with it sense." It won't leave until I've signed the final papers. *Odd how this part of me functions.*

A year to complete my Act of Power. *Where do I start? How much can I afford to pay? Good starting point that.*

I found an accountant and set up an appointment. I started to look at properties on September 11. My fingers indicated that the choice of location was between Quebec and the area to the west of Ottawa. Not taking any chances, I also checked the area east of Ottawa first. I felt much more at home in the west. More woods for one thing but it also felt more like northland, less sophisticated. There was one house and setting on the Galetta Sideroad to which I was particularly attracted. *Does it have some acreage? There isn't any open area at present for a garden, except perhaps close to the road. That's not good.*

The following weekend Sue and I visit the Galetta sideroad home. There are huge white pines towering everywhere. The real estate agent hasn't arrived. We walk on the gravel path between the house and the garage to peek a look out back. A small area of grass with a blue jay calling at a pole feeder. But I hardly even notice the blue jay. There are tall white birches, varying sizes of spruce trees, maples too. Mature mixed woods right on the property and far more woods behind. My heart thumps wildly, my insides churn with excitement. I gasp. I can hardly contain myself. Over beyond the house there is even a small vegetable garden. I am in love.

The agent arrives. The house is small and a little dark, but pleasant, with a wood stove to supplement electric heating. I barely notice all that. It is more than adequate, but my heart and soul are still outside, caught in the immediate access to Nature.

I visited a variety of homes and also returned to the Galetta Side Road home with Carmen and Louise. I was more and more convinced that this was the house I wanted, not that my heart needed any convincing at all.

My first offer went in on September 29 and I left for Toronto to arrange for the financing. The counter offer came back that evening and my new offer was faxed the following morning. I went to the Edwards Gardens and walked. No tension in my body, relaxed. In fact, I'm fully confident that I'll have the house that day, with a good possibility of its being under the price I had put out to the Universe. Calm, pleased. Glad to be out in Nature, smelling the rich fall leaf smell, rustling the fallen red and yellow maple leaves as I walk. I kick some deliberately and smile, appreciating life and Nature, the very reason I'm doing all this!

On the way back I notice a large dragonfly on a bush, bring my hand under the large, rough leaf to look at it better. The wings are black but the body has sky blue and forest green flecks. The eye lobes seem enormous, as though I could gaze right down into their depths of a green hue. Very beautiful and there to reinforce all that is going on for me. It allows me to encourage it on to my hand and stays with me several minutes before flying off. Dragonfly, my Seawall ceremony symbol for my brother. Tears come. *Was it he, acknowledging this step that brings me back to woods such as I had as a child when he was alive??*

My agent called later that day to say the offer had been accepted. She congratulated me but I wasn't excited. It was merely confirmation of what I already knew. My Act of Power was achieved hardly six weeks after I had made the commitment.

I can't bring *Nature Speaks: I Listen* to an end without taking you to my Power Place in the Enchanted Forest and to the Nature Spirit's plot. I took possession of my new home on November 1, 1993 and arrive with my first carload of belongings shortly after noon.

I start unloading and notice the empty bird feeders as I head to the house. Winged Ones Invite her Essence's head drops. *Need to remedy that next trip.*

The first load inside, I'm pulled out to the back. Enter the woods and sing "Send me a Voice" at the top of my lungs to the accompaniment of my tape and the barking of the neighbours' dogs. Give a prayer of thanks to the Nature Spirits and ask for their help.

I'm champing at the bit to seek out my Power Place. Has to be a white pine at its centre, has to be just into the wood. Narrow it down to one of two pines and my fingers help choose between them. I crane my neck to look up it, my heart ever so full. Run my fingers slowly over its well-grooved bark. Put my arms around it, not quite able to reach all the way. Pine needles are soft under foot and my feet slide slightly. Rub my cheek against the warm, rough bark, and smell its faint aroma. That coming home feeling washes over me.

And so I had my new Power Place.

I moved on November 12 but didn't have my first full day at the house, on my own, until the 18th.

In the afternoon I have a strong urge to ask the Nature Spirits to guide me to their special area. This is more of a challenge than in the vegetable garden. There's an eager anticipation to my step as

I don my jacket and head outside. Having no idea where the Nature Spirits will want to be, I divided the property into four quadrants and use my fingers to guide me. This takes time but it can't be rushed. Back half of the property. *Thought that was likely.*

Much to my surprise, however, the Nature Spirits, guide me to Sister Pine of my Power Place. I pull back in disbelief but they confirm that I share a circle with them, my Power Place and their special territory. *Wow!!*

I'm thrilled, want to jump for joy but restrain myself. I'm overwhelmed too. Tears come to my eyes and I hug Sister Pine. *Talk about wanting Oneness and then being invited to their spot, theirs and mine in union.*

I go to my car to retrieve the rocks from the summer vegetable garden and lovingly carry them back to Sister Pine. I place them at the edge of the Nature Spirit plot in the four directions, with the clearer quartz reserved for the centre at the foot of Sister Pine. My heart is bursting with pleasure. As I stand there, so satisfied with the undertaking, Dee, with a bit of fat from the nearby feeder, flies in, hovers a moment of acknowledgement and continues on her way. Enchanted Forest it truly is.

I turn, cold now from the November nip in the air, and walk back to the house.

And so my stated Act of Power was completed, opening the way for new growth, new learning, more lessons flowing from this Act of Power. I asked that I might learn from a place of wisdom, not one of fear and doubt and I vacillated between the two. I was caught in delight in moving wood from the wood pile to the shelter by the house. I was trapped in fear that I didn't have enough wood, that it wouldn't last the winter, that I wouldn't learn to use it efficiently, that wood costs would be as exorbitant as the electrical heating they assisted. Finally I let go, enjoyed the fire, grateful to the wood, trusting that Great Spirit had looked after me in that respect too. All had been in place throughout the search and the move. It was meant to be. *So accept, enjoy, trust my path.*

Thank you Brooke, thank you Great Spirit, thank you sleeping bag that slipped down that slope, that kept me awake that Vision Quest night. Thank you Shooting Star that lit up my thinking, my intuition to grasp the message, see it clearly, reach out with open arms. I hug myself, I hug the Universe.

33

Afterwards

THERE WERE still loose threads for me and, no doubt, for you the reader too. What has come of my first Vision Quest vision of a healing centre? Well, in 1995 a friend and his son built me a screened-in porch on the side of the house. One day, shortly after it was completed, I returned to the house from my new vegetable garden. I looked admiringly at what I now call my Music Room, since it is there that I listen to bird song, frog and cricket choruses, and the sigh of leaves in the wind. Looking at the shape of the cedar frame above the screen windows I suddenly saw the arch of my first overnight ceremony vision of the Nagai Earthwalk Centre. My heart thumped awake. *Is this the beginning of the healing centre vision?*

Since then I have offered my first workshop here, "Moccasin Walking in Nature," and an astrologer friend from Brooke's camp, has also done readings and given workshops here. Thus in a small way my Bear Tribe vision is finally off the ground.

Timba, the dog who used to live next door, is now a full-time resident with me. She has become the country dog I didn't think she could be and I the country woman I also had doubts about. And the dragonfly that held my attention the day my house offer was accepted must have been Jon. Why I even call this space The Enchanted Forest, the forest we walked together with Winnie-the-Pooh.

As for the outcome of my handclapping ceremony in July and my relationship with Sue, on the surface nothing much seems to have happened. No human has arrived on the scene to join me in bringing the healing centre vision more alive. And yet The Enchanted Forest and Timba have offered the support I needed to set off on that dream in those initial ways.

And as for the other hand that held Sue. On the surface that hasn't changed either. We are still limited to short visits during the year and a longer stretch in the summer. But somehow as time has gone on I have come to see it all in a different light. My path is here in The Enchanted Forest for now and the visits from Sue are moments to enjoy to the fullest. Her support of my path and my writing are nurturing me, as are Timba and The Enchanted Forest. And Sue's spiritual path, stirred in so many ways by connections with mine, moves forward too. How natural it is for us to hold hands and pray with gratitude as we begin a meal. So much comes down to seeking to see in a new way what we already do in our lives, learning to appreciate openly many of the day-to-day moments and gifts. In so doing our focus comes back to the moment. And it is only in the moment that we truly walk our spiritual paths.

Would Sue or I ever have believed in 1987 that she would take one of her spiritual tools, Angel cards, small cards with an angel and a single word such as Persistence, Flexibility, Gentleness on each, to the schools she administers as principal? The cards are a tool she uses with staff at the end of the year to give them a focus for the school year that lies ahead. And the willow outside one of her schools has a special place in her heart. Our paths in so many ways nurture each other. And we leave what lies ahead to the plans of Great Spirit.

And how do I now view my spiritual path, Grasshopper's path to spirituality? As this book has come together so have my thoughts about this path I walk. In case it may help you to put this story of mine into a perspective useful to you, let me show you how I map it myself.

I view oneness with "all my relations" as what is described as enlightenment in some religions, and what is elsewhere described as the love that binds all. Oneness and enlightenment is what I attempt to attain on my spiritual path in moment-by-moment day- to-day life. This Spirit is within and around us at all times and we touch in to it the more our hearts are open and we become centred and focused.

As we walk our spiritual paths, our spiral dance brings us closer and closer to this central core of oneness and we touch in to it more and more often. (See Illustration 1)

I now like to imagine the path that Grasshopper leads me along as comprised of flagstones that vary in size and shape. Not only does the path spiral in closer and closer to the central core of enlightenment as I progress along my path, but also anywhere along the path, the flagstones may be more centred or off kilter. (See Illustration 2)

My personal flagstones are five in number. I consider focused intent and balance as the central stone. The better it is in place, the more the other flagstones can expand and flourish.

The flagstone of reciprocal relationship with Nature is a direct link with oneness and highlights the role that Nature plays on my spiritual path.

My third flagstone represents intuition, inner vision or knowing. The more I am focused and in balance, the more I can open myself to this inner wisdom within. At times this inner wisdom flows as a channel through the connection with oneness.

My fourth flagstone is appreciation of and gratitude for the magic of and in life. This flagstone colours the way I view Nature and my world and spontaneously leads to gratitude for all Nature's gifts that come my way.

Finally, the fifth flagstone is creativity and serving. Creativity is freed when the other flagstones are in place. And joyful creativity is central to providing what I can then share, and, in doing so, I serve. (See Illustration 3)

Many of the spiritual tools I have acquired as I have been walking my path are useful for more than one of my flagstones. In Illustration 4, I have shown which tools I tend to apply to each of the flagstones. I find that there are reciprocal relationships between flagstones and between flagstones and the tools. For example, in my Power Place I become more balanced and focus my intent more clearly. That may then amplify the energy of the Power Place and add to the effect of any ceremony that I carry out there.

I have sometimes written of the ebbs and flows that I encounter as I walk my path. Once again, my spiritual tools come to my aid not only as I seek guidance and answers to problems that arise but also as I seek to bring about change or face the battlefield of doubts. (See Illustration 5)

Finally, in Illustration 6, I have listed my spiritual tools. Two are more recent additions that came from the discovery of Julia Cameron's *The Artist's Way*. She offers a program to release blocks to creativity. The core tools for this are the daily writing of three pages each morning and a weekly date with one's artist child. The date, taken alone, is a way to refill the artist's well. These morning pages and artist dates have become well-used tools in my spiritual tool kit. May you enjoy your tool kit as much as I enjoy mine.

1. GRASSHOPPER'S PATH TO SPIRITUALITY

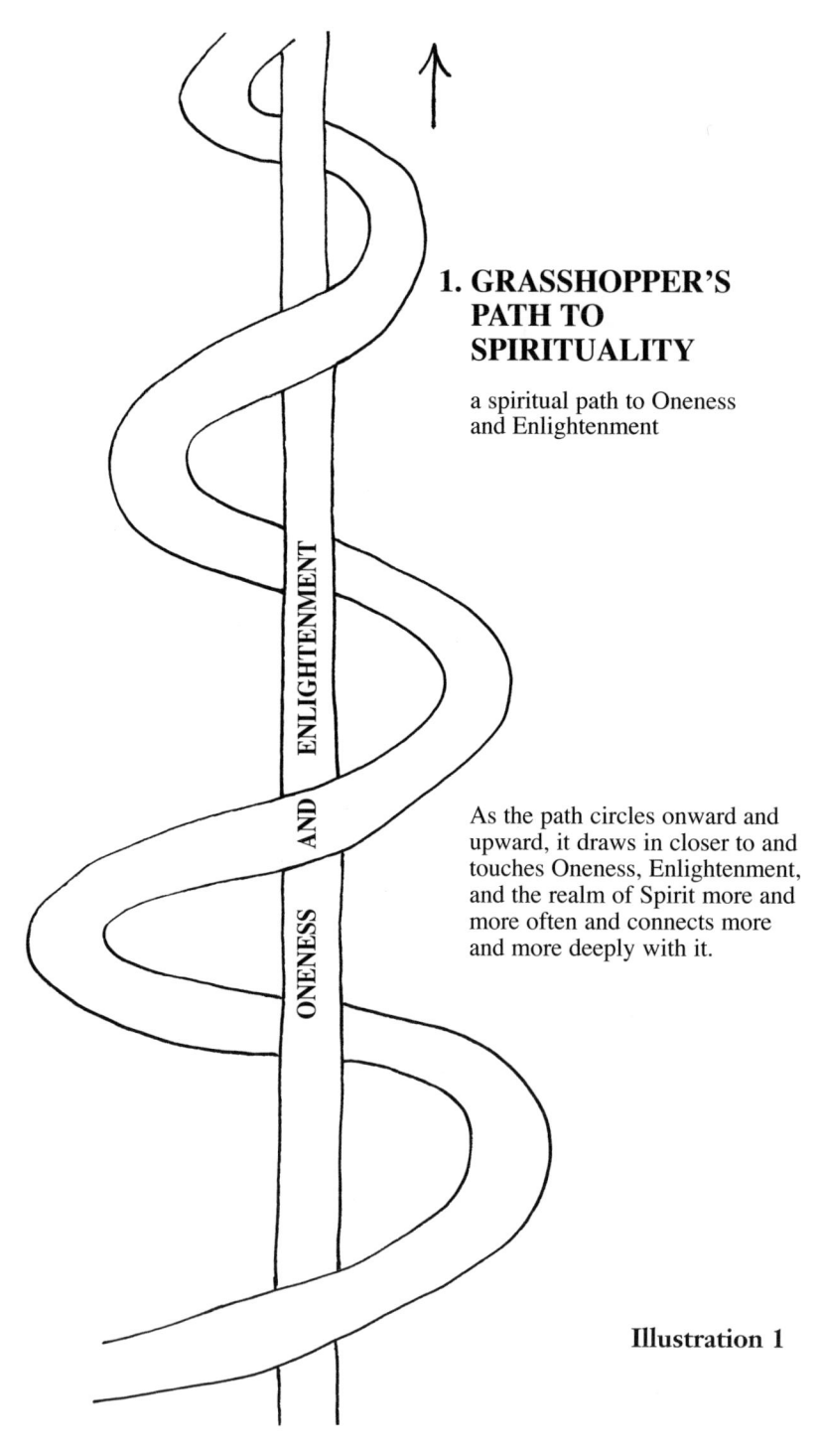

a spiritual path to Oneness and Enlightenment

As the path circles onward and upward, it draws in closer to and touches Oneness, Enlightenment, and the realm of Spirit more and more often and connects more and more deeply with it.

Illustration 1

2. COMPOSITION OF THE SPIRITUAL PATH

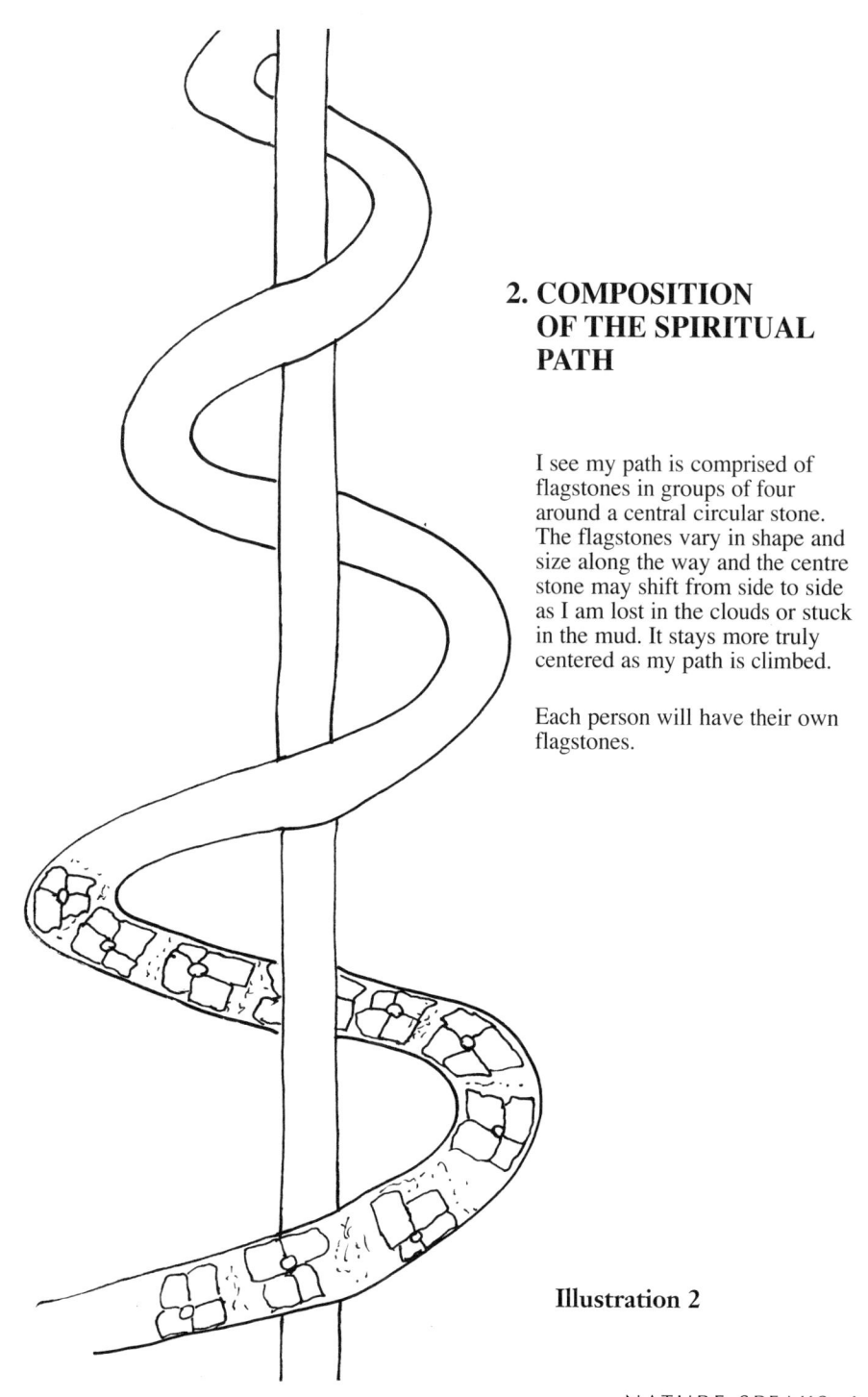

I see my path is comprised of flagstones in groups of four around a central circular stone. The flagstones vary in shape and size along the way and the centre stone may shift from side to side as I am lost in the clouds or stuck in the mud. It stays more truly centered as my path is climbed.

Each person will have their own flagstones.

Illustration 2

Reciprocal Relationship with Nature

Intuition, Inner Vision or Knowing, Channel

Focused Intent & Balance

Creativity, Serving

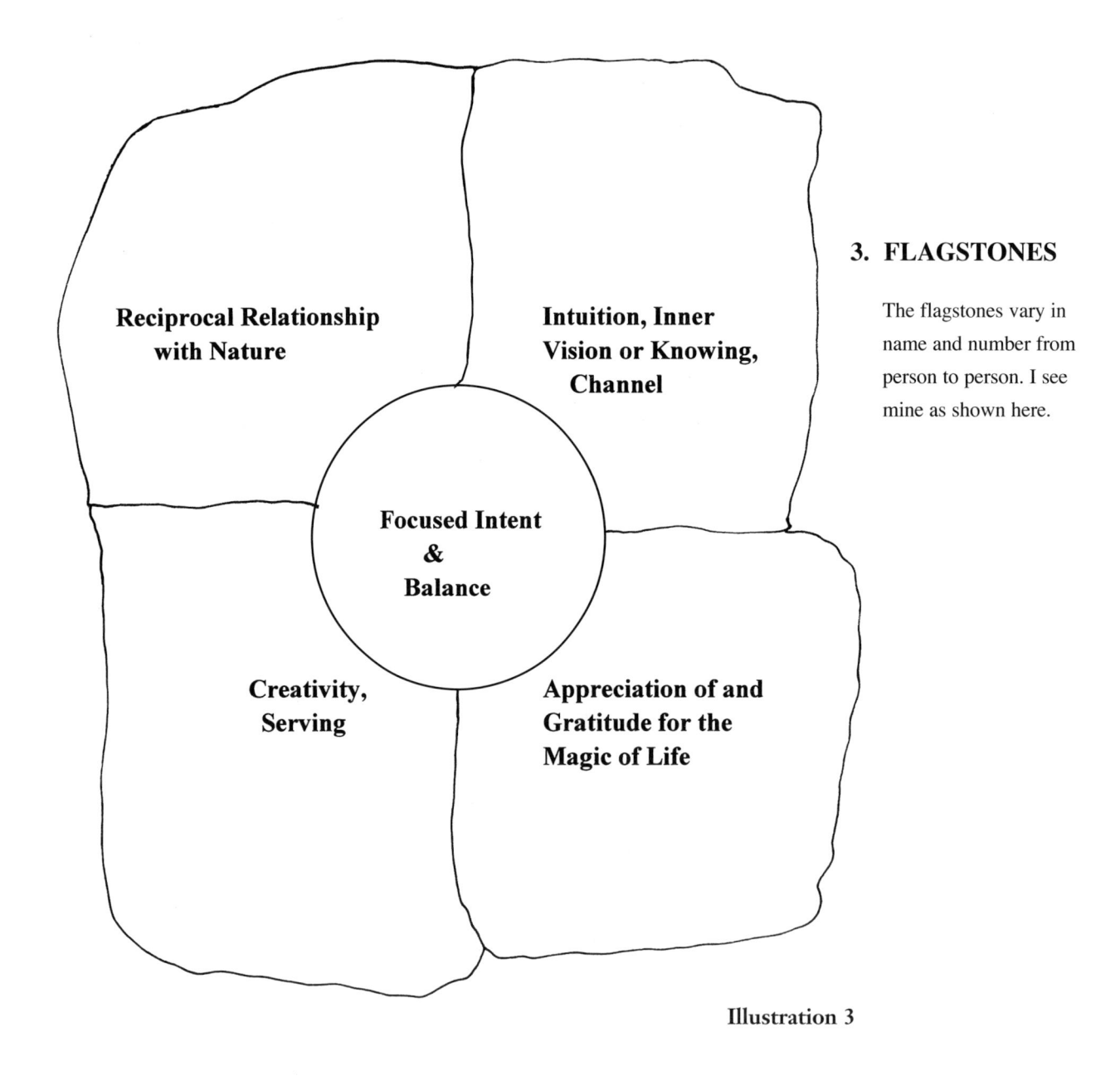

Appreciation of and Gratitude for the Magic of Life

3. FLAGSTONES

The flagstones vary in name and number from person to person. I see mine as shown here.

Illustration 3

4. FLAGSTONE TOOLS

Each flagstone is chipped out and put in place by a variety of spiritual tools, which may change from flagstone to flagstone and from time to time. A sample of mine is shown here.

I imagine the tools as being part of my Spiritual Tool Kit.

There is a reciprocal relationship between the tools and the flagstones and between the flagstones, particularly the central one.

Reciprocal Relationship with Nature
Tools:
Nature as symbols
Medicine Wheel
Conversations with Nature
Gardening
Dreams
Animal Medicine Cards

Appreciation of and Gratitude for the Magic of Life
Tools:
Ceremony
Medicine Walks
Sweat Lodge
Prayer
Communication with Nature
Nutrition

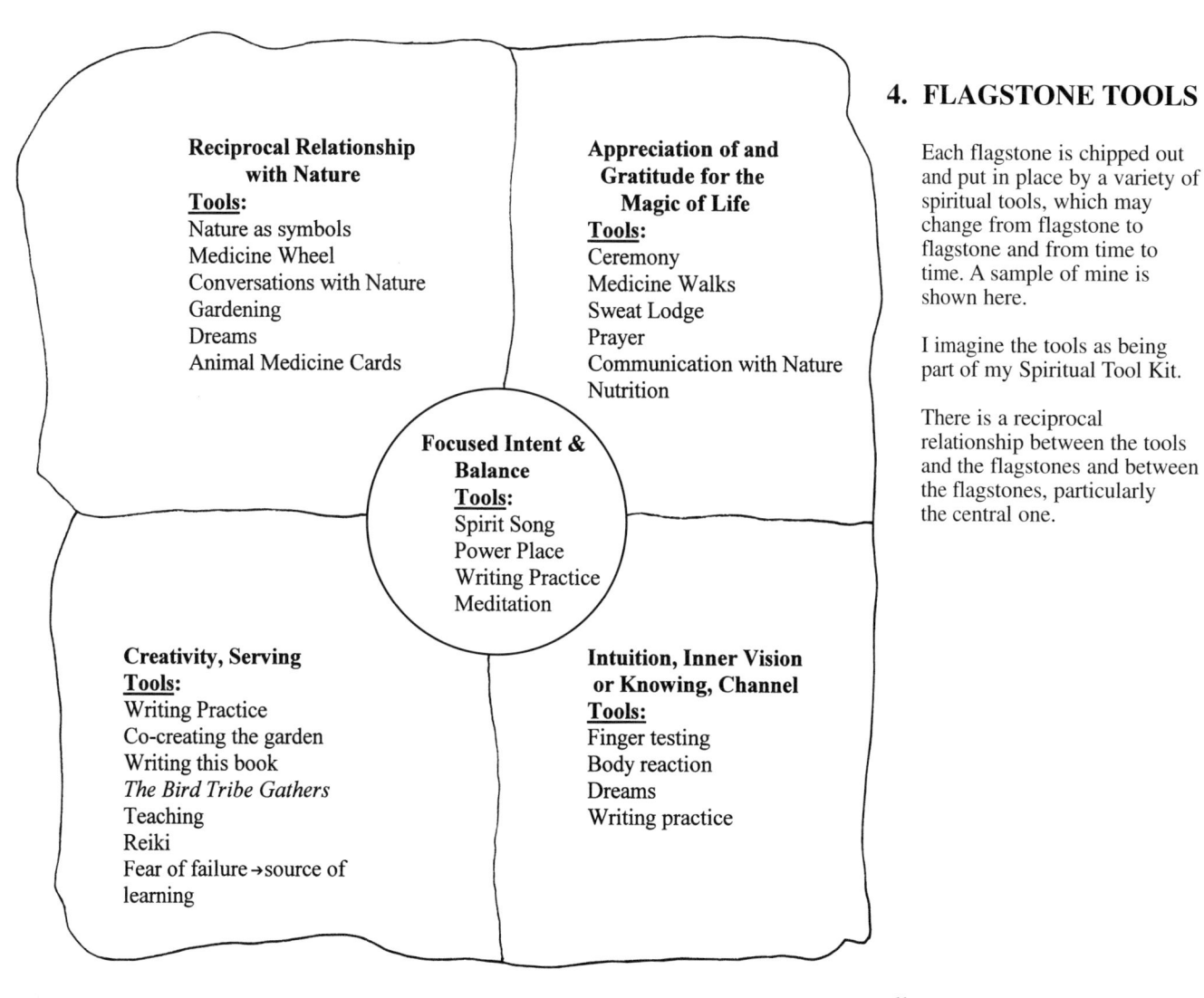

Focused Intent & Balance
Tools:
Spirit Song
Power Place
Writing Practice
Meditation

Creativity, Serving
Tools:
Writing Practice
Co-creating the garden
Writing this book
The Bird Tribe Gathers
Teaching
Reiki
Fear of failure → source of learning

Intuition, Inner Vision or Knowing, Channel
Tools:
Finger testing
Body reaction
Dreams
Writing practice

Illustration 4

NATURE SPEAKS: I LISTEN 165

5. ALONG THE WAY

Seeking Guidance and Answers

<u>Tools:</u>
Spiritual guides
Dreams
Medicine walks
Vision Quest
Sacred Path cards
Animal Medicine cards
Runes
I Ching
Power place
Writing practice

Aiding and Abetting Change

<u>Tools:</u>
Ceremony
Pipe
Prayer
Sweat Lodge
Dreams
Medicine walks

Keeping the Faith

<u>Tools:</u>
Asking for signs
Progress reviews
some of the spiritual
Teachers & programs

There are three aspects which help me to keep on moving along the path. Each is aided by tools.

6. SPIRITUAL TOOL KIT

The items in my spiritual tool kit during the time of which I have written are listed in alphabetical order. Two that have become important more recently are listed with an asterisk.

Animal Medicine Cards
Artist date*
Aware of presence of something - calling it in
Conversations with Nature & Animals
Creating ceremony
Finger testing
Gardening
Medicine Walks
Medicine Wheel
Morning pages*
Nature as symbols
No fear of failure but see it as learning
Nutrition
Pipe
Power Place

Sweat lodge
Prayer
Progress reviews
Reciprocal relationship with Nature
Reiki
Spirit Song
Timba
Vision quest
Writing
Writing practice

Illustrations 5 & 6

Epilogue

Epilogue

July 1995, I returned to another of Brooke Medicine Eagle's camps at Blacktail Ranch in Montana. I was out on my Vision Quest site, lying out as flat as I ever lie. Heard you, Grasshopper, off by the side, remembered reading of each of you having your own unique song. Hard for me to believe that's true, but never mind. It's what I was thinking right then. And then there you were, right before my eyes, just far enough off to be fully in focus for someone who needs glasses for reading. You were facing me, obviously there to speak to me. I held my breath, watched, heard your leg voice. Then you turned to face west. You sang again and then your mighty leap, up and out. Such a wondrous leap you made! I got part of your message right then: a leap like yours was in store for me. It took morning alertness to tune me in to the rest: you came to show me my Act of Power, the leap to put forth our book, my voice, *Grasshopper's Path to Spirituality*. What a messenger. Grasshopper yourself to tell me to take the leap.

I've been so blessed with messengers. I slip into expectations of beings like Eagle or Bear or Elk but fortunately I'm open to whoever comes; let you be as mighty a messenger as any of those. Not one of them could mean as much as you yourself bringing that message to me. Spirit that Moves in all Things has a better perspective by far than I. Oh Grasshopper, thank you for the lessons you bring me. Big leaper, not frequent leaper. I watched long hours in '91, witnessed how little you jumped. I'm honoured you've chosen to come yourself to guide me to my Act of Power. Would you like to speak to me?

Grasshopper: I get a kick out of how I brought that message to you. It was I who suggested you lie down, get down to my level to watch my show. You heard and responded. There's another example of the listening you say you can't do. Once I had you seated so to speak, I got you thinking of me and my voice so you'd be ready. Again you heard well.

So the stage was set. Not often I'm centre stage like that. Looked into the depths of those blue eyes of yours and sang to you. That's the first time I've chosen to sing to a human. Not often I'm part of a book title that puts me in such a spiritual light. So now it was my turn to honour you, then turn and show you your Act of Power. I told you too but it didn't sink in. As usual, you were too excited by my presence. Never mind, you got it soon enough and you're using the energy of an Act of Power once again and using it well. I'm with you, proud of our work together. Ho!

Act of Power:

> To complete the initial writing of my book, *Grasshopper's Path to Spirituality*, edit and revise it, and submit it to two publishers and/or initiate self-publication within a year.

And so this, my unique song is now sung, as commanded by Grasshopper. May it cast new light on your path and stir you to seek the enjoyment and growth that is waiting out there for you. That is the dream we share, Grasshopper and I.

Glossary

3rd dimension
The physical reality in which we normally operate.

5th dimension
The dream world and world of spirit.

All my relations
All living beings, including animals, trees, stones, etc.

Ceremony
Existing rituals, a spiritual observance in which instructions are followed, or a self created spiritual observance

Channeling
An opening of a person who is often in a trance state that allows messages to come of which the person is not directly aware. The channeling may come through voice or writing.

Dream Warrior
A wise warrior being of the spirit and dream reality

Finger testing
A technique that alerts us to negative energy that does not maintain the balance of an individual. It can also be used to obtain yes/no answers to questions.

Focused intent
A state of mind in which one is fully centred and concentrating on a specific intention

Medicine
Anything that improves one's connection to the Great Spirit and/or anything which brings personal power, strength, and understanding.

Medicine walk
Seeking guidance from Nature through focusing on a particular issue and then walking out in Nature alert for the signals and symbols that bring clarity to the issue.

Medicine Wheel
A symbolic wheel of life containing all directions, aspects, attributes, things and beings.

Pish Make a soft noise that sounds like the word "pish," with the "sh" drawn out. Some birds respond by approaching.

Reiki A way of channeling energy from the universe through our body and out our hands to another person.

Sacred Path cards
Cards and text of native American teachings whose purpose is to show us steps in our spiritual development in a way that allows us to discover our own truths.

Smudge
The burning of sacred plants such as sage and sweet grass for the purpose of smudging.

Smudging
Brushing the smoke of smudge over a person in order to cleanse the person of negative thoughts and energy.

Spirit shield
Every person carries within us two spirit shields of the opposite sex to our physical self. One is the small spirit child, capable of doing anything, the other the adult spirit shield or Dream Warrior, our wise warrior and perfect mate.

Spirit song
A song that comes to you that helps you to centre yourself and be more in tune with your Inner Being.

Substance shield
Every person carries within two substance shields, the adult shield, how we manifest ourselves to the outside world, and the child shield, the shield of our childhood that lingers with us as adults. Both are the sex of our physical self.

Sweat lodge
A dome-shaped structure made of arched poles covered with blankets and tarps that has a pit in the ground in the centre to hold red hot rocks.

Sweat Lodge Ceremony
The ceremony is one of purification of mind, body and spirit through prayer and cleansing, a time for discarding what is no longer needed and asking assistance to bring in the new for oneself and others. Sometimes used for specific healing purposes.

Synchronicity
Non-coincidental timing of two events, or of a thought and an event.

Talking stick
A ceremonial stick, usually either carved or with ornaments attached to it that is used in group settings. The holder of the stick speaks without interruption, except for clarification, and the stick is passed from person to person.

Transformation game
A board game in which you pass through 4 levels, physical, emotional, mental and spiritual. Your progress is determined by rolling dice and dealing with setbacks, insights, etc. that relate to the space on which you have landed.

Vision Quest
An ancient rite of dying, passing through, and being reborn through the experience of fasting alone in the wilderness